The Sedevacantist Delusion

The Sedevacantist Delusion

WHY VATICAN II'S CLASH WITH
SEDEVACANTISM SUPPORTS
EASTERN ORTHODOXY

John C. Pontrello

Copyright © 2015 John C. Pontrello
All rights reserved.

ISBN: 1511768746
ISBN 13: 9781511768740
Library of Congress Control Number: 2015906489
CreateSpace Independent Publishing Platform
North Charleston, South Carolina
Cover image Denniro/Shutterstock & Pontrello

Contents

	Clarification of Terms Used	xi
	Preface	xv
	Introduction	xxxvii
	They Call Themselves "Brothers"	xlvii
Chapter 1:	**On Indefectibility**	1
	Objection One	3
Part I:	Indefectibility Defined	5
	Indefectibility Compared	14
Part II:	Essential Constitution of the Church	19
	Essence	19
	Foundation	21
	Hierarchy and Sacraments	30
	Four Marks	35
Part III:	Defection of Rome	37
	Barque of Peter	37
	Metamorphosis	39
	Defection of the Hierarchy and Sacraments	45
	Two Schools of Sedevacantists	46
	Remnant Church Heresy	48
	Essential Constitutions Compared	50
	Summary	53
	Objections	58

Chapter 2: On the Vicoration of Christ · **67**
                Objection Five · 69
Part I: Interregnums · 71
                Defection in Disguise · 71

Part II: Glitches in the System · 83
                Passing the Torch · 87
                Why Inheritance Works · 90
                Ascension of Power · 92
                Vicar of Peter · 93
                Summary · 98
                Objections · 101

Chapter 3: The First Vatican Council (1869–1870) · · · · · · · · · · · · · **107**
                Objection Six · 110
Part I: *Pastor Aeternus*: First Dogmatic Constitution on
                the Church of Christ · 111
                Overview · 111
                Dimond's Ark · 117
Part II: The Papacy of Desire · 121
                Passage One · 122
                   a. Office of the Papacy—Some Clarifications · · · · · · 125
                   b. The Papacy of Desire versus the Holy See · · · · · · · 130
                   c. Conversions to Dimond's Ark · · · · · · · · · · · · · · · · · 131
                   d. Papacy of Desire Ends in Schism · · · · · · · · · · · · · · 132
                Passage Two · 133
                Passage Three · 135
                   a. Vicar without a See · 139
                   b. Peter's Real Successors · 143
                   c. The Reversal · 145
                New Classification of Heretic—*Honest* · · · · · · · · · · · · · 147
                Summary · 150
                Objections · 155

Chapter 4:	**Visibility of the Church** ························· **173**	
	Objection Fifteen ···························· 175	
Part I:	Visible Unity ································ 177	
	Visible Unity of Hierarchy···················· 183	
	Visible Head································· 185	
Part II:	False Teachers ······························ 191	
	Arianism and Indefectibility ·················· 195	
	Invisible Church Ecclesiology ················· 196	
Part III:	...and Apostolic Church ······················ 205	
	Una Cum Antichrist? ························· 223	
	Summary ···································· 226	
	Objections ··································· 229	
	Conclusion··································· 239	
	Afterword ··································· 245	
	Appendix···································· 251	
	The Sedevacantist Argument in Brief ·········· 252	
	A Doctrinal Catechism ······················· 253	
	Mortalium Animos ···························· 254	
	Bibliography ································ 265	

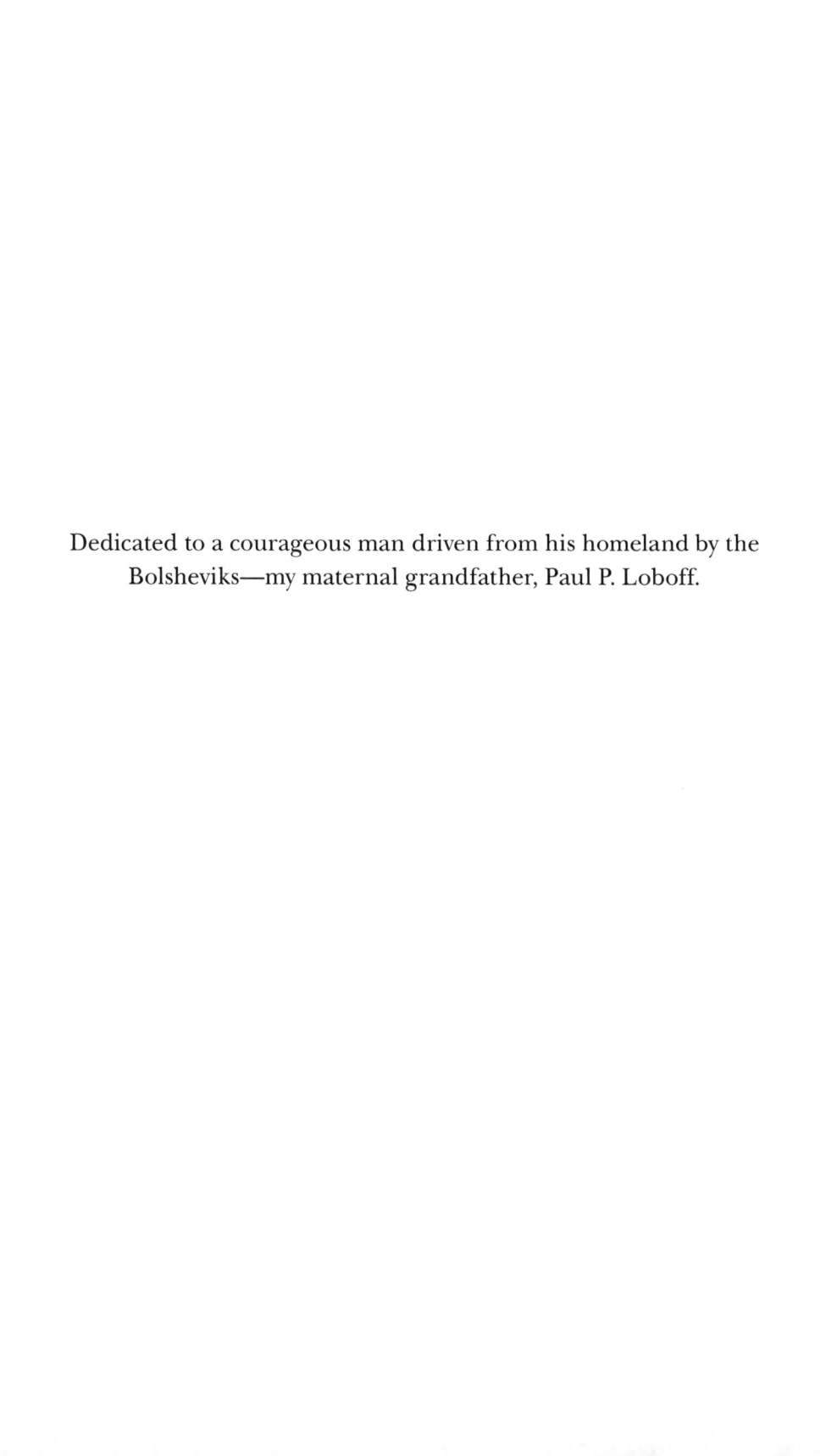

Dedicated to a courageous man driven from his homeland by the Bolsheviks—my maternal grandfather, Paul P. Loboff.

Clarification of Terms Used *

Catholic- universal.

Church/Catholic Church—the Roman Catholic Church.

Conciliar/post–Conciliar/Vatican II Catholic—the Catholic Church and its membership since Vatican II, also referred to as the *modern Church*.

Eastern Orthodox Church/Eastern Orthodoxy—the world's second largest Christian Church. It is a family of self-governing Churches united in doctrine, liturgy, and government, commonly identified by ethnicity or country (e.g., Russian, Greek, Serbian, Ukrainian, etc.). Like the Roman Catholic Church it also considers itself the one, holy, Catholic, and apostolic Church founded by Jesus Christ. Originally, the Eastern Orthodox Church and the Roman Catholic Church were one Church until the great schism of AD 1054 between the apostolic sees of Rome and Constantinople. Following the schism Rome represented Western Christianity while Antioch, Alexandria, Constantinople, and Jerusalem represented Eastern Christianity.

Traditional Catholicism—the Catholic Church as it existed in its worship, doctrine, and discipline up until Vatican II and the post–Conciliar reforms. Traditional Catholicism most notably identifies itself by the celebration of the Latin Mass.

Clarification of Terms Used *

Traditional Catholic—generally denotes any Catholic who finds fault with Vatican II and the post–Conciliar reforms of the Church. Although *traditional Catholic* includes both the Sedevacantists and the non-Sedevacantists, the term is mostly used to distinguish those who do *not* accept the Sedevacantist position.

Traditional Catholic Movement—a very broad movement of traditional Catholics who desire to believe and worship as the Church believed and worshipped up until Vatican II and the post–Conciliar reforms. Various theories and means are employed for that end.

Sedevacantists—a traditional Catholic sect that believes Vatican II was an invalid council and that Pope Francis is not a true/valid pope. Most Sedevacantists also believe that all of the popes dating to Pope John XXIII (1958) were invalid. The basic tenets of the movement are referred to as *Sedevacantism*.

Papacy—the Roman Catholic Church's foundation composed of the following mutually dependent, constituent parts: the Apostle Peter, the primacy, Rome (Holy See), and the Roman Pontiff.

Roman Church/Holy See/Roman See/Rome/Apostolic See—interchangeable terms that specifically refer to the Diocese of Rome, where the Catholic Church's central government is located. The *Roman Church* includes the Roman Pontiff and all of the important departments and ministries that assist him in governing the Church (e.g., congregations, tribunals, and the offices of the Curia).

Vatican I/First Vatican Council—the twentieth ecumenical council of the Catholic Church (1869–1870). This council defined important dogmas on the papacy, including papal infallibility.

Vatican II/Second Vatican Council—the twenty-first ecumenical council of the Catholic Church (1962–1965).

* **Note:** Clarification of terms used is how the author defines and uses these terms in this work, not necessarily how they are defined and used elsewhere.

Preface

I BECAME A SEDEVACANTIST EIGHT years ago. My conversion followed an exploration of historical revisionism and a skeptical inquiry of the September 11, 2001, acts of terrorism on American soil. That important period of discovery expanded my vision and reshaped my world paradigm. Hence at the time I did not find it too difficult to accept that a series of papal pretenders could occupy Saint Peter's chair in Rome and revolutionize the Catholic Church. After all, that a revolution in Rome transpired with Vatican II was self-evident; what remained obscure was a convincing explanation for how such a feat was pulled off in the one true Church of Jesus Christ.

My exploration of the Vatican II controversy began with certain presuppositions about the Catholic Church, and naturally I set out to align myself with the theory that best conformed to them. My initial reaction to the Sedevacantist thesis was that it was untenable according to what I believed to be true about the Catholic Church in general, as Sedevacantism certainly appeared to suggest that some kind of defection of the Church must have occurred in order to be correct. At that time, however, I was not sufficiently versed in the doctrine of the indefectibility of the Church to dispute the Sedevacantists' claims.

On the other hand, the Sedevacantists amassed a sizable arsenal of facts over the course of several decades to wage an impressive war against the post–Vatican II Church, essentially proving that *it* defected from core tenets of the Catholic faith. Because a question concerning the fallibility of the Catholic Church was not an acceptable consideration for the Catholic faithful, the logical assumption was that one of these two groups represented the true Catholic Church. Ostensibly the Sedevacantists presented the most compelling case, and I began to sell all I had for the one pearl of great price. I did not foresee that I was about to embark on a wild-Church chase that would conclude precisely where it began- Rome.

The prevailing mind-set among the Sedevacantists is that longstanding prophecies were fulfilled with Vatican II. Purportedly it was around that time that powers of darkness secured control of the Church, struck the shepherd, and scattered the flock so that only a remnant of the faithful remains—*them*. Understandably the Sedevacantists believe they are involved in a battle of epic proportions for the freedom of the one true Church of Jesus Christ and the salvation of souls. In light of the devastations that continue to befall the post–Vatican II Church[1] as well as the rapid de-Christianization of global societies over that time span, the Sedevacantists' vision can be alluring to idealistic Catholics who would aspire to become warriors and martyrs for Christ. Undeniably I was one.

After approximately five years of involvement in the Sedevacantist movement that culminated with leaving behind a successful career and entering a seminary to commence studies for the priesthood, I eventually found my way back to the Vatican II Church for theological reasons, many of which have been refined and incorporated into the present writing. Following Sedevacantism, my stint reunited with the local diocese was short-lived, lasting approximately nine months. During that time I mostly commiserated with the diocesan-sponsored Latin Mass community, where the last bastions of Vatican II holdouts huddled every Sunday

---

[1] Following the Second Vatican Council, enrollments in seminaries and religious orders plummeted, Mass attendance drastically declined, long-standing parishes were forced to merge or close, and scandals continuously plagued the Church. Interestingly the popes and bishops have managed to keep up appearances while extolling the so-called "spirit of Vatican II" and a "new springtime" in the Church. Fifty years after Vatican II, the hierarchy is preaching a "new evangelization," an initiative aimed primarily toward the Catholic faithful. Thoughtful Catholics may rightfully inquire why a "new evangelization" might be necessary in the first place.

morning. Exiled to the far outskirts of the diocese, where we could not infect modern Catholics with our *disease* and where deprivation of liturgical necessities prevailed (e.g., priests who could read Latin), it became obvious that our presence in the diocese was barely tolerated and expected to wither away in due time. It also became apparent that the problems this particular Latin Mass community faced were a microcosm of those that others throughout the universal Church experienced, as the modern hierarchy has patiently awaited Vatican II resistance groups to complete the assimilation process into the modern structure of the Church and the remaining holdouts to flatline.

My journey through traditional Catholicism came to an abrupt halt one particular evening after carefully reading a debate between a Sedevacantist and a Vatican II Catholic. For whatever reason it was at this time that I had my epiphany moment: *both sides were wrong and right.* Most importantly I saw the reason as being that the "true" Catholic Church promulgated contradictory doctrines, some of which qualified as infallible.

I did not see Vatican II in the proper context until I began to understand that the Catholic Church could actually contradict itself and remain the Catholic Church. With this understanding I began to speculate on the possibility that some of the changes of Vatican II may have been intended, at least initially, to correct the Church's gradual departure from orthodoxy over the course of a millennium, particularly concerning the papacy and Rome's propensity to complicate the Church with cumbersome laws and dogmatic formulas.[2] Moreover, because I now understood that the Catholic Church could contradict itself, other controversies began to make sense, including those predating Vatican II.

The present writing began as a series of letters to acquaintances involved in the Sedevacantist movement during the period when I had begun to openly question the movement's tenability. The first of those letters explaining my decision to leave the Sedevacantist movement and

---

[2] Traditional Catholics often say, "Either the Church was right for two thousand years until Vatican II or else the Church was wrong all along, and Vatican II corrected it." In reality the Church was wrong and right throughout its history.

return to the Church of Rome carried a theme—"the Church is still the Church"—that drew impassioned criticism from the Sedevacantist crowd I had mingled with. Convinced that I was correct, I was driven to continue building on that premise, which eventually formed the substance of objection one on the indefectibility of the Church and the analogy to the Barque of Peter.

Throughout this writing project, several factors kept me motivated to see it through to completion. First, I wanted to answer my own question: What drove me from the Vatican II Church, where I had belonged since my youth, into the dark underworld of traditional Catholicism, then back to the modern Church of Rome and finally to where I am today? Having changed my position on a matter previously declared with certainty and for which I was willing to sacrifice many important things, I felt this deserved an explanation.

Today I wish to impart to the reader that I was correct on both sides of the divide and simultaneously wrong. What exactly do I mean when I say I was right and wrong on each side of the divide? I mean it is correct to say that from a Sedevacantist perspective, the post–Vatican II Church is not the true Catholic Church on the grounds that it has excommunicated itself for heresy, yet it is quite wrong to say that the post–Vatican II Church is not the Catholic Church on the grounds that it cannot be anything else. In fact a Vatican II controversy can never be satisfactorily resolved so that one side irrefutably proves it is not contradictory because each side *is* contradictory, which renders both vulnerable to their opponents' refutations and debunking. Hence it is not the credibility of Catholics who discover they must change their positions while attempting to navigate the Vatican II dichotomy that one should question but rather the credibility of those Catholics who do not.

And so the answer to my question—what drove me to hold more than one position in this controversial debate on Vatican II?—is that an earnest search for an infallible and indefectible Catholic Church turns up contradictions on all sides. Today I have no doubt that the reason is that such a Church never existed.

Contrary to the Sedevacantist thesis I had previously championed, it is my present conviction that the modern Church, headed by Pope Francis, is in fact the real Roman Catholic Church. There is no such thing as a "real" Roman Catholic Church prior to Vatican II as distinct from a "false" Roman Catholic Church presently ruling the Roman See and its corresponding dioceses throughout the world. Even so, it is not my interest to defend the Vatican II Church from the Sedevacantists' accusations of heresy and apostasy. I am not an apologist for the modern regime in Rome any more than I am for the Sedevacantists. I am a critic of both.

My second interest in writing on this subject was to retrace the road map I followed to arrive at my conclusions. This will allow critics an opportunity to challenge my ideas and like-minded thinkers to expand on them. Supporters of either side who believe they can refute my conclusions are welcome to have a go at it. I maintain that what will emerge in the process is precisely what I have already stated: Each side can effectively debunk the other side. Still, as my conclusions are no more infallible than the Church I criticize, I must remain open minded to opposing viewpoints. In that, I believe, there is far more to gain from approaching this subject than there is to lose, and that also applies to my readers.

Unlike the Sedevacantists, who remain convinced God will eventually exonerate their side and see them unto victory, I hold no expectations that God will sanction my conclusions, nor do I have expectations that what I write will transform a single person, let alone the world. But self-assurance of God's approval and changing the way the world works are not ambitions of mine; my ambition is only to remain true to myself. That I can no longer side with the Sedevacantists or the post–Vatican II Church is because they both fall short of what they claim themselves to be—the real manifestation of an infallible and indefectible Church.

Initially, one of the more difficult aspects about writing on this subject was deciding whether I really wanted to tangle with the Sedevacantists in their ecclesiastical arena again.[3] In choosing to do so, I am reentering a world that is not even real, yet it is comprised of people who perceive it is real to such an extent that only martyrdom or a miracle is all their future holds. Obviously, then, our stakes in this matter are worlds apart, yet I still felt a need to confront and inter an antiquated and, in some cases, dangerous ideology that has consumed some of the most promising years of my life. I doubt that I am the only former Sedevacantist to wish he knew then what he knows now. Having said that, I also recognize that most Sedevacantists are good people forced into a theological dead end through no fault of their own and who remain in desperate need of a way out that does not necessitate espousing contradictions. I know this because I was one of them.

I can attest to how painful it is to learn that important things we uphold and value are based on myths. Contradictions discovered in an idealized belief system result in cognitive dissonance. If the stress does not serve its intended purpose as a defense mechanism and trigger a necessary confrontation of and process of deconstructing illusions, irrational thinking is bound to follow. One example of irrational thinking I will emphasize in this work is that all Sedevacantists deny the *possibility* of a defection of the Church while simultaneously proving that a defection has occurred *in fact*. Their confusion is the consequence of recognizing a clear defection of the Church while "knowing" it could never happen. However, once a defection has been proven, there are no countertheories that can be proposed and no movements that can save the Church.

Is it correct to say the Sedevacantists have successfully proven a defection of the post–Vatican II Church? In my opinion, yes. Traditional Catholicism in all of its forms and variations, most especially

---

3 It has been fifty years since Vatican II, and the Sedevacantists are understandably desperate and frustrated. On one hand the contradictory and untenable aspects of their position back them into a corner, and on the other hand the Catholic majority discounts even the noncontradictory and tenable aspects of their position. These factors, combined with the perception that infallible truth and eternal damnation are at stake, can see a debate with a Sedevacantist quickly regress into a personal affair.

Sedevacantism, has proven the defection of the Roman Catholic Church, but no Catholic can admit this because to do so would expose the Church's fallibility and undermine a fundamental belief system that is perceived to be vital to their existence.[4] That is why the Sedevacantists had to base their arguments upon a theory of two Churches: an apostate Church in Rome and themselves. The supposition of the two Churches allows the Sedevacantists to perpetuate their belief system in spite of Rome's defection.

This phenomenon bears similarities to *splitting* in cases of child abuse, when a child creates two versions of an abusive primary caregiver in order to fulfill a fundamental need to believe he or she is loved. As there is, of course, only one real version of the parent, splitting is only a defense mechanism that allows the abused child to avoid the painful reality of the situation. Here, the Sedevacantists need the illusion of another Roman Catholic Church to offset the painful reality of defection of the real one. What Sedevacantists must come to understand is identical to what adult children who have been abused must come to understand: Neither needs the illusion to survive anymore.

When considering the contradictions of Sedevacantism that I will expose here, it should become apparent that when doctrinal controversies arose following Vatican II, traditional Catholics did not ask the right questions or look for answers in the right places. For example, what if arriving at the correct conclusions on matters pertaining to contradictions between infallible doctrine A and infallible doctrine B is not an either/or process after all? What if arriving at the correct answer is

---

4 Though reduced to insignificance in the post–Conciliar Church, one of the difficult emotions with which traditional Catholics must constantly contend is fear—above all, fear of a vengeful God who will punish them for their failures. It may help to consider that if any religious system from which dogmatic beliefs derive is demonstrably contradictory (i.e., fallible), fear should begin to diminish. I submit that *any* Church that contradicts itself even once in matters pertaining to its self-ascribed infallibility automatically forfeits credibility. Vatican II was a "get out of jail free" card for the Catholic faithful, but traditional Catholics opted instead to uphold the infallibility myth. The infallibility myth is directly responsible for heightened states of fear and anxiety among traditional Catholics because it demands that they espouse contradictions in order to preserve an idealistic conception of the Church and secure God's favor.

really contingent upon the truthfulness or falsity of infallibility itself? Unfortunately the Church does not allow the Sedevacantists to question its infallibility, which makes it impossible to reconcile their theory with the Church's own doctrines of infallibility and indefectibility without stepping into other contradictions. Only if one is not restricted to forming conclusions with the presupposition of the Church's infallibility and indefectibility can one avoid these contradictions.

Unfortunately Catholics have selective memories. While traditional Catholics rightfully criticize Vatican II Catholics for failing to realize that the Church did not suddenly begin with Vatican II, they in turn deserve criticism for failing to realize that Vatican II was not the first time Rome assumed a prerogative to change previously defined doctrines of the faith and got away with it. For example, let us never forget that it was the *Roman branch* of the Catholic Church that added the *filioque*[5] clause to the Nicene Creed *after* it had been formulated in ecumenical councils. We must ask the question: How could

---

5 *Filioque* (Ecclesiastical Latin: [fili'ɔkwe]), Latin for "and (from) the Son," is a phrase included in some forms of the Nicene Creed but not others and which has been the subject of great controversy between Eastern and Western Churches. The controversial phrase is shown here in italics: "We believe in the Holy Spirit, the Lord, the giver of life, who proceeds from the Father *and the Son*, who with the Father and the Son is adored and glorified." Whether one includes that phrase, and exactly how the phrase is translated and understood, can have important implications for how one understands the central Christian doctrine of the Holy Trinity. To some the phrase implies a serious underestimation of the Father's role in the Trinity; to others denial of what it expresses implies a serious underestimation of the role of the Son in the Trinity. Over time the phrase became a symbol of conflict between East and West, although (see below) there have been attempts at resolving the conflict. Among the early attempts at harmonization are the works of Maximus the Confessor, who notably was sainted independently by both Eastern and Western Churches. The filioque is included in the form of the Niceno-Constantinopolitan Creed used in most Western Christian Churches since at least the 6th century. It was accepted by the popes only in 1014 and is rejected by the Eastern Orthodox Church and Oriental Orthodox Churches. It was not in the Greek text of this Creed, attributed to the Second Ecumenical Council (the First Council of Constantinople), which says that the Holy Spirit proceeds "from the Father" without additions of any kind, such as "and the Son" or "alone." ("Filioque," last modified November 12, 2014, http://en.wikipedia.org/w/index.php?title=Filioque&oldid=599606019.)

the members of these holy councils not have formulated such an important doctrine correctly and completely under the guidance of the Holy Ghost? Moreover, if the early ecumenical councils did not receive something as important as the creed of faith correctly or in its entirety then how are Roman Catholics to know with certainty that they have it now?

The early Church surely thought they had the creed right, and even as late as the ninth Century Pope Leo III censured the addition of the filioque.[6] Because the Catholic Church later formally adopted the filioque as an article of faith, who can say with certainty that in five hundred years henceforth Her Holiness, Pope Mary Magdalene III, will not declare that the Holy Ghost proceeds from the Father, Son, Holy Ghost, and Blessed Virgin Mary? The point is if Rome had the power to change an article of the faith way back then, let the Sedevacantists do a better job of explaining why Rome did not have that same power to change constant teachings of the faith at Vatican II, for such doctrinal changes are essentially the same in principle. In each case the living Roman magisterium claimed the power to alter what a prior magisterium had declared and did so. Furthermore, in both cases, Catholics who disagreed with Rome became known as heretics and schismatics.

A more recent example of a mutation of a previously defined doctrine that predates Vatican II involved a controversy between Jesuit

---

6 The interpolation in the creed had, nevertheless, some advocates, who, five years later, proposed, in a council Aix-la-Chapelle, to solemnly authorize the Filioque. They met with opposition, and it was decided to refer the question to Rome. Leo III was then Pope. He compromised the matter. Without positively rejecting the doctrine of the procession from the Father and from the Son, he censured the addition made to the creed. He even saw fit to transmit to posterity his protest against any innovation by having the creed engraved upon two tablets of silver that were hung in St. Peter's Church, and under which was written the following inscription: "I, Leo, have put up these tablets for the love and preservation of the orthodox faith." [Abbé Guettée, *The Papacy: Its Historic Origin and Primitive Relations with the Eastern Churches* (Blanco, TX: New Sarov Press, 1866), 329.]

theologian Father Leonard Feeney[7,8] and Rome regarding the Church's well-known dogma *extra Ecclesiam nulla salus*[9] that erupted in the 1950s. To his credit Father Feeney was one of the first to recognize that the dogmatic formula on who could be saved had softened in latter centuries and taken on an entirely new meaning in the decades leading up to Vatican II. The central issue of the controversy concerned whether the sacrament of baptism as celebrated with real and natural water was *absolutely* necessary for salvation. Fr. Feeney held the affirmative position in accordance with specific canons "infallibly" decreed by the Council of Trent as well as the explicit words of Jesus in the Gospel of John,[10] but Rome derailed him. The problem was that the Church had long since promulgated other doctrines that allowed substitutions for the actual sacrament of baptism. In order to explain the Church's gradual mutation of infallible teachings while ostensibly preserving the Roman system, Father Feeney was forced to name an enemy—"liberals"—and a new cult movement that many referred to as "Feeneyites" began. The zealous movement persists in various forms to the present day.

---

7 Father Leonard Edward Feeney (February 18, 1897–January 30, 1978) was a US Jesuit priest, poet, lyricist, and essayist. He articulated and defended a strict interpretation of the Roman Catholic doctrine *extra Ecclesiam nulla salus* ("outside the Church there is no salvation"). He took the position that baptism of blood and baptism of desire are unavailing and that therefore no non-Catholics will be saved. Fighting against what he perceived to be the liberalization of Catholic doctrine, he came under ecclesiastical censure. ("Leonard Feeney," last modified November 11, 2014, http://en.wikipedia.org/w/index.php?title=Leonard_Feeney&oldid=602557677.)

8 Father Feeney was an extraordinary priest. History recounts how he lived with great zeal for the Catholic Church, preached the Gospel in crowded streets, and fearlessly called out the enemies of the Catholic Church by name. Father Feeney inspired countless Catholics with his strong faith and helped solidify a Catholic identity in an increasingly secular world. To Feeney the purpose and necessity of the Church and membership through the saving font of baptism were ideals of the highest and most urgent importance. Today the Church in Rome considers "going green" and recycling plastics of that same caliber, and deems priests such as Father Feeney fanatical, bigoted, and anti-Semitic.

9 Latin phrase meaning "outside the Church there is no salvation."

10 "Jesus answered: Amen, amen I say to thee, unless a man be born again of water and the Holy Ghost, he cannot enter into the kingdom of God." (John 3:5)

The persistence of the Feeneyites among today's traditional Catholics compels a nonbiased answer to the question "was Father Feeney right?" In a similar fashion to Vatican II's clash with Sedevacantism, the doctrine of infallibility takes center stage. Like both sides in the Vatican II controversy, Father Feeney was indeed right...and simultaneously wrong.[11] To understand this more clearly, one must realize that the maker of the rules (the Church) is not always obliged to play by them. Although it is historically infrequent, at times the Church can and does contradict itself but always remains the Church. It is important to understand that when contradictions in teachings do occur (e.g., Vatican II), the final arbiter of any ensuing debates is not a prior magisterial teaching, nor is it the precise wording of a dogmatic formula, as many among today's Sedevacantists incorrectly believe. The final arbiter of all controversies is the *living* Roman Catholic magisterium, irrespective of any departures it may take from past magisterial teachings, infallible or not. And so the most relevant question one can ask is not "which side contradicted the Roman Catholic Church?" but rather "which side is the only side that allows one to remain a member of the Roman Catholic Church?" As Father Feeney learned the hard way, and, as we shall see later, as applies equally to the Sedevacantists, the answer is always that side that stands with Rome and its appointed bishop.

Although the Church's gradual expansion of its salvation formula so as to include heretics, schismatics, and unbaptized non-Christians

---

11 Any of the following sources is a good starting place to understand why both sides of the baptism controversy are correct: *Outside the Catholic Church There Is Absolutely No Salvation* by Brother Peter Dimond (www.mostholyfamilymonastery.com); Griff Ruby's refutation of the aforementioned book (www.the-pope.com/BOB_BOD_BOK.html); and Fr. Cekada's article "Baptism of Desire and Theological Principles" (www.traditionalmass.org/images/articles/BaptDes-Proofed.pdf). Again, the Church's so-called "infallibility" is the culprit that precludes a definitive resolution to the debate. For example, the Church could not infallibly declare that the sacrament of baptism is necessary for salvation on one hand while infallibly teaching that the sacrament of baptism is not always necessary on the other. Errors such as this have forced theologians to play the part of double-talking lawyers and politicians, in this case by defining "necessary" according to degrees. If infallibility were not a myth, the Church's "infallible" organs would remain consistent, and its doctrines would always square up.

officially culminated with the documents of the Second Vatican Council, "liberals" were only a scapegoat for the transgression of the dogma that required actual membership in the Roman Catholic Church for salvation. The truth is that long before Father Feeney's time, the Church itself promulgated contradictory doctrines by way of ecumenical councils and its ordinary magisterium,[12] each of which is an organ of the Church's infallibility. Thus the infamous twentieth-century Boston controversy concerning one of the Church's fundamental dogmas was already in the making several centuries before Father Feeney's time; it was only a matter of where, when, and by whom it would be exposed. Predictably that individual would take the fall. Failing the ultimate test of obedience, Father Feeney was a victim of a flawed system and became martyred on its altar of infallibility.

Tragic stories such as Father Feeney's will persist for as long as Roman Catholics remain blind to their real causes. This will necessitate a constant supply of enemies on whom to lay blame for the sins of the Church. Liberals, Jews, Freemasons, progressives, Communists, bureaucrats, and modernists are all examples of scapegoats traditional Catholics use today in order to protect the system. Despite all evidence pointing directly to a *fallible* magisterium as the real culprit for Vatican II's contradictions and heresies, those who cannot come to terms with this explanation would sooner sacrifice canonized popes and ecumenical councils than let go of their idealisms. Splinter the Catholic Church into a thousand warring factions if they

---

12 The bishops exercise their infallible teaching power in an ordinary manner when they, in their dioceses, in moral unity with the Pope, unanimously promulgate the same teachings on faith and morals. The Vatican Council expressly declared that also the truths of Revelation proposed as such by the ordinary and general teaching office of the Church are to be firmly held with "divine and catholic faith" (d 1792). But the incumbents of the ordinary and general teaching office of the Church are the members of the whole episcopate scattered over the whole Earth. The agreement of the bishops in doctrine may be determined from the catechisms issued by them, from their pastoral letters, from the prayer books approved by them, and from the resolutions of particular synods. A morally general agreement suffices, but in this the express or tacit assent of the Pope, as the Supreme Head of the Episcopate, is essential. [Ludwig Ott, *Fundamentals of Catholic Dogma*, 2nd ed. (Cork, Ireland: The Mercier Press, Limited, 1957), 300.]

must—whatever it takes, just as long as the system itself is never acknowledged as being at fault. With the advent of Sedevacantism, this has all come to pass.

The architects of the Vatican II revolution provided the faithful with an excellent opportunity to see their Church for what it is and always has been, but the Sedevacantists chose instead to exchange one illusion for another. Fueled by desperation to protect and perpetuate a romanticized perception of the Church, the Sedevacantists are not about to concede the hard truth that certain tenets of Roman Catholicism were officially discontinued by the *true* Roman Catholic Church in virtue of the twenty-first ecumenical council. Eventually they will have to accept this if they hope to remove the tag of schism. If they refuse, a hundred years from now their successors will be viewed as the Old Catholics continue to be viewed by Rome today—as a schismatic group that broke away from the Holy See in a prior century. To avoid this outcome Sedevacantists should accept the Church for what it really is—fallible—or else consider another religion. For what it is worth, the Sedevacantists are not the first Catholics to experience betrayal from Rome…not by a long shot. Nor will they be the last.

Another reason for embarking on this writing project was my interest in Vatican II Catholics and the council's overall implications to their Church. After all this Church is where I belonged most of my life. While I am no longer compelled to challenge peaceful Vatican II Catholics content with the modern Church with the heresies they are now forced to espouse, the fact is many modern Catholics will eventually find their way into the Vatican II controversy, just as I did. Even if the subject matter of traditional Catholicism and Sedevacantism is still unfamiliar territory for the modern faithful under Pope Francis, those who do elect to read this should discover there is something in it for them. Anyone who identifies himself or herself as Catholic has an interest in Vatican II as the threshold between the *old* Church and the *new* Church whether or not they realize it. Engaging this subject should provide modern Catholics with solid doctrinal reasons why the Sedevacantists are quite wrong to accuse them of not being Roman Catholics anymore. However, before taking comfort in the fact and proceeding to scoff at the Sedevacantists, they should quickly realize why they are anything but in the clear.

To begin with, inquisitive Vatican II Catholics who have begun deeper searches for answers about their Church should be careful not to dismiss the Sedevacantists before attempting to understand what they believe and why they even exist.[13] The fact is the Sedevacantists have a legitimate basis for many of the theological and moral positions they hold, and they deserve to be taken seriously. To treat this important movement flippantly simply because Sedevacantists are small in numbers or because they stand in opposition to popular post–Conciliar popes is an affront to their extraordinary Catholic devotion and love for the Church. With this understanding, perhaps the Sedevacantists' greatest fault lies in having believed too much. When one delves into the Vatican II controversy with a genuine openness to understand it, he or she cannot fail to see why traditional Catholicism persists today and why traditional Catholics ought to be commended for defending their perception of the "true" Church. In fact certain groups like the Sedevacantists have been so effective in exposing the post–Vatican II Church's contradictions that it should be difficult, if not impossible, for the Catholic faithful to look at the Church in the same way again. As long as Sedevacantism persists,

---

13 In most cases Vatican II Catholics are no match for the Sedevacantists doctrinally. The Sedevacantists' mastery of Church teachings before Vatican II, combined with the strengths of the Sedevacantist thesis, has secured many conversions to the Sedevacantist cause throughout the years. For that reason I would be remiss to write about this subject without issuing a warning that many if not all Sedevacantist groups meet the criteria of being mind-control cults to one degree or another, and the dangers typically associated with cults are every bit as real throughout traditional Catholicism as can be found anywhere. The reason for the strong tendency toward cultlike circumstances among the various Sedevacantist sects is that there is no recognized, regulatory authority in Rome—each Sedevacantist is his or her own authority. Lack of authority invites a host of problems including abuses, bizarre practices, and antiquated thinking. Some examples include administering the sacrament of confession via the telephone, backwards walking in chapels, foregoing medical care and criminal justice for excorcisms, and brainwashing techniques to reinforce loyalty and compliance. Vatican II Catholics who choose to learn about Sedevacantism are warned to keep a healthy distance from the various Sedevacantist sects; the answers they ultimately seek will not be discovered there. However, understanding Sedevacantism can be an important means to an end.

more and more Vatican II Catholics will be forced to come to terms with the fact that the Catholic Church has been caught contradicting itself. Just a few examples should suffice to demonstrate the sort of doctrinal contradictions that necessitated the creation of a resistance movement in the first place.

I have already touched on one of the Church's important doctrinal transitions pertaining to the dogma *extra Ecclesiam nulla salus* (outside the Church there is no salvation), exposed by Father Feeney just prior to Vatican II. Let us briefly return to that dogma by considering the following authoritative, pre–Vatican II teaching and recognizing its unmistakable transition in our times, specifically with respect to the requirements necessary for salvation and also with what constitutes the unity of the Catholic Church:

> It (the Roman Catholic Church) firmly believes, professes, and proclaims that those not living within the Catholic Church, not only pagans, but also Jews and heretics and schismatics cannot become participants in eternal life, but will depart "into everlasting fire which was prepared for the devil and his angels," (Matt 25: 41), unless before the end of life the same have been added to the flock; and that the unity of the ecclesiastical body is so strong that only to those remaining in it are the sacraments of the Church of benefit for salvation, and do fastings, almsgiving and other functions of piety and exercises of Christian service produce eternal reward, and that no one, whatever almsgiving he has practiced, even if he has shed blood for the name of Christ, can be saved, unless he has remained in the bosom and unity of the Catholic Church.[14]

The above is an excerpt from the papal bull *Cantate Domino*, authored by Pope Eugene IV in AD 1444 at the Council of Florence, and it qualifies as an infallible declaration (i.e., dogmatic). According to the nature

---

14 Henry Denzinger, *The Sources of Catholic Dogma* (Fitzwilliam, NH: Herder & Co., 1954), sec. 714.

of dogmatic truths, this declaration is immutable, which means it cannot change throughout the course of centuries, nor may it be understood any differently today than at the time of its declaration. In simple layman's terms, the Council of Florence declared that one must be an actual member of the Roman Catholic Church to be saved and that even martyrdom for Jesus Christ is insufficient for salvation in and of itself.[15] Try as they might, it is difficult even for the most skilled modern Catholic apologists to deny that the Church teaches something very different today, particularly concerning salvation for Jews and members of other non-Christian religions.

Let us now have a look at one of Vatican II's more controversial documents, *Lumen Gentium*, to understand how the dogma "outside the Church there is no salvation" officially mutated by the addition of a few choice words:

"Therefore, those could not be saved who refuse either to enter the Church, or to remain in it, *while knowing* that it was founded by God through Christ as required for salvation."[16] [Italics added.]

The new catechism of the Catholic Church followed suit with this explanation of the dogma "outside the Church there is no salvation": "Hence they could not be saved who, *knowing* that the Catholic Church

---

15 Prior to Vatican II, Pope Pius XII explained what constitutes actual membership in the Roman Catholic Church in his encyclical letter *Mystici Corporis Christi*: "Actually only those are to be included as members of the Church who have been baptized and profess the true faith, and who have not been so unfortunate as to separate themselves from the unity of the Body, or been excluded by legitimate authority for grave faults committed. 'For in one spirit' says the Apostle, 'were we all baptized into one Body, whether Jews or Gentiles, whether bond or free.' As therefore in the true Christian community there is only one Body, one Spirit, one Lord, and one Baptism, so there can be only one faith. And therefore if a man refuse to hear the Church let him be considered—so the Lord commands—as a heathen and a publican. It follows that those are divided in faith or government cannot be living in the unity of such a Body, nor can they be living the life of its one Divine Spirit." [Pius XII, "*Mystici Corporis Christi* (On the Mystical Body of Christ)," in *The Papal Encyclicals* (Raleigh: McGrath Publishing Company, 1981), 41.]
16 Vatican Council II, "*Lumen Gentium* (Dogmatic Constitution on the Church)," in *Vatican Council II: the Basic Sixteen Documents*, ed. Austin Flannery (Northport, NY: Costello, 1996), 20.

was founded as necessary by God through Christ, would refuse either to enter it or to remain in it."[17] [Italics added.]

As can be seen, the Church simply added new language to the dogmatic formula that many recognize as being irreconcilable with the infallible and immutable declaration from the Council of Florence.[18] Not only does the new language alter Cantate Domino's unambiguous meaning, but it is an illogical addition, for obviously, "whosoever would refuse to enter into the Church or to remain in it" could also be considered "unknowing that it was founded as necessary by God through Christ." This could include *all* non-Catholics (i.e., those who leave the Church as well as those who never entered it).

Whereas Cantate Domino can be seen as an *all-exclusive* salvation doctrine, *Lumen Gentium* should be seen as an *all-inclusive* doctrine of salvation that opened the door wide to the post–Conciliar concepts of universal salvation and a new ecumenism. Only now, thanks to the Internet and traditional Catholicism, are authoritative teachings like Cantate Domino being introduced to Vatican II Catholics, many for the very first time. What often follows is a great deal of embarrassment on the part of modern Catholics that their Church once taught something so strict and cold hearted, especially in light of the so-called "Spirit of Vatican II." But there is much more.

Arguably, no single document has done more to undermine the Roman Catholic Church and its authority than Vatican II's Decree on Ecumenism and the so-called *ecumenical movement*[19] as championed by the

---

17 *Catechism of the Catholic Church*, 2nd ed., 846.

18 The new language effectively redefined who could be considered members of the Church (i.e., anyone) even if a person rejects fundamental tenets of the Catholic faith (e.g., the papacy, real presence of Jesus through the consecration of bread and wine, etc.).

19 Ecumenism is an interdenominational initiative aimed at greater Christian unity or cooperation. The term is used predominantly by and with reference to Christian denominations and Christian Churches separated by doctrine, history, and practice. Within this particular context, ecumenism is the idea of a Christian unity in the literal meaning: that there should be a single Church. ("Ecumenism," last modified November 24, 2014, http://en.wikipedia.org/w/index.php?title=Ecumenism&oldid=617151791.)

post–Conciliar popes. What is important to realize is that the magisterium had previously condemned Vatican II's version of ecumenism and even considered the ecumenical movement's prescribed activities mortally sinful.

Why did the Church previously condemn these ideas and practices? Because according to the teaching of the pre–Vatican II Church, Christ founded exactly one faith, one baptism, one Church, and *they are it*. The Church taught that it alone possessed the truth and that any participation in false worship was to deny or at least compromise that truth and offend God. The Church was also mindful that participation in interdenominational faith activities would unnecessarily expose the faithful to a myriad of heretical doctrines and false worship that could pose grave dangers to their faith. The concept of Roman Catholics participating in interfaith services among Christians from dozens of denominations that teach contradictory and heretical doctrines and non-Christian religions *used to be* unthinkable. But all of this changed with Vatican II. In fact many Sedevacantists have argued that the new ecumenism was the real purpose for the Second Vatican Council and that the ecumenical Church that emerged from it has overshadowed the real Roman Catholic Church of the ages.

Modern Catholics who are inclined to doubt my assertions and who are genuinely interested in reading what the constant teaching of the Catholic Church *was* on the subject of religious unity and ecumenism prior to Vatican II are invited to read Pope Pius XI's brilliant encyclical *Mortalium Animos*,[20,21] penned in 1928, and compare that with Vatican II's Decree on Ecumenism—*Unitatis Redintegratio*,[22] authored only thirty-six

---

20 *Mortalium Animos* is a papal encyclical letter promulgated in 1928 by Pope Pius XI on religious unity, condemning certain presumptions of the early ecumenical movement. ("Mortalium Animos," last modified August 5, 2014, http://en.wikipedia.org/w/index.php?title=Mortalium_Animos&oldid=550013375.)

21 "Mortalium Animos," Papal Encyclicals Online, accessed April 29, 2015, http://www.papalencyclicals.net/Pius11/P11MORTA.HTM.

22 *Unitatis Redintegratio* is the Second Vatican Council's Decree on Ecumenism. The title in Latin means "restoration of unity," which in itself has been a cause for contention with traditional Catholics, who point out that the constant teaching of the Church is that Christian unity is already inherent and whole in the Catholic Church and therefore could never need restoration. See *Mortalium Animos* in the appendix.

years later. How one can possibly engage such a comparative study and come away unconvinced of the Church's about-face on its own perennial teachings[23] would exemplify man's extraordinary capacity to deceive himself. Readers will find the short papal encyclical *Mortalium Animos* included in the appendix.

The new ecumenism bred a slippery slope of doctrinal heresies such as a new concept of Christian unity—*partial or imperfect communion*—with the Church of Christ.[24,25] Because of this novel teaching, *anyone* can now be considered a member of the Roman Catholic Church—even if they reject many of the Church's infallible dogmas. Yet according to pre-

---

23 Consider the following lesson found in a widely distributed catechism prior to Vatican II:
> 205. How does a Catholic sin against faith?
> A Catholic sins against faith by apostasy, heresy, indifferentism, and by taking part in non-Catholic worship.
> 206. Why does a Catholic sin against faith by taking part in non-Catholic worship?
> A Catholic sins against faith by taking part in non-Catholic worship when he intends to identify himself with a religion he knows is defective. *This is why I was born,* and why I have come into the world, to bear witness to the truth. Everyone who is of the truth hears my voice. (John 18:37) ["The First Commandment of God," Catholicity.com, accessed March 14, 2015, http://www.catholicity.com/baltimore-catechism/lesson16.html.]

Who can reconcile the Catechism with Vatican II's ecumenism? Should Catholics who took their catechisms to heart not be confused, resistant, or angry? More importantly, can a sin that is deemed mortal to the soul suddenly become a virtue? If so then what would preclude the same for sins such as homosexuality, artificial contraception, or adultery?

24 *Unitatis Redintegratio #3* states: "But in subsequent centuries much more serious dissentions appeared and large communities became separated from *full communion* with the Catholic Church...For those who believe in Christ and have been properly baptized are put in some, *though imperfect, communion* with the Catholic Church." [Emphasis added.] [Vatican Council II, " *Unitatis Redintegratio* (Decree on Ecumenism)," in *Vatican Council II: the Basic Sixteen Documents*, ed. Austin Flannery (Northport, NY: Costello, 1996), 502.]

25 "The Church has many reasons for knowing that it is joined to the baptized who are honored by the name of Christian, but do not profess the faith in its entirety or have not preserved unity of communion under the successor of Peter." (Vatican Council II, *Lumen Gentium*, 20–21.)

Vatican II teaching, there is no such a thing as unity that is not whole and entire. Either one was fully in the Catholic Church or fully out; there was no in-between or partial state of membership.

Let us read how Pope Leo XIII explained this in his encyclical letter, *Satis Cognitum*:

> Every revealed truth, without exception, must be accepted.
> 9. The Church, founded on these principles and mindful of her office, has done nothing with greater zeal and endeavour than she has displayed in guarding the integrity of the faith. Hence she regarded as rebels and expelled from the ranks of her children all who held beliefs on any point of doctrine different from her own. The Arians, the Montanists, the Novatians, the Quartodecimans, the Eutychians, did not certainly reject all Catholic doctrine: they abandoned only a certain portion of it. Still who does not know that they were declared heretics and banished from the bosom of the Church? In like manner were condemned all authors of heretical tenets who followed them in subsequent ages. "There can be nothing more dangerous than those heretics who admit nearly the whole cycle of doctrine, and yet by one word, as with a drop of poison, infect the real and simple faith taught by our Lord and handed down by Apostolic tradition."

The practice of the Church has always been the same, as is shown by the unanimous teaching of the Fathers, who were wont to hold as outside Catholic communion, and alien to the Church, whoever would recede in the least degree from any point of doctrine proposed by her authoritative Magisterium. Epiphanius, Augustine, Theodore:, drew up a long list of the heresies of their times. St. Augustine notes that other heresies may spring up, to a single one of which, should any one give his assent, he is by the very fact cut off from Catholic unity. "No one who merely disbelieves in all (these heresies) can for that reason regard himself as a Catholic or call himself one. For there may be or may arise some other heresies, which are not set out in this work of ours, and, if any one holds to one single one of these he is not a Catholic."[26]

The consequences of Vatican II's *Lumen Gentium* and *Unitatis Redintegratio* should be clear to all who have eyes to see. Membership in the one true Church founded by Christ is no longer understood as necessary for salvation, as was declared by the Council of Florence, but rather only a matter of personal preference. The outcome of Vatican II's watered-down doctrines is religious indifferentism (i.e., one Church is as good as another Church)[27] and fragmented Catholic identities.

Vatican II should also explain the epidemic phenomenon known as *cafeteria Catholicism*.[28] No longer are Catholics required to submit to the Church's authoritative teachings, and no longer are they considered heretics for denying them, provided they fully accept Vatican II. Is it any wonder, then, that so many among today's Catholics feel at liberty to disagree with the Church on any number of issues yet consider themselves Roman Catholics in good standing? This is not their fault; it is the direct consequence of the "infallible" magisterium leading by example. Since Vatican II everyone, regardless of what they believe or practice, is welcomed at the Lord's Supper; this is unprecedented teaching in the history of Roman Catholicism and overtly contradictory to the Church's past teachings as explicated in councils, papal encyclicals, canon law, and catechisms distributed to the faithful for several centuries. There are numerous other examples of Vatican II's contradictions, but this is

---

26 Leo XIII, "*Satis Cognitum* (Encyclical Letter on the Unity of the Church)," in *The Papal Encyclicals* (Raleigh: McGrath Publishing Co., 1981), 393.
27 See Pope Gregory XVI's encyclical *Mirari Vos* # 13 and 14 for the Church's condemnation of religious indifferentism. ("Mirari Vos," Papal Encyclicals Online, accessed April 29, 2015, http://www.papalencyclicals.net/Greg16/g16mirar.htm.)
28 "A cafeteria Catholic is typically defined as one who picks and chooses what Catholic teaching he wants to believe. Catholics are not free to choose which teachings (on faith and morals) to obey. Even when the Church has not spoken on a matter of faith or morals definitively (infallibly), the faithful must give a religious submission of the intellect and will to its teachings." ("What Is a Cafeteria Catholic?" last modified December 3, 2014, http://www.catholic.com/quickquestions/what-is-a-cafeteria-catholic.)

neither the time nor the place to cite them. All that is important for Vatican II Catholics to know with certainty is that they exist.

Finally I began to realize much deeper personal implications of this writing project only after I commenced. Today, more so than ever, I recognize how my spiritual odyssey has cost me considerably in all aspects of life and that it did not begin or end with Sedevacantism. As I am especially mindful of the foul side of dogmatic religion and its immense sphere of influence, I have found this writing to be remedial and liberating. Nevertheless, recovery from impassioned ideologies such as Sedevacantism can be an arduous and slow-moving process, often accompanied by a feeling of internal emptiness. Such is a likely consequence following all unhealthy attachments, especially those defined by unrealistic expectations and demands. But the disquiet that follows deconstructed illusions must be endured, not relieved by another illusion, for it is the only path to the true self.

What I hope shines through most in this writing is that my loyalty to truth is the engine that drives me, even during those times when I lose sight of it. Invariably such times have been when I surrendered the critically important capacity we humans possess to trust our own instincts and intuitions and freely handed it over to that which is presumed good simply because it claims to represent God. In the search for the truth about the world we live in, there is nothing more important than beginning that search within and about ourselves and learning to trust our innate instincts, which are incapable of lying and deceiving us like ideologies, gurus, and the latest movements often do. In my spiritual journey, few of the people, places, or things who bid for my trust, my time, my sacrifices, my loyalty, and my financial resources ever deserved any of those things and even less possessed the truth I had hoped to discover in return. For the most part, I learned what I needed to know on my own and paid a high premium.

Introduction

Many important things have changed in the Roman Catholic Church because of the Second Vatican Council (1962–1965). Some of the post–Conciliar changes in doctrine, worship, and discipline were supposed to be ineligible for modification or mutation; as a result the traditional Catholic movement was born. From Archbishop Marcel Lefebvre's Society of St. Pius X (SSPX) to independent chapels across the world, traditional Catholic societies and dissident groups have formed for the purpose of preserving the integrity of the Roman Catholic faith that has been severely compromised since Vatican II.

During the past thirty years, no dissident group has assaulted the modern Roman Catholic Church with greater vigor than the Sedevacantists, whose intense scrutiny of everything Catholic has opened a gigantic can of worms that encompasses far more than Vatican II and its popes. The Sedevacantists fall under the larger umbrella of traditional Catholicism,[29] but they stand apart from the traditional mainstream by their claim that the Catholic Church is currently without a legitimate pope. Most Sedevacantists also claim the last six popes, dating to John

---

29 Non-Sedevacantists comprise a large arm of the traditional Catholic movement. Unlike the Sedevacantists most traditional Catholics recognize the legitimacy of the post–Conciliar hierarchy but advocate disobedience and resistance to its authority. The most notorious traditional Catholic society is the Society of St. Pius X (SSPX).

Introduction

XXIII (successor to Pope Pius XII, 1958), have been antipopes[30] fronting what became a *new Church* following Vatican II. The Sedevacantists have assumed the responsibility of defending the "real" Roman Catholic Church (i.e., themselves) against what they perceive as a false Church standing in its place from the local parishes all the way to the Holy See in Rome.[31]

It is important to mention that I do not contest some of the teachings and laws used to support Sedevacantism, for example the 1559 papal bull *Cum ex Apostolatus Officio*[32] as well as the 1917 Code of Canon Law. Consider for a moment that according to the 1917 Code of Canon Law, which remained in effect until John Paul II promulgated the new code in 1983, officials who publicly defect from the Catholic faith automatically forfeit their offices, including the office of the papacy. Canon 188 n.4 reads as follows: "Through tacit resignation, accepted by the law itself, all offices become vacant ipso facto and without any declaration if a cleric:…n.4. Has publicly forsaken the Catholic Faith."[33]

Examples of the Vatican II hierarchy publicly forsaking doctrines of the Church as they had been previously established are legion, yet the Vatican II reforms and popes march unabated into the twenty-first century with more than a billion members, many of whom are enamored with the spirit of Vatican II and the post–Conciliar transformation. For traditional Catholics loyal to the pre–Vatican II teachings of

---

30 Antipope: a false claimant to the Holy See in opposition to the pope canonically elected. There have been more than thirty in the Catholic Church's history. [John Hardon, *Modern Catholic Dictionary* (Garden City, NY: Doubleday and Company, Inc., 1980), 31.] Note: Other sources list approximately forty-one antipopes.
31 For a brief summary of the Sedevacantist position, see Father Cekada's "The Sedevacantist Argument in Brief" in the appendix.
32 *Cum ex Apostolatus Officio* is the name of a papal bull issued by Pope Paul IV on February 15, 1559, as a codification or explication of the ancient Catholic law that only Catholics can be elected Popes, to the exclusion of non-Catholics, including former Catholics who have become public and manifest heretics. ("Cum ex apostolatus officio," Wikipedia, The Free Encyclopedia, last modified October 4, 2013, http://en.wikipedia.org/w/index.php?title=Cum_ex_apostolatus_officio&oldid=575778370.)
33 "Canon 188.4 or Where is the Church," TraditionalMass.org, accessed December 1, 2013, http://www.traditionalmass.org/articles/article.php?id=12&catname=10.

the Church, this is a perplexing phenomenon. To make sense of this, traditional Catholic groups such as the Sedevacantists often look to apocalyptic prophecies, dubious Marian apparitions, and a scriptural reference to a great deception that is to take place near the end of the world that will culminate with the reign of the Antichrist.

Although Vatican II was the immediate cause for the formation of the Sedevacantist movement, a controversy between the Sedevacantists and the Vatican II Church persists fifty years after Vatican II in virtue of the First Vatican Council (1869–1870),[34] not the reforms imposed by Vatican II. Without the First Vatican Council's dogmas on the papacy, such as infallibility, primacy of jurisdiction, and the Roman Pontiff's supreme authority over the whole Church, the Sedevacantist movement as it exists today would have been unnecessary. Instead traditional Catholics could oppose the post–Conciliar reforms without contradicting infallible authority in the same way that US citizens can oppose and protest decisions of their government. However, the First Vatican Council's dogmas on the papacy render all *non-Sedevacantist* traditional Catholic positions against Vatican II and the reigning magisterium obsolete. In other words infallibility is *the* issue, and those who style themselves Sedevacantists are the only traditional Catholic groups that make serious attempts to account for it.[35]

Non-Sedevacantist traditional Catholics who resist Vatican II are overtly contradictory because in essence they are attempting to oppose the Church's infallibility. For one thing most of the Vatican II reforms that traditional Catholics oppose qualify as infallible just by the *ordinary*

---

34 The First Vatican Council (Vatican I) was convoked by Pope Pius IX on June 29, 1868, and it was the twentieth ecumenical council of the Catholic Church. The council is best known for its definition of papal infallibility.
35 Sedevacantist bishop Donald Sanborn satirized the position of non-Sedevacantist traditional Catholics: "The Catholic Church is infallible except when it is wrong." ("Response to Bishop Williamson: On the subject of the vacancy of the Roman See," traditionalmass.org, accessed April 30, 2015, http://www.traditionalmass.org/images/articles/williamson_response.pdf.) Note: The Sedevacantist bishop is quite correct, yet can it really be argued that the Sedevacantist position is any better? "The Catholic Church is indefectible except when it becomes another Church" or "The Catholic Church is indefectible except when heretics embody the Holy See."

universal magisterium[36,37] alone. More importantly the ratification of an ecumenical council by a pope qualifies as an act of papal infallibility, which essentially guarantees that a council is free from error. Because the reigning pope at the time, Paul VI (1963–1978), officially ratified Vatican II, those who resist or reject Vatican II and its reforms must contend with the serious charge of schism from the Holy See.

The Sedevacantists, on the other hand, present what appears to be a solution to the infallibility problem by taking the position that Pope Paul VI was not a true pope and thus lacked authority to ratify Vatican II. In this way Vatican II would have to be considered an invalid council.[38] The Sedevacantists do not agree on whether Pope Paul VI never became the pope[39] or if he lost the papal office at some point because of heresy.[40] Either way Sedevacantists ingeniously attempt to deflect the charge of schism away from themselves and back on the entire Vatican II hierarchy, which continues to acknowledge the validity of Pope Paul VI's papacy, Vatican II, and all of the ensuing post–Conciliar reforms. Thus Sedevacantism effectively avoids certain contradictions of mainstream traditional Catholicism and *appears* to be the most plausible explanation

---

36 "A truth of faith or morals is then infallible by the very fact of being proclaimed by the episcopate in universal agreement as binding, and not only when it is formally declared to be infallible." [Hans Küng, *Infallible? An Inquiry* (Garden City, New York: Doubleday & Company, Inc., 1983), 72.]

37 One of the errors many Catholic apologists commit is downplaying or ignoring the infallibility of the ordinary universal magisterium when the Church flip-flops, errs, or promulgates contradictory teachings. A few historical examples include baptism of desire, geocentrism and Copernicus's cosmology, usury, religious liberty, the new ecumenism, and at least one case where the Church revoked an ancient canonization. In each example it may indeed be said the Catholic Church was infallible—except when it was wrong.

38 Some Catholics may not be aware that the Catholic Church has held seventeen councils that were later deemed illegitimate, the first dating to Antioch in AD 341. Many traditional Catholics remain hopeful that a future Church council will rule Vatican II illegitimate. This is wishful thinking because such a ruling would contradict infallibility of general councils and require espousing at least some tenets of Sedevacantism. But as we shall learn later, the price one must pay for the Sedevacantist solution is the doctrine of indefectibility.

39 A heretic cannot be validly elected to the papacy (*Cum ex Apostolatus Officio*).

40 A heretic cannot retain ecclesiastical office (1917 Code of Canon Law).

for Vatican II and the sweeping changes of the post–Conciliar Church. Nevertheless, as we shall see, Sedevacantism is not without its own contradictions, and many there are.

In order for Sedevacantism to be tenable, it is not sufficient that *some* doctrines and laws of the Church support the theory if *others* repudiate it. If Sedevacantism could be true, it cannot contradict any infallible doctrines and laws of the Church. My objective in this work is to prove that Sedevacantism violates fundamental doctrines of the Church and is therefore a heretical theory. In addition I will propose an alternative explanation to the doctrinal problems the Church has created that does not necessitate espousing the contradictions of both the Sedevacantists and the non-Sedevacantist traditional Catholics. This will entail entertaining the following five premises about the Catholic Church that I hold and upon which this work is based:

1. The Sedevacantists have successfully proven the defection of the Catholic Church at or subsequent to Vatican II.[41]
2. The Church can defect and remain the Church.
3. The post–Vatican II Church is the real Catholic Church, and Francis is the real pope.
4. Infallibility is a myth.
5. The papacy is not the original foundation of the Roman Church.

Francis is indeed the legitimate pope but not because the Sedevacantists' arguments have all failed—rather because the Roman Church says so despite the fact that he is not even a Catholic according

---

[41] Traditional Catholicism has existed in various forms since the close of Vatican II in 1965. The movement has produced an exhaustive array of evidence demonstrating the contradictions and heresies of the post–Vatican II Church. My work is based on numerous years of studying this controversy and the premise that the Sedevacantist movement has inadvertently proven the defection of the Catholic Church. However, I will not present the proofs of the Roman Church's defection in this work. Interested readers may find their time well spent studying traditional Catholicism, Sedevacantism, and post–Vatican II apologetics and decide for themselves whether such proofs exist.

to pre–Vatican II standards of the faith. Therefore the secondary objective of this work is to present my criticisms of the papacy.

By criticizing the papacy, I hope to show the reader a very different perspective of the Vatican II controversy as well as Church history. If Catholics objectively consider criticisms of the papacy without prejudice or bias, they could discover a legitimate way out of their conundrum, which is that regardless of which side of Vatican II they are on they must necessarily espouse numerous contradictions. What I am suggesting is that the real reason the Church called for and implemented contradictory reforms with Vatican II is that the Church is not now, nor has it ever been, the infallible institution it claims to be.

It is my position that the doctrines on the papacy are false, and I believe historical evidence lends support to my belief, especially during the first eight centuries. Although it is far beyond the scope of this work to argue historical proofs against the supremacy of the Roman Pontiff over all Christian Churches or the fallibility of the Church's claim to infallibility, the concept of a Western innovation of the papacy is the key to solving the problem of what really happened to the Catholic Church after Vatican II. By reconsidering the papacy's origin, historical development, and doctrinal contradictions from a non-Catholic perspective, we can discover a more realistic explanation for the controversies between traditional Catholicism and Vatican II. In this way readers will understand how I can use the doctrine of the indefectibility of the Church to disprove Sedevacantism while glossing over how Sedevacantists also use that same doctrine convincingly to support their claims against the Vatican II Church.

Two things stand out from this paradox. First, one of the Church's fundamental doctrines can disprove the legitimacy of the "true" Church from either perspective. For Vatican II Catholics and Sedevacantists, this presents a difficult problem but one that is easily explained when the papacy is recognized as a mythical innovation of the Western Church that gradually evolved over many centuries.

Only a manmade papacy can defect and fail according to its own terms.

Second, just because the doctrine of indefectibility can be used against the legitimacy of the Vatican II Church does not automatically justify Sedevacantism; in fact, as I will demonstrate in chapter one, the doctrine of indefectibility methodically repudiates Sedevacantism. Therefore the fallacious Sedevacantist argument that says "we *must be* the real Church, since the post–Vatican II Church cannot be" is shot down, leaving the Sedevacantists in need of another explanation that does not necessitate contradictions essentially present throughout the entire traditional Catholic movement—which, I contend, will never be found as long as one is confined to search within a rigid, dogmatic system governed by authority that is presumed to be infallible. Although it is not my objective to disprove papal infallibility, the proposition must be entertained if one is sincerely interested in understanding the new face of Roman Catholicism introduced at the Second Vatican Council and its most antagonistic enemy since the Protestant Reformers: the Sedevacantists.

Concerning the five premises of this work, what do they mean for the Sedevacantists and the Catholic Church in general? Simply stated they mean that the only principle of Catholic unity is obedience and submission of the faithful to the living albeit fallible magisterium of their respective age. Consequently, what defines a Roman Catholic is not fidelity to the unchanging faith of the fathers because, as Church history demonstrates, the magisterium may change it, contradict it, or disclaim it at will, all under the pretext of defining and clarifying the original deposit of faith.[42] In reality what defines full membership in the Church[43] is one's submission to the living magisterium in his own time regardless of what it teaches, and *that* is the real lesson Vatican II teaches. By choosing to stand in opposition to the only criterion that really

---

42 The deposit of faith entrusted to the Catholic Church is immutable (except when it changes).

43 According to Vatican II teaching we must now distinguish membership in the Church as partial or full.

Introduction

matters, Sedevacantists are engaged in a fight they can never win—even when they are right.

In 2007 Sedevacantist brothers Frederick and Robert Dimond (aka the Dimond Brothers) began marketing their book *The Truth about What Really Happened to the Catholic Church after Vatican II*. The Dimonds' book is an exhaustive effort condemning Vatican II and the post–Conciliar hierarchy while advancing their particular version of Sedevacantism. Chapter twenty-one of the Dimonds' book is titled "Answers to the Most Common Objections against Sedevacantism,"[44] and it consists of nineteen objections to Sedevacantism in total, followed by the Dimonds' answers to each. For this work I selected four of the nineteen objections to address. My reason for choosing these four in particular is that each pertains to the Church's indefectible, essential constitution and, as such, they closely overlie. Because I am in agreement with each of the stated objections, I refute the Dimonds' answers and expose Sedevacantism's heresies. The four objections to Sedevacantism I chose to address are as follow:

- **Objection one:** The gates of hell cannot prevail against the Church, as Christ said. He said he would be with his Church all days until the end of the world. What you are saying is contrary to the promises of Christ.[45]
- **Objection five:** The Church cannot exist without a pope, or at least it cannot exist for forty years without a pope, as Sedevacantists say.[46]
- **Objection six:** Vatican I's definition of the perpetuity of the papal office contradicts the claims of the Sedevacantists.[47]

---

44 Michael Dimond and Peter Dimond, *The Truth about What Really Happened to the Catholic Church after Vatican II* (Fillmore, NY: Most Holy Family Monastery, 2007), 298–347.
45 Ibid., 298–299.
46 Ibid., 308–310.
47 Ibid., 310–315.

- **Objection fifteen:** The Church and the hierarchy will always be visible. If the Vatican II Church is not the true Catholic Church, then the Church and hierarchy are no longer visible.[48]

Although Sedevacantism involves numerous contradictory positions that will emerge in this work, I have identified five that stand apart as principal heresies. Each of the five heresies I have identified corresponds to each of the four objections stated above. The five principal Sedevacantist heresies are as follow:

1. A defection of the Church occurred in fact (objection one).
2. The Vicar of Christ is accidental to the Church (objection five).
3. "Papacy of desire" is sufficient for membership in and visible unity of the Church (objection six).
4. Visible hierarchical unity is accidental to the Church (objection fifteen).
5. Apostolic authority is accidental to the episcopal order (objection fifteen).

The format the Dimonds employed in response to each objection was to state the objection first and immediately follow it with their answer. In this work I will begin with a brief introduction to the chapter followed by the stated objection and each of our respective answers. Each chapter will end with a summary and an Objections and Answers section. Where merited, I will even incorporate some of the Dimonds' best arguments as objections to which I will respond.

Last, because I am not loyal to either side in the ongoing war waged by traditional Catholics against Vatican II Catholics, I am free to move at will in order to expose each side's weaknesses and contradictions. Although I will argue my points from a Roman Catholic perspective, at times I will switch to an outside perspective such as Eastern Orthodoxy, especially in the Objections and Answers section at the conclusion of

---
48 Ibid., 331–334.

each chapter. An Eastern Orthodox perspective proves to be extremely valuable to the two main subjects of this work, especially when the Sedevacantists attempt to argue that historical events such as Arianism or the Great Western Schism demonstrate a precedent to the Sedevacantist thesis when, more fittingly, these historical events only undermine the papacy.

Similarly an Eastern Orthodox perspective is important when Sedevacantists cite quotations or prophecies they believe support Sedevacantism but that more likely indicate the early Church's ignorance of the divine prerogatives of the papacy that should have been well known since the foundation of the Church. If the later version of the Roman papacy was unknown to the early Catholic Church, and I believe this to be true, inconsistencies and contradictions should be expected to surface. Interested readers are invited to search beyond the present work for a myriad of issues that call into question the legitimacy of the claimed origins of the papacy. For those who do, my hope is they will examine the Eastern Orthodox Church's claims with the same objectivity with which they scrutinize the Vatican II/Sedevacantist controversies. In this work all I will conclusively demonstrate is that the Vatican II countermovement known as Sedevacantism is refuted by the very Church it intended to defend.

They Call Themselves "Brothers"

~~~~

A Note about the Dimond Brothers[49]

It is my understanding that Frederick Dimond, aka Brother Michael, and Robert Dimond, aka Brother Peter, are natural siblings who have assumed religious names and identities in what they claim to be the legitimate Order of St. Benedict (OSB) in the Roman Catholic Church. The Dimond siblings operate under the name Most Holy Family Monastery (MHFM), located in Upstate New York. Throughout this work I refer to the brothers as "Dimond" despite the fact that they are both acknowledged as the authors of the book upon which my refutation of Sedevacantism is primarily based. I refer to them in the singular only for the sake of simplicity.

---

49 The late Father James Wathen wrote, "The two 'Brothers' Dimond are two worrisome little men. Without any authorization and without proper theological training, they have endeavored to establish themselves as teachers of the faithful and 'certifiers' of all priests in this country. They make a lot of money with their misleading publications, tapes, etc., and they spend much time on the phone persuading people to stay away from the Masses of non-Sedevacantist priests. Who knows how many Catholics of good will have been persuaded to stay home for months on end, even years, rather than attend Mass, confess their sins, and receive Holy Communion? I urge everyone to give these men a wide berth; do not buy or circulate their materials, even those which are acceptable. Do not send them money. Beware of wolves in monk's habits." (Father James Wathen, *I Know Mine and Mine Know Me: The Voice of a Faithful Catholic Priest to His Flock* (Louisville, KY: The James F. Wathen Traditional Catholic Foundation, 2012), Vol. I, 49.

Additionally, because neither the Roman Catholic diocese in which jurisdiction the Dimond siblings operate nor I recognize MHFM as legitimate, I choose not to acknowledge or respect their religious names, titles, or monastery in this work.[50] For more information about the Dimond brothers and MHFM, readers may refer to *Wikipedia*.[51]

---

[50] Wathen also wrote, "They call themselves 'brothers,' but neither of them has ever made a standard novitiate, which the Code says is strictly necessary for professed religious. They call themselves 'brothers' because this lends prestige to their opinions… The two brothers do not pretend to live a monastic life. Their vocation, as they see it, demands that they busy themselves in controversy…Neither of the brothers has had the opportunity for normal catechetical instruction, let alone theological training. They imagine this does not matter, and it does not to the uninstructed. To those of us who have 'taken all the courses,' their inadequacy is a glaring reality." (Wathen, *I Know Mine*, 46.)

[51] "Most Holy Family Monastery," *Wikipedia*, accessed February 27, 2015, http://en.wikipedia.org/w/index.php?title=Most_Holy_Family_Monastery&oldid=627871630.

Delusion:

An erroneous belief that is held in the face of evidence to the contrary.[52]

---

52 "Delusion," WordNet Search 3.1, accessed April 17, 2015, http://wordnetweb.princeton.edu/perl/webwn?s=delusion.

CHAPTER 1

On Indefectibility

⁂

> There had been at the time of the deluge only one ark of Noah, prefiguring the one Church, which ark, having been finished to a single cubit, had only one pilot and guide, i.e., Noah, and we read that, outside of this ark, all that subsisted on the earth was destroyed.
>
> — Boniface VIII[53]

Objection one is that Sedevacantists deny or at least contradict the Catholic Church's doctrine of indefectibility of the Church. My position is agreement with this objection; the Sedevacantists absolutely contradict numerous aspects of the doctrine of indefectibility, especially as pertaining to the Church's essential constitution. This chapter comprises my rebuttal to Dimond's defense of the Sedevacantist position as we encounter the first principal Sedevacantist heresy: a defection of the Church occurred in fact.

The Sedevacantists believe that the current Church under Pope Francis is a substantially different organism than the Roman Catholic Church. They maintain that the post–Conciliar Church is a counterfeit sect, at least from the commencement of the reforms called for at the

---

[53] "Unam Sanctam," Papal Encyclicals Online, accessed April 30, 2015, http://www.papalencyclicals.net/Bon08/B8unam.htm.

Second Vatican Council, and that the true Church exists elsewhere in a remnant of faithful. All of this is what many Sedevacantists believe to be the real-time fulfillment of a great apostasy or falling away[54] from the Catholic faith as the sign that the second coming of Jesus Christ is imminent.

Whether or not the world is in its final stages and whether or not the Roman Catholic Church is enduring a great apostasy is not the subject of this work. The issue at hand is whether or not the Sedevacantists can have both a great apostasy of the Catholic Church *and* the doctrine of indefectibility; as we shall see, that would be impossible. The truth is that either the Church is in a period of *sede vacante* because of a defection or the present Church headed by Pope Francis is still the Church because of indefectibility.

---

54 2 Thess. 2:3–5.

Objection One

❦

The gates of hell cannot prevail against the Church, as Christ said (Matthew 16). He said he would be with his Church all days until the end of the world (Matthew 28). What you (i.e., all Sedevacantists) are saying is contrary to the promises of Christ.[55]

---

55 Dimond, *The Truth*, 298.

Part I

Indefectibility Defined

❦

LET US BEGIN OUR JOURNEY into the surreal world of Sedevacantism by delving into the meaning of the doctrine of indefectibility of the Church. What does it mean when Roman Catholics refer to their church as *indefectible*? As with many other doctrines of the Catholic Church, there is both a short answer and a long answer. Dimond begins his defense to objection one by providing his readers with the short answer. Let us turn to Dimond's opening statement, where he presents the following definition of indefectibility:

> ...indefectibility (the promise of Christ to always be with his Church, and that the gates of Hell will not prevail against it) means that the Church will, until the end of time, remain essentially what she is. The indefectibility of the Church requires that at least a remnant of the Church will exist until the end of the world, and that a true pope will never authoritatively teach error to the entire Church.[56]

Although there is nothing erroneous about Dimond's definition, it is by no means a comprehensive description of the Church's indefectibility. Because Dimond is defending himself against the serious charge that his Sedevacantist theory contradicts the doctrine of indefectibility,

---
56 Ibid.

one would expect a more honest effort, including precision in terminology, but Dimond fails to deliver. Instead he relies upon a partial definition of indefectibility and then confidently makes the following assertion:

> There is not one teaching of the Catholic Church that can be quoted which is contrary to the fact that there is presently a counterfeit sect which has reduced the true Catholic Church to a remnant in the days of the Great Apostasy, which is presided over by antipopes who have falsely posed as popes. Those who assert that the Vatican II sect is the Catholic Church assert that the Catholic Church officially endorses false religions and false doctrines. This is impossible and would mean that the gates of Hell have prevailed against the Catholic Church.[57]

Dimond does not invite the reader to examine the doctrine of indefectibility to see whether it is congruent with Sedevacantism; instead he presumes readers will accept his word that it is. He then employs a diversion strategy to lure the reader away from what could easily emerge as problematic to the Sedevacantist defense by focusing on what he terms "the Vatican II sect." Admittedly it is easy to be led astray by the accusations against the post–Vatican II Church, but we must remember that Dimond is really selling Sedevacantism. For our purposes, then, it is necessary to demonstrate only that Sedevacantism contradicts indefectibility, and Dimond's assertion, true or not, becomes irrelevant.

Having seen Dimond's definition of indefectibility, let us now review three explanations of the doctrine of indefectibility and then compare them with Dimond's definition. We begin with "The Creed Explained" by the Rev. Arthur Devine.

---

57 Ibid., 299.

Section 5. (Article IX.)
The Properties of the Church

Besides the four Notes or marks, the Church has many other properties inherent in and essential to her. The principal of these are indefectibility in being or existence; infallibility in teaching; and authority or power in ruling or governing. These three properties or attributes are denied by all non-Catholic sects, because otherwise they could not account for their existence, or assign any plausible reason for not belonging to the one true Church. We have now to explain separately these properties or attributes.

INDEFECTIBILITY
1. This is a property by which the Church cannot fail; it is that by which she cannot either lose or have diminished any of her divine qualities or gifts even for a short time.

The doctrine of the indefectibility of the Church may be comprised in the following propositions:

(a) The whole Church is indefectible.
(b) One part of the Church, namely the Apostolic See, is indefectible.
(c) The particular Church of this or that particular diocese or this or that particular nation may fail and fall away.

Perpetuity is included in indefectibility. Although, rigorously speaking, unless God had ordained otherwise, the Church could be perpetual, without being in all respects indefectible; as a man remains the same human being even to death, although he fails in many respects, both in soul and body. Perpetuity imports continuation without interruption, but indefectibility imports duration and immutability as well.

On Indefectibility

Indefectibility means more than infallibility. Infallibility extends only to those things which concern the Church's teaching in matters of faith and morals, but it does not imply that she is to continue always, or to the end of the world, but that as long as she exists, she cannot err in these matters.

2. Heretics, in regard to the indefectibility of the Church, err on two points.

   (1) As to the possibility of defection.
   (2) As to the fact of defection.

They have held various opinions as to the possibility of defection.

   (a) Some have held that the whole Church can fail entirely for a time.
   (b) Some say the visible Church can fail, but not the invisible Church, as if these were two distinct Churches.
   (c) Others affirm that, although the Church cannot fail entirely, she can do so in part, at least for a time, and even always by losing this or that attribute or perfection, or retaining it, but maimed and vitiated.

As to the fact of defection. All heretics of every sect hold that the Church has, in some way or other, failed; otherwise, as I have said, they cannot assign any reason for their separation from her; but as to the time of her defection, they are not agreed. On this point there are two extreme opinions. The first dates the defection of the Church from the Council of Constance, in the year 1414. The second holds that defection began in the very time of the Apostles; in their time, they say, and in every age since, the Church was affected by a number of errors. This latter opinion is held by a great number of recent Protestant writers, such as Goode, Whately, and some Puseyites, as Palmer.

Against all these errors, Catholics hold the indefectibility of the Church, as above explained, and the proofs of it, and of her infallibility, may be said to be the same; and I shall therefore prove both at the same time, after I explain the nature and meaning of Infallibility.

(Continuation with proofs of indefectibility)

We may now assert the proposition, and assign the proofs which are given in support of the doctrine explained in this Section.

6. The Church is indefectible and infallible. Both parts of this proposition are so closely connected that the reasons for one prove the other; we may, however, for the sake of order, take them separately.

The Church is indefectible. This may be proved—

(a) From the promises of Christ. He promised (1) that the gates of hell would not prevail against her.* (2) That He would be with her all days, even to the consummation of the world, &c.† From which we may conclude that, should the Church fail, the promises of Christ would not be fulfilled. The gates of hell would prevail, and Christ would cease to be with his Church. Therefore, the Church cannot be said to fail, but must be indefectible.

(b) The properties and attributes which are essential to the Church, and flow from her original constitution, cannot fail, or the Church cannot lose them, or suffer them to be impaired. For if in any of them she did fail, or if any of them should be wanting in time, then she should cease to be that Church which was founded by Christ. For Christ founded his Church, that in all times and places she could supply men with the due means of salvation; and, therefore, she ought always to be, and to be capable of being deemed, the true

Church of Christ, which would not be the case were she at any time to fail even in part, or lose any of her essential attributes. Men might then be deceived, as they would not be able to recognise any longer that which is the true Church established by Christ on earth. They would, therefore, be destitute of those means which would guide men in that affair which is the most excellent and necessary of all, namely, in the knowledge of the true religion. And all this would be at variance with the end, which Christ had in view in establishing his Church. Against the fact of her defection, we can say that the present state of the Catholic Church, after so many ages, is an incontrovertible argument that she possesses the prerogative of indefectibility. "The Church," says St. Augustine, "will not be conquered, nor eradicated, nor will she yield to any temptation or trial until the end of the world comes."[58]

St. Matt. xvi. t Ibid. xviii. See also St. Matt. lii. 25; Eplies. tv. 18.[59]

As we can see, Dimond's definition did not include many of these important distinctions to the property of indefectibility. The next explanation of indefectibility I will present is an excerpt from *Christian Apologetics, a Defense of the Catholic Faith* by the Rev. W. Devivier:

---

[58] Some Sedevacantists may see in Augustine's words an opportunity to interpret the meaning in favor of Sedevacantism in a similar fashion as Protestants interpret Matthew 1:25 ("And he knew her not *till* she brought forth her firstborn son: and he called his name Jesus"; emphasis added) to deny the perpetual virginity of Mary. In both instances the context of the words as interpreted by the Church indicates continuance or perpetuity. From a papist perspective the Sedevacantists may not interpret Augustine's words—"until the end of the world comes"— as meaning that the Church will be conquered, be eradicated, or yield to any temptations or trials at the end of the world, as the Sedevacantist thesis presupposes.

[59] Arthur Devine, *The Creed Explained; or, an Exposition of Catholic Doctrine According to the Creeds of Faith and the Constitutions and Definitions of the Church* (New York: Benziger Bros.,1903), 289–292.

ART. I.—INDEFECTIBILITY OF THE CHURCH.

Taken in its broadest acceptation the indefectibility of the Church is the duration that Jesus Christ promised her until the end of the world, with the maintenance of her interior constitution and her exterior form, with the preservation of all her properties and her prerogatives. The Church can, of course, admit, in the series of centuries, disciplinary changes required for the good of souls, but she will never be deprived of one of her constituent elements (her members, her chiefs, her organization), nor of any of her essential properties (unity, sanctity, catholicity), nor of her divine prerogatives (authority, infallibility)...Let us observe at the same time that this promise of indefectibility is made to the universal Church, and not to each of her parts, or to particular Churches. The latter may fall away or disappear; but despite these shipwrecks the true Church of Christ will always remain, ever the same; these defections, moreover, will be compensated by the conquest or the foundation of new Churches. Protestants, sometimes openly, sometimes covertly, reject this indefectibility. No doubt the invisible Church, many of them say, cannot fail, but it is quite otherwise with the visible Church, which may disappear from the world for a greater or shorter time; and this they allege is what has taken place.[60]

The final explanation I chose to include for our review comes from *The Catholic Encyclopedia.*

"Church" X. Indefectibility

Among the prerogatives conferred on his Church by Christ is the gift of indefectibility. By this term is signified, not merely that the Church will persist to the end of time, but further, that it will preserve unimpaired its essential characteristics. The Church can never undergo any constitutional change which will make it, as a social organism,

---

[60] W. Devivier, *Christian Apologetics: A Defense of the Catholic Faith* (New York: Benziger Brothers, 1903), 391–393.

On Indefectibility

something different from what it was originally. It can never become corrupt in faith or in morals; nor can it ever lose the Apostolic hierarchy, or the sacraments through which Christ communicates grace to men. The gift of indefectibility is expressly promised to the Church by Christ, in the words in which He declares that the gates of hell shall not prevail against it. It is manifest that, could the storms which the Church encounters so shake it as to alter its essential characteristics and make it other than Christ intended it to be, the gates of hell, i.e., the powers of evil, would have prevailed. It is clear, too, that could the Church suffer substantial change, it would no longer be an instrument capable of accomplishing the work for which God called it in to being. He established it that it might be to all men the school of holiness. This it would cease to be if ever it could set up a false and corrupt moral standard. He established it to proclaim His revelation to the world, and charged it to warn all men that unless they accepted that message they must perish everlastingly. Could the Church, in defining the truths of revelation err in the smallest point, such a charge would be impossible. Nobody could enforce under such a penalty the acceptance of what might be erroneous. By the hierarchy and the sacraments, Christ, further, made the Church the depositary of the graces of the Passion. Were it to lose either of these, it could no longer dispense to men the treasures of grace.

The gift of indefectibility plainly does not guarantee each several part of the Church against heresy or apostasy. The promise is made to the corporate body. Individual Churches may become corrupt in morals, may fall into heresy, may even apostatize. Thus at the time of the Mohammedan conquests, whole populations renounced their faith; and the Church suffered similar losses in the sixteenth century. But the defection of isolated branches does not alter the character of the main stem. The society of Jesus Christ remains endowed with all the prerogatives bestowed on it by its Founder. Only to One particular Church is indefectibility assured, viz. to the See of Rome. To Peter, and in him to all his successors in the chief pastorate, Christ committed the task of confirming his brethren in the Faith (Luke 22:32); and thus, to the Roman Church, as Cyprian says, "faithlessness cannot gain access (Epistle 54).[61]

Let us now compare Dimond's description with what we know to be true about indefectibility according to the above Catholic sources. The following charts demonstrate how Dimond's description of the Church's indefectibility stacks up against the three descriptions provided.

---

61 G. H. Joyce, *The Catholic Encyclopedia* (New York: Robert Appleton Company, 1913), Vol. III, 756.

Indefectibility Compared

The Creed Explained (CE)

Indefectibility includes…	Dimond	CE
Indefectible in being/existence		√
Indefectible in authority/power in governing		√
Cannot lose divine qualities for a short time		√
Cannot have diminished gifts for a short time		√
The whole Church is indefectible		√
The Apostolic See is indefectible		√
Doesn't extend to particular Churches		√
Perpetuity	√	√
Immutability	√	√
Essential constitutional properties and attributes:		√
Cannot fail	√	√
Cannot be lost		√
Cannot be impaired		√
Cannot be wanting in time		√
Supplies men with means of salvation in all times/places		√
Always recognizable as true Church of Christ		√
Indefectibility precludes deception		√
Cannot be conquered or eradicated		√
Cannot succumb to any temptation or trial		√
Heresies:		√
The whole Church can fail entirely for a time		√

	Dimond	CA
Visible Church can fail but not invisible Church		√
The Church can fail in part for a time		√
Church can lose attributes or perfections		√
Church can retain maimed and vitiated attributes		√

CHRISTIAN APOLOGETICS (CA)

Indefectibility includes…	Dimond	CA
Maintenance of Church's interior constitution:		√
Exterior form		√
Preservation of all properties and prerogatives		√
The Church cannot be deprived of constituent elements:		√
Members		√
Chiefs		√
Organization		√
Essential properties:		√
Unity		√
Sanctity		√
Catholicity		√
Divine prerogatives:		√
Authority		√
Infallibility	√	√
Not applicable to particular Churches		√

Heresies:

	Dimond	CA
Invisible Church cannot fail; visible Church can fail for a short time		√

The Catholic Encyclopedia

Indefectibility includes…	Dimond	Encyclopedia
Essential characteristics unimpaired		√
Church cannot undergo any constitutional change		√
Church cannot become corrupt in faith or morals		√
Church cannot lose apostolic hierarchy or sacraments		√
The gates of hell shall not prevail against the Church	√	√
The Church cannot suffer substantial change		√
The Church cannot err in defining the truths of revelation	√	√
Pertains only to corporate body not individual Churches		√
Defection of branches does not alter the main stem		√
Only to one particular Church, viz. to the See of Rome		√
Must remain endowed with all original prerogatives		√
Faithlessness cannot gain access to the Roman Church		√

As can be observed, indefectibility is much more than a continuance of believers sharing the same faith until the end of time, as some Sedevacantists would have us believe. Yes, the members of the Church body are important; however, the Church's essential, indefectible constitution includes numerous other components.

Before moving on, let's pause for a moment and consider an important question. Is it possible to credibly defend Sedevacantism against the accusation that it contradicts indefectibility if any of the following is true? (a) The apologist's understanding of the doctrine of indefectibility is deficient; (b) the apologist's understanding of indefectibility is erroneous; (c) the apologist unintentionally misses critical points in its defense; or (d) the apologist intentionally conceals critical points from the reading audience.

Part II

Essential Constitution of the Church

~~~~~

ESSENCE

As seen in the comparison charts at the end of part I, numerous attributes, properties, and characteristics belong to and identify the Church. But when talking about the Church's essential constitution, what exactly is meant by *essential*?

> In philosophy, essence is the attribute or set of attributes that make an entity or substance what it fundamentally is, and which it has by necessity, and without which it loses its identity. Essence is contrasted with accident: a property that the entity or substance has contingently, without which the substance can still retain its identity.[62]

There are attributes of all human beings that make them unique persons. Remove or change these attributes and a person will cease to exist or lose his or her identity. Like human persons the Catholic Church also has fundamental attributes that make it what it is and that it must have by necessity. We will always identify that Church by these essential items as long as the world exists. Just as a human person cannot become another person, neither can the Church become another Church. The

---

62 "Essence," last modified November 12, 2014, http://en.wikipedia.org/w/index.php?title=Essence&oldid=601926247.

Church must remain that same entity *in being* for the duration of her existence.

> Besides the four Notes or Marks, the Church has many other properties inherent in and essential to her. The principal of these are indefectibility in being or existence…[63]

> Although, rigorously speaking, unless God had ordained otherwise, the Church could be perpetual, without being in all respects indefectible; as a man remains the same human being even to death, although he fails in many respects, both in soul and body. Perpetuity imports continuation without interruption, but indefectibility imports duration and immutability as well.[64]

> In saying that the Church is indefectible we assert both her imperishableness, that is, her constant duration to the end of the world, and the essential immutability of her teaching, *her constitution* and her liturgy. This does not exclude the decay of individual "Churches" (i.e., parts of the Church) and accidental changes.[65]

In our study it is concerning the Church's essential constitution that the theory of Sedevacantism contravenes indefectibility. Because Sedevacantists assert that the Church that emerged from the Second Vatican Council is no longer the Roman Catholic Church, but more importantly that the Sedevacantists are that Church, it is important to answer the question "of what is the Catholic Church principally composed?" Once we have answered this key question, we shall see whether any Sedevacantist sect can make a credible claim of being that same Church. As with any structure, we begin by identifying the first and most important part of its essential constitution—the foundation. Let

---

63 Devine, *The Creed Explained*, 289.
64 Ibid., 289–290.
65 Ott, *Fundamentals of Catholic Dogma*, 296.

us now verify that the Catholic Church does in fact have a foundation and identify it because whatever it is, it cannot be removed or divided without destroying the Church.

Foundation

In Roman Catholicism neither Jesus Christ nor Peter's profession of faith in Christ is the foundation of the Church. Although the Church's foundation is revealed by Peter's profession of faith, his faith per se is not it; otherwise a great schism with the Eastern Churches in AD 1054 could have been avoided. Interestingly, the foundation of Roman Catholicism is not a doctrine directly pertaining to God or Jesus Christ such as the Blessed Trinity, the Incarnation, or the Resurrection. In fact from a Roman Catholic perspective, the foundation of the Church must have been so firmly established and so well known and accepted by all Christians that it was not even included in original creeds of Catholic faith as formulated at the First Council of Nicaea (AD 325) and the First Council of Constantinople (AD 381). So what could the Church's foundation upon which the whole edifice rests be? To answer this question definitively, we turn to the First Vatican Council (1869–70).

A careful study of Vatican I's First Dogmatic Constitution of the Church of Christ as well as various other teachings[66] of the magisterium identifies the Church's divinely laid foundation. The First Vatican Council's First Dogmatic Constitution of the Church of Christ states:

> ...he set blessed *Peter* over the rest of the apostles and instituted in him the permanent principle of both unities and their visible foundation.[67]

---

66 A search for the precise identity of the Catholic Church's foundation turns up several nominees. These include Christ, Peter, the primacy, Rome, the Roman Pontiffs, the apostles, and Peter's profession of faith. Confusion about this core doctrine is even found among the fathers and doctors of the Church. I believe we can attribute contradictory findings, complexities, and historical ambiguities to Rome's gradual mutation of the Church's original Christocentric foundation to that of the Roman papacy.

67 Denzinger, *The Sources of Catholic Dogma*, 1821.

On Indefectibility

> For no one can be in doubt, indeed it was known in every age that the holy and most blessed Peter, prince and head of the apostles, the pillar of faith and the foundation of the catholic Church...[68]

The Catholic Encyclopedia states:

> The episcopal body is infallible also, but only in union with its head, from whom moreover it may not separate, since to do so would be to separate from the foundation on which the Church is built.[69]

> ...the ultimate touchstone is to be found in communion with the Holy See. On Peter Christ founded his Church. Those who are not joined to that foundation cannot form part of the house of God.[70]

So we have now identified the first component of the Church's foundation, and it is human; his name is Peter. But there is more to the divinely laid foundation than just Peter. Vatican I's First Dogmatic Constitution of the Church of Christ also speaks of something called the "sacred primacy."

> And, since the gates of hell, to overthrow the Church, if this were possible, arise from all sides with ever greater hatred against its divinely established foundation, We judge it to be necessary for the protection, safety, and increase of the Catholic flock, with the approbation of the Council, to set forth the doctrine on the institution, perpetuity, and nature of the Sacred Apostolic Primacy, in which the strength and solidarity of the whole Church consist, to be believed and held by all the faithful, according to the ancient and continual faith of the universal

---

68 Ibid., 1824.
69 Jean Bainvel, *The Catholic Encyclopedia* (New York: Robert Appleton Co., 1912), Vol. XV, 10.
70 Joyce, *The Catholic Encyclopedia*, 755.

Church, and to proscribe and condemn the contrary errors, so pernicious to the Lord's flock.[71]

Ott describes the primacy as follows:

> Primacy means first in rank. A primacy may be one of honour, of control, of direction (*primatus directionis*), or of jurisdiction, that is, of government. A primacy of jurisdiction consists in the possession of full and supreme legislative, juridical and punitive power.[72]

For our purposes the "Sacred Apostolic Primacy" is *authority* that ranks the bishop of Rome first in honor, control, direction, and jurisdiction in the Church. By its institution it is to be understood that an authoritative government belongs to the Church's essential constitution.

Twenty-six years after the First Vatican Council, Pope Leo XIII wrote:

The Universal Jurisdiction of St. Peter

> 12. From this text it is clear that by the will and command of God the Church rests upon St. Peter, just as a building rests on its foundation. Now the proper nature of a foundation is to be a principle of cohesion for the various parts of the building. It must be the necessary condition of stability and strength. Remove it and the whole building falls. It is consequently the office of St. Peter to support the Church, and to guard it in all its strength and indestructible unity. *How could he fulfil this office without the power of commanding, forbidding, and judging, which is properly called jurisdiction?*[73] [Emphasis added.]

---

71 Denzinger, *The Sources of Catholic Dogma*, 1821.
72 Ott, *Fundamentals of Catholic Dogma*, 279.
73 Leo XIII, "*Satis Cognitum*," 397.

On Indefectibility

We have now determined that the Church's divinely laid foundation consists of both material and immaterial components, which the First Vatican Council *initially* identified as:

a. Blessed Apostle Peter
b. The primacy (authority)

Following the naming of the Church's foundation in Peter and the primacy, the council goes on to name additional members to the Church's foundation. In chapter two we learn of the third member:

c. Rome

Watch how the First Vatican Council dogmatically bound the primacy to Rome:

…and he up to this time and always lives and presides and exercises judgment in his successors, *the bishops of the holy See of Rome*, which was founded by him and consecrated by his blood.[74]

Therefore, *whoever succeeds Peter in this chair,* he according to the institution of Christ himself, holds the primacy of Peter over the whole Church.[75]

For this reason *it has always been necessary because of mightier pre-eminence for every Church to come to the Church of Rome, that is those who are the faithful everywhere, so that in this See, from which the laws of "venerable communion" emanate over all, they as members associated in one head, coalesce into one bodily structure.*[76]

---

74 Denzinger, *The Sources of Catholic Dogma*, 1824.
75 Ibid.
76 Ibid.

Wherefore we teach and declare that the Roman Church, by the disposition of the Lord, holds the sovereignty of ordinary power over all others...[77]

But what exactly does the Church mean by "Rome"? Rome's relationship to the Catholic Church can be understood in at least three distinct ways:

1. Rome the city (capital of Italy)
2. Rome the Diocese (Holy See)
3. Rome the independent country (Vatican City State)

When considering both the First Vatican Council's Dogmatic Constitution and the doctrine of indefectibility, it is with number two that we are concerned. A defection of a particular Church or territory occurs when its governing see defects. The Church teaches that a defection can occur in virtually any diocese or territory in the world except one: Rome. The doctrine of indefectibility is very specific on this, and so Roman Catholics have been assured by the promises of Christ as well as the First Vatican Council that the Holy See cannot leave the Church because essentially *it is* the Church.

So that there is no confusion, let us briefly make note that the following terms are interchangeable: *Roman See, Apostolic See, Roman Church, See of Rome,* and *Holy See*,[78] so that when one reads, "Only to One particular Church is indefectibility assured, viz. to the See of Rome..."[79] it will be understood that indefectibility belongs in a particular way to the Roman Church. Furthermore the Holy See also includes the entire ensemble of departments and ministries that assist the bishop in the government of

---

77 Ibid., 1827.
78 Holy See: In this canonical and diplomatic sense, the term is synonymous with Apostolic See, Holy Apostolic See, Roman Church, and Roman Curia. [P. M. Baumgarten, *The Catholic Encyclopedia* (New York: Robert Appleton Company, 1910), Vol. VII, 424.]
79 Joyce, *The Catholic Encyclopedia*, 756.

the Church. Important members of this governmental body include the congregations, the tribunals, and the offices of the Curia.[80]

The Holy See includes the central government of the Catholic Church and so belongs to the Church's essential constitution. The Code of Canon Law reads:

CHAPTER IV: THE ROMAN CURIA

Can. 360. The Supreme Pontiff usually conducts the business of the universal Church through the Roman Curia, which acts in his name and with his authority for the good and for the service of the Churches. The Curia is composed of the Secretariat of State or Papal Secretariat, the Council for the public affairs of the Church, the Congregations, the Tribunals and other Institutes. The constitution and competence of all these is defined by special law.[81]

Can. 361. In this Code the terms Apostolic See or Holy See mean not only the Roman Pontiff, but also, unless the contrary is clear from the nature of things or from the context, the Secretariat of State, the Council for the public affairs of the Church, and the other Institutes of the Roman Curia.[82]

All of the above comprises the Roman Church, which by definition is indefectible. But lest I am accused of ascribing infallibility to individual governmental members such as the Curia, I remind the reader that I am addressing whether the Sedevacantists contradict indefectibility, not infallibility. Whereas infallibility extends to those things that concern faith and morals, indefectibility belongs to all of the material and

---

80 Benedetto Ojetti, *The Catholic Encyclopedia* (New York: Robert Appleton Company, 1912), Vol. XIII, 147.
81 "Chapter IV: The Roman Curia," last modified August 26, 2007, http://www.intratext.com/IXT/ENG0017/_P19.HTM.
82 Ibid.

immaterial components, attributes, and properties covered in Part I, beginning with the Holy See.

Let us now read about the great significance of Rome—the Eternal City—to the Holy See:

> *The significance of Rome lies primarily in the fact that it is the city of the pope. The Bishop of Rome, as the successor of St. Peter, is the Vicar of Christ on earth and the visible head of the Catholic Church. Rome is consequently the centre of unity in belief, the source of ecclesiastical jurisdiction and the seat of the supreme authority which can bind by its enactments the faithful throughout the world.* The Diocese of Rome is known as the "See of Peter," the "Apostolic See," the "Holy Roman Church" the "Holy See"—titles which indicate its unique position in Christendom and suggest the origin of its preeminence. Rome, more than any other city, bears witness both to the past splendour of the pagan world and to the triumph of Christianity. It is here that the history of the Church can be traced from the earliest days, from the humble beginnings in the Catacombs to the majestic ritual of St. Peter's. At every turn one comes upon places hallowed by the deaths of the martyrs, the lives of innumerable saints, the memories of wise and holy pontiffs. From Rome the bearers of the Gospel message went out to the peoples of Europe and eventually to the uttermost ends of the earth. To Rome, again, in every age countless pilgrims have thronged from all the nations, and especially from English-speaking countries. With religion the missionaries carried the best elements of ancient culture and civilization which Rome had preserved amid all the vicissitudes of barbaric invasion. To these treasures of antiquity have been added the productions of a nobler art inspired by higher ideals, that have filled Rome with masterpieces in architecture, painting, and sculpture. These appeal indeed to every mind endowed with artistic perception; but their full meaning only the Catholic believer can appreciate, because he alone, in his deepest thought and feeling, is at one with the spirit that pulsates here in the heart of the Christian world. [83] [emphasis added]

---

83 U. Benigni, *The Catholic Encyclopedia* (New York: Robert Appleton Company, 1912), Vol. XIII, 164.

Finally, just as the sacred primacy was a power Christ instituted in the person of Peter so he might exercise it for the sake of the government and unity of the Church, it must also continue in Christ's Church exactly as he instituted it. Hence the foundational relationship of Peter to his sacred primacy as instituted by the Lord remains unchanged in that *human persons must continue to exercise it*. This brings us to the fourth component of the Roman Church's divinely laid foundation:

d. Roman Pontiff

Ott wrote:

> In the Encyclical "Satis Cognitum," which ex professo treats of the unity of the Church, Leo XIII comments: "As her Divine founder willed that the Church should be one in faith, in government and in communion, He appointed Peter *and his successors to be the foundation and, as it were, the center of its unity.*"[84]

The importance of the Roman Pontiff as successor to Peter to this foundation cannot be minimized, as all Sedevacantists are forced to do on account of the Church's defection at or near the time of Vatican II. Just as a human person has a physical head and body, likewise does the Church. A visible head belongs to the essential constitution of the Church because although Peter's life would come to an end, the Church's unity and its government as established by Christ must continue in perpetuity. Again, Pope Leo XIII provided a meticulous explanation:

> The Roman Pontiff Possesses Supreme Jurisdiction in the Church Jure Divino.
>
> 13. It was necessary that a government of this kind, since it belongs to the constitution and formation of the Church, as its principal

---

[84] Ott, *Fundamentals of Catholic Dogma*, 302–303.

element that is as the principle of unity and the foundation of lasting stability—should in no wise come to an end with St. Peter, but should pass to his successors from one to another. "There remains, therefore, the ordinance of truth, and St. Peter, persevering in the strength of the rock which he had received, hath not abandoned the government of the Church which had been confided to him." For this reason the Pontiffs who succeed Peter in the Roman Episcopate receive the supreme power in the Church, jure divino.[85]

Bishops Separated from Peter and His Successors, Lose All Jurisdiction

15. From this it must be clearly understood that Bishops are deprived of the right and power of ruling, if they deliberately secede from Peter and his successors; *because, by this secession, they are separated from the foundation on which the whole edifice must rest.* They are therefore outside the edifice itself; and for this very reason they are separated from the *fold*, whose leader is the Chief Pastor; they are exiled from the *Kingdom*, the keys of which were given by Christ to Peter alone.[86] [Italics added.]

Leo XIII wrote that the form of authoritative government established by Christ "belongs to the constitution and formation of the Church"[87] and that it is the Church's "principal element."[88] He also stated that the office of Peter would have ended with Peter's death had Christ not arranged for its transmission. Please note that *human successors* are essential to the principle of unity of the Church and foundation of lasting stability; Peter's primacy in and of itself is insufficient without additional members c and d (Rome and successor Roman Pontiffs). Thus the

---

85 Leo XIII, "*Satis Cognitum,*" 398–399.
86 Ibid., 400–401.
87 Ibid., 398.
88 Ibid.

answer to the original question "of what is the Church's essential constitution principally composed?" is the Catholic Church's divinely laid foundation comprised of the following components:

a. Blessed Apostle Peter
b. The primacy (authority)
c. Rome (Holy See)
d. Roman Pontiff

The constituent parts of this foundational structure are mutually dependent; they cannot be divided without frustrating the end for which they exist—unity of the Church. Their symbiotic relationship as pertaining to the Sedevacantist thesis will become much clearer later on, but for now let us put a name to this foundation: the papacy. The papacy is the foundation of Roman Catholicism; remove it or divide it and the whole institution crumbles to earth.

Hierarchy and Sacraments

As a human cannot survive the loss of its body since the body contains components vital to the life of its head, the Church's body is likewise essential. Indefectibility pertains to the hierarchy and sacraments:

> ...nor can it ever lose the Apostolic hierarchy, or the sacraments through which Christ communicates grace to men...By the hierarchy and the sacraments, Christ, further, made the Church the depositary of the graces of the Passion. Were it to lose either of these, it could no longer dispense to men the treasures of grace.[89]

Ott wrote of the Church's hierarchical constitution:

---

89 Joyce, *The Catholic Encyclopedia*, 756.

Christ gave his Church an hierarchical constitution. (de fide.)[90]

Hierarchy—The successors of the Apostles under the Pope as successor of St. Peter. Three powers are included under the Catholic hierarchy: teaching, pastoral, and sacerdotal. They correspond to the threefold office laid on Christ as man for the redemption of the world; the office prophet or teacher, the pastoral or royal office of ruler, and the priestly office of sanctifying the faithful. Christ transferred this threefold office, with the corresponding powers, to the Apostles and their successors. A man enters the hierarchy by episcopal ordination when he receives the fullness of the priesthood. But he depends on collegial union with the Bishop of Rome and the rest of the Catholic hierarchy for actually being able to exercise the two other powers of teaching divine truth and of legitimately ruling the believers under his jurisdiction.[91]

The Council of Trent stated:

> If anyone says that in the Catholic Church a hierarchy has not been instituted by divine ordinance, which consists of the bishops, priests, and ministers: let him be anathema.[92]

> The bishops who succeeded in the place of the Apostles belong by excellence to the hierarchical order…[93]

---

90 *De fide*: a term meaning "of Faith," used to identify those doctrines of the Church which are infallibly true. Their infallible certitude derives ultimately from divine revelation, but proximately from the fact that they have either been solemnly defined by the Church's magisterium or have been taught by her ordinary universal teaching authority as binding on the consciences of all the faithful. (Hardon, *Modern Catholic Dictionary*, 149.)
91 Hardon, *Modern Catholic Dictionary*, 249.
92 Denzinger, *The Sources of Catholic Dogma*, 966.
93 Ibid., 960.

The Church body is comprised of two parts, the *ecclesia docens* and the *ecclesia audiens*. However, only one of these belongs to the Church's essential constitution:

> Roman Catholics now define the Church as: The congregation of all the Faithful, who, being baptized, profess the same faith, partake of the same sacraments and *are governed by their lawful pastors, under one visible head on earth*. They make a distinction between the *ecclesia docens* and the *ecclesia audiens*, that is, between "the Church consisting of those who rule, teach, and edify" and "the Church which is taught, governed, and receives the sacraments." *In the strictest sense of the word it is not the ecclesia audiens but the ecclesia docens that constitutes the Church.* The latter shares directly in the glorious attributes of the Church, but the former is adorned with them only indirectly.[94]

The First Vatican Council stated: "Just as He sent the Apostles whom He had elected for Himself from the world, as He Himself was sent by the Father (John 20, 21,), so He wishes that there should be pastors and teachers in his Church to the end of time."[95]

The Catholic Encyclopedia states:

> *The teaching Church is essentially composed of the episcopal body*, which continues here below the work and mission of the Apostolic College. It was indeed in the form of a college or social body that Christ grouped His Apostles and it is likewise as a social body that the episcopate exercises its mission to teach."[96]

---

94 Louis Berkhof, *Systematic Theology* (Grand Rapids, MI: W M. B. Eerdmans Publishing Company, 1953), 562.
95 Denzinger, *The Sources of Catholic Dogma*, 1821.
96 Bainvel, *The Catholic Encyclopedia*, 10.

Because Christ established the episcopacy in the persons of the Apostles from the foundation of the Church, any Church claiming it is Roman Catholic must readily be able to account for a visibly unified hierarchy. Notice also that the episcopacy must retain the ordinary power of the apostles. Ott wrote:

> The Powers bestowed on the Apostles have descended to the bishops. (De fide.)[97]

> The perpetuation of the hierarchical powers follows necessarily on the indefectibility of the Church desired by Christ.[98]

> The hierarchical magisterial powers of the Church embrace the teaching power, the pastoral power (legislative, juridical and punitive power), and the sacerdotal power.[99]

Pius XII, in the Encyclical "Mystici Corporis" (1943), rejected the distinction between "a Church shaped by charity," and "a Church consisting of juridical elements," for such a distinction postulates that the Church founded by Christ was originally merely one kept together by the invisible bond of charity, a religious society endowed with charisma, which only gradually, under the influence of external conditions, developed into a legally organized society with an hierarchical constitution (juridical Church). The distinction rests on the thesis of R. Sohms, according to which the essence of the Church law contradicts the essence of the Church. In the last analysis, this thesis of R. Sohms harks back to the view of the Reformers that the Church is an invisible, that is, not a divinely established community of believers in Christ. According to the teaching of the Church, there belongs to the Mystical Body of Christ an external, visible, juridical element (i.e., the

---
97 Ott, *Fundamentals of Catholic Dogma*, 278.
98 Ibid.
99 Ibid., 276.

legal organization), and an inner, invisible, mystical element (i.e., the communion of grace), just as in Christ, the Head of the Church, there is the visible human nature, and the invisible Divine nature, and in the Sacraments, the outward signs and the inward grace. [100]

Pope Leo XIII wrote:

Bishops Belong to the Essential Constitution of the Church

14. "…and just as it is necessary that the authority of Peter should be perpetuated in the Roman Pontiff, so, by the fact that the bishops succeed the Apostles, *they inherit their ordinary power, and thus the episcopal order necessarily belongs to the essential constitution of the Church.*"[101]

It must be said that not once in the history of the Catholic Church has a situation existed that the Church was left with an impotent episcopacy, not even temporarily. Being that authority belongs to the Church's essential, indefectible constitution, it follows that the sacraments must continue *licitly*[102] and without interruption until the end of time. If a controversy involving the liceity of sacraments persists and cannot be definitively resolved, it is assuredly only because the Church suffered a defection in its hierarchy—precisely the problem occurring on both sides of the Sedevacantist/Vatican II controversy.

---

100 Ibid., 277–278.
101 Leo XIII, "*Satis Cognitum*," 400.
102 Liceity: The legitimacy of a human action and its consequences, e.g., administration of a sacrament or a contract. It is commonly distinguished from validity, since an action may be valid but not licit, as a layman conferring baptism without urgent necessity. (Etym. Latin *licentia*, license, freedom to act.) (Hardon, *Modern Catholic Dictionary*, 319.)

FOUR MARKS

Indefectibility of the Church specifically includes the Church's four notes or marks: unity, holiness, universality, and apostolicity.[103]

> The Church can, of course, admit, in the series of centuries, disciplinary changes required for the good of souls, but she will never be deprived of one of her constituent elements (her members, her chiefs, her organization), *nor of any of her essential properties (unity, sanctity, catholicity), nor of her divine prerogatives (authority, infallibility).*[104]

> Among the prerogatives conferred on his Church by Christ is the gift of indefectibility. By this term is signified, not merely that the Church will persist to the end of time, *but further, that it will preserve unimpaired its essential characteristics.*[105]

So far indefectibility tells us that for any Church even to be considered Roman Catholic, it must be identifiable by all of the aforementioned essential components beginning with the correct foundation, the Roman papacy—*even if this Church were reduced to a remnant.* The church that claims to be Roman Catholic must also possess a central government, a visibly unified hierarchy, authority, and apostolicity from which valid and licit sacraments flow without interruption. All of these things belong to the Church's essential, indefectible constitution on the grounds that they were instituted by Jesus Christ from the foundation of the Church. Most importantly, let the reader observe that what Christ originally instituted must remain in his Church until the end of the world:

---

103 Because Sedevacantism most noticeably stands in opposition to the Church's marks of unity and apostolicity, I will not specifically address the marks of sanctity and universality in this work. I address unity of the Church in all chapters and apostolicity in part III of this chapter and again in chapter four. Additionally, because unity of the Church cannot exist without the property of visibility, we will explore what the Church's visibility entails at length in objection fifteen.
104 Devivier, *Christian Apologetics*, 392.
105 Joyce, *The Catholic Encyclopedia*, 756.

On Indefectibility

It follows then that the Church of Christ not only exists to-day and always, but is also exactly the same as it was in the time of the Apostles, unless we were to say, which God forbid, either that Christ our Lord could not effect His purpose, or that He erred when He asserted that the gates of hell should never prevail against it.[106]

---

106 Pius XI, "*Mortalium Animos* (Encyclical Letter on Religious Unity)," in *The Papal Encyclicals* (Raleigh: McGrath Publishing Company, 1981), 314.

Part III

Defection of Rome

※

BARQUE OF PETER

FROM ANTIQUITY CATHOLICS HAVE PORTRAYED the Catholic Church as a great ship at sea. Most Catholics refer to this image as "the Barque of Peter." This portrayal of the Catholic Church as a barque conveys several meanings, one of which is that the Church is something more than its crew and passengers; the ship itself has a very special significance. The barque gives an important identity to her crew and passengers and, in a certain way, carries on a life of its own. One can visualize this ancient vessel's majesty, with masts and topsails triumphantly towering high above the seas and her hull that boasts of many victories in battle. Her keel is the consecrated earth of the Apostles Peter and Paul; the captain's cabinet and quarterdeck are the royal offices of the papacy; and the apostolic college and her cabins filled with passengers are the faithful. Her hold is lined with relics of her saints, her decks are stained with the blood of her martyrs, and aboard this vessel looms a prevailing sense that their spirits still dwell there. Neither enemy nor incompetence can cause this vessel to sink or veer off course from her destination. The Barque of Peter is material, perpetual, indestructible, and unique from all other vessels. Thus can we romanticize the Catholic Church.

If the Barque of Peter were really the Roman Catholic Church, the material vessel would belong to the essence of that Church so that if the barque could ever be lost or sunk, the Church would cease to exist, and if the barque could ever change substantially the faithful would lose their identities. In this analogy *barque* signifies *Church* and *of Peter* signifies *of Rome* so that if her crew and passengers left the ship, they could no longer be identified as belonging to the Church of Rome.

This analogy should make it obvious why most Catholics accuse the Sedevacantists of contradicting the doctrine of indefectibility. Sedevacantists consider the barque inessential or accidental to the existence and perpetuation of the Church so that in times of peril, when passengers fear the ship is bound to sink or that enemies have invaded and conquered her, they can abandon ship without severing connection to the foundation of their faith. However, the Sedevacantists fundamentally err in assuming that any barque can potentially be a Barque of Peter depending only on the faith of its passengers. This is because the Sedevacantists fail to acknowledge the Church's human and material foundational components identified earlier, in part II.

By considering the Church's foundation as something merely spiritual, the Sedevacantists have unwittingly adopted a central tenet of Protestantism. But consider this: If an intangible or purely mystical foundation comprised the whole essence of the Church, as Dimond and many Sedevacantists erroneously believe, the Sedevacantist theory would carry considerably more weight. Like the Eastern Orthodox Church, they could then condemn the Roman Church for falling into heresy or apostasy without contravening indefectibility of the universal Church. However, the Roman Catholic teachings on the Holy See pose an insurmountable and demoralizing problem for all Sedevacantists. By condemning the Roman Church, Sedevacantists are condemning her divinely laid foundation and simultaneously revealing their particular Sedevacantist churches as having counterfeit foundations. Metaphorically speaking, Sedevacantists do not have the barque. At best they sail a foreign ship, and at worst they have crew and passengers at large on the open seas. That is how we can know with certitude that all Sedevacantists fly false flags when attempting to identify their groups as the Roman Catholic Church; they do not have the correct foundation. If the papacy is the foundation of the Church, Rome is the foundation of the papacy, and the Sedevacantists definitively do not have either one.

What the Sedevacantists fail to understand is that because the barque belongs to the Church's constitution, they cannot sever connection to it without losing their own identities. This, of course, is what all Sedevacantists have inadvertently done. Most of the Roman Catholic faithful whom the Sedevacantists approach and present with their tracts and literature instinctively know this, which explains why the majority of traditional Catholics do not support the Sedevacantists despite the overwhelming evidence that the post–Vatican II Roman Pontiffs have been manifest heretics. Contrary to the charge levied by some of the more aggressive/bullying Sedevacantist types, those who refuse to accept Sedevacantism after recognizing the theory's inherent contradictions should not be assumed to be liars, nor should it be said that they have been punished by God with a spiritual blindness for not loving the truth. The real truth is that these Catholics are caught in a doctrinal quandary through no fault of their own and realize why they are damned if they do and damned if they don't. Consequently they choose to remain attached to the Roman-based structure as opposed to independent chapels and their self-constituted configurations.

Metamorphosis

All Sedevacantists agree that the characteristics, attributes, and properties of the Church as defined earlier were clearly identifiable until a counterfeit sect allegedly assumed control of Rome. However, the Sedevacantists do not agree on how or when the supposed transformation occurred. Remember the pertinent words of the Reverend Divine:

> All heretics of every sect hold that the Church has, in some way or other, failed; otherwise, as I have said, they cannot assign any reason

for their separation from her; but as to the time of her defection, they are not agreed.[107]

When considering the Church's indefectibility of essence, it should become clear why it is impossible that the Barque of Peter could set sail from point A in 1962 and become another barque by the time she reached her destination, point B, in 1965. All of the elements that constitute the Catholic Church, and which were identifiable at the beginning of 1962, had to remain intact and identifiable at the close of Vatican II in 1965 and to the present day. Indefectibility in being or essence means that *if* the Church that entered into the Second Vatican Council was the real Roman Catholic Church, then the Church that emerged from that council *is still* the Roman Catholic Church unless it can be shown to have stood in opposition to the false church that emerged from and illegitimately ratified the council. If we cannot account for such a "true" Church then the Catholic Church suffered a defection.

Similarly, if the Church that entered into the Second Vatican Council was *not* the real Church, then the real Church must be accounted for immediately preceding the council. Moreover, that Church's departure from Rome must be traceable from that time to the present day, or again the Catholic Church would have suffered a defection. Perhaps a better way to expose the problem is to pose a multipart question: Where was the Roman Church, and who comprised its offices before Vatican II, at the time of the council, immediately following the council, and to the present day? Let those who endeavor to answer this question take care to specifically address the Church's foundational component that comprise the Roman papacy and not merely pockets of faithful, scattered priests or bishops.

Let us now look at two prevailing theories proposed by the Sedevacantists that attempt to explain *how* this transposition of Churches

---

107 Devine, *The Creed Explained*, 290.

allegedly occurred and notice the clear defection involved in each. The two prevailing theories are as follow:

1. The Roman Church, Vicar of Christ, and episcopal body defected from the Catholic faith and formally espoused heresy at some arbitrary point in time.
2. Non-Catholic infiltrators overthrew the Roman Church and replaced her visible head, central government, episcopal body, and seven sacraments with counterfeits at some arbitrary point in time.

The commonality in both theories is that on some arbitrary day, all of the essential components of the Roman Church identified her as the true Church, but on some subsequent day they did not. Whether this transformation or transposition of Churches occurred according to the first or second theory is inconsequential. The actual date or time of this transformation is also inconsequential. What is of consequence is the belief that either theory could occur at all. It is this actual transformation of a living, visible organism from *being* the Roman Catholic Church into *not being* the Roman Catholic Church that I want to zero in on because I am certain that the Sedevacantists cannot explain it without contradicting indefectibility of the Church. In fact it is this belief that stands out as the first principal heresy in the Sedevacantist theory—that a defection of the Roman Church occurred in any capacity. So if one were to state Sedevacantism's fundamental premise, it would sound like this: On some arbitrary date or period of time, the Roman Catholic Church, Barque of Peter, Mystical Body of Christ, metamorphosed into the end-times, apostate Church of the Antichrist.

At this point some Sedevacantists will accuse me of misrepresenting what they believe. Recognizing the problem in what I have stated as being their *real* premise, they will tend to migrate toward the second theory stated above, which says the Roman Church did not transform into another Church; rather another Church has usurped the place of the real Roman Church. In an attempt to conserve indefectibility and infallibility, they will claim that the "true" Church exists elsewhere. But in truth I did not misrepresent Sedevacantists by either theory. Contrarily, the Sedevacantists misrepresent themselves. Out of desperation to preserve an idealized concept of the Church, Sedevacantists do not realize that for Sedevacantism to be true by any theory, a defection of the Church had to come first. Take your pick of the two prevailing theories offered for the transposition of Churches; it makes no difference to the point. Though differing in methodology, both theories directly involve a defection of the foundation of the Roman Church, one *actively* and the other *passively*. I will explain.

In the first theory, Sedevacantists have the Holy See and entire episcopal body defecting and leading the rest of the Church into a great apostasy. This is an *active/positive defection* of the Church because the hierarchy would have done the defecting. Going back to the analogy of the Barque of Peter, the legitimate captain and crew would have sabotaged the barque and passengers so it could not arrive at its destination.

In the second theory, Sedevacantists have the Church's enemies orchestrating a successful coup d'état of the Roman Church to its foundation. This is a *passive/negative defection* from the faith because the hierarchy would have allowed a coup d'état to occur. In such a case, the legitimate captain and crew could have been mugged, drugged, murdered, or imprisoned while their counterfeits sabotaged the barque and deceived her passengers. Again, with counterfeits in control of the barque, it would not be possible for the vessel to arrive at her destination.

Furthermore, for the second theory to be true, an active/positive defection would have preceded the passive defection because the "true" Church would have been responsible for elevating enough non-Catholic infiltrators (Communists, Marrano Jews, Freemasons, etc.) into positions of power that they could eventually overthrow the Church at Vatican II or whenever. Nevertheless, *allowing* a defection is still a defection. Sedevacantists subscribing to the second theory claim that the infiltration and coup d'état were successful, but were they? We must remember that indefectibility assures the faithful that even if the enemy successfully attained influential positions in the hierarchy, they could only fail in their attempt to overthrow the Roman Church; otherwise the gates of hell would have prevailed. The mind-set of the Church is clear on this point:

> The gift of indefectibility is expressly promised to the Church by Christ, in the words in which He declares that the gates of hell shall not prevail against it. It is manifest that, could the storms which the Church encounters so shake it as to alter its essential characteristics and make it other than Christ intended it to be, the gates of hell, i.e., the powers of evil, would have prevailed.[108]

> ...And, since the gates of hell, to overthrow the Church, if this were possible, arise from all sides with ever greater hatred against its *divinely established foundation*, We judge it to be necessary for the protection, safety, and increase of the Catholic flock, with the approbation of the Council, to set forth the doctrine on the institution, perpetuity, and nature of the Sacred Apostolic Primacy, in which the strength and solidarity of the whole Church consist...[109]

Remember, the foundation Vatican Council I is referring to above is the papacy, *not* articles of faith as recited in the Nicene Creed.[110] Moreover, if counterfeits replaced the legitimate officials, departments, and ministries of the Catholic Church's government, what happened to them?

---

108 Joyce, *The Catholic Encyclopedia*, 756.
109 Denzinger, *The Sources of Catholic* Dogma, 1821.
110 I find it especially revealing that the creeds of faith (Nicene and Niceno-Constantinopolitan) formulated in council while East and West were still one Church mention nothing about Peter, the primacy, Rome, or the Roman Pontiffs. If the papal dogmas of the Church were true from the foundation of the Church, this would have to be one of the most significant omissions of the ancient Church. After all, even Pontius Pilot made his name into the creed, yet not a word about Peter or Rome despite the fact that Christ purportedly founded the Church on Peter and bound his primacy to Rome in perpetuity.

On Indefectibility

According to indefectibility they could not be overthrown; they could not be rendered impotent; they could not become invisible; they could not *all* simultaneously defect from the faith. So where did they go?

Let us also remember another important point concerning the Roman Church: indefectibility precludes deception.

> Men might then be deceived, as they would not be able to recognise any longer that which is the true Church established by Christ on earth. They would, therefore, be destitute of those means which would guide men in that affair which is the most excellent and necessary of all, namely, in the knowledge of the true religion. And all this would be at variance with the end, which Christ had in view in establishing His Church.[111]

It is supposed to be impossible for the Catholic faithful to be deceived when doing and believing what they are obliged to do and believe in accordance with Catholic doctrines (i.e., maintaining communion with Rome). If the Roman Church could be the source of such a deception, the Church would have defected according to its own terms. No matter how Sedevacantists theorize the transformation or transposition of Churches, indefectibility is violated because of one incontrovertible flaw in their premise: Sedevacantism directly involves a defection or failure of the Holy Roman See. "Only to One particular Church is indefectibility assured, viz. to the See of Rome..."[112]

In an obvious contradiction to the doctrine of indefectibility and the dogmas of the First Vatican Council, the Holy See is the vital organ of the Catholic Church that Sedevacantists claim either apostatized or was overthrown by her enemies over half a century ago and which has not been legitimately accounted for since. As to the whereabouts of the "true" Catholic Church, even the brightest Sedevacantist minds cannot account for a single Church that could indisputably be identified as

---

111 Devine, *The Creed Explained*, 292.
112 Joyce, *The Catholic Encyclopedia*, 756.

Roman Catholic. According to all Sedevacantists, faithlessness has not only gained access to the foundation of Roman Catholicism; faithlessness has conquered it.

Defection of the Hierarchy and Sacraments

The Barque of Peter would have defected without a crew because the barque's founder (Jesus Christ) instituted a crew from the outset. Therefore the Church must always retain a legitimate, visibly unified, apostolic hierarchy and the means to sanctify the Church through the sacraments:

> "...*nor can it ever lose the Apostolic hierarchy, or the sacraments through which Christ communicates grace to men*...By the hierarchy and the sacraments, Christ, further, made the Church the depositary of the graces of the Passion. Were it to lose either of these, it could no longer dispense to men the treasures of grace."[113]
>
> Thesis.—Jesus Christ Wished his Church to Endure without any Essential Change until the End of Time. b. *Christ, sole mediator between God and man, has confided the fruits of His Redemption and the means of salvation to the Church.* Now there will always be souls to be saved by these means; hence Christ, in sending the apostles to teach and to baptize, promises to be with them all days, even to the consummation of the world (Matth. xxviii. 20). *But this perpetual indefectibility of the apostolic ministry, on which everything depends in the Church, evidently entails that of the Church itself.*[114]

There are many branches of Sedevacantism, and not one of them has the complete package of essentials the doctrine of indefectibility *should have* protected. Let us now look at how Sedevacantists consider the indefectibility of the apostolic hierarchy and sacraments.

---

113 Ibid.
114 Devivier, *Christian Apologetics*, 392–393.

Two Schools of Sedevacantists

For the sake of simplicity, there are two schools of Sedevacantists (not to be misconstrued with the two prevailing theories used to explain the transformation/transposition of Churches addressed earlier):

1. The apostolic hierarchy and sacraments continued after Vatican II by way of self-constituted men
2. The apostolic hierarchy and sacraments have been lost indefinitely

Proponents of these two schools are at constant war with each other, each claiming it is *they* who represent the "real" Catholic Church while the other is in schism. The truth is that both involve contradictory positions, hypocrisy, and violation of immutable doctrines of the Church. For example, school one erroneously proposes:

- *The formal and material* elements of apostolic succession are inessential to apostolicity.[115]
- Apostolic succession is not severed when the Church must supply deficiencies in the human transmission of apostolic power.
- Visibility of a Sedevacantist bishop, priest, chapel, or congregation suffices for visible, hierarchical unity of the Church.

School one mutilates the indefectibility of the Church by reducing her hierarchical structure to scattered, headless churches, none of which can be shown to possess all of her essential characteristics, attributes, and properties. Furthermore, by disclaiming the formal element of succession, school one is forced to accept an impotent episcopacy that lacks teaching power and most conspicuously pastoral (legislative, juridical, and punitive) power. Assuming that some deficiencies of apostolicity are

---

115 Formal and material elements of apostolic succession are covered in chapter four.

supplied by the Church still severs the means Christ instituted for succession—human succession.

The fact is a self-constituted apostolic hierarchy does not exist in the Church founded by Jesus Christ, and every Sedevacantist is self-constituted. Furthermore the Church can never reach a crisis stage that warrants a self-constituted apostolic authority unless the proponents of this heretical position are prepared to admit that the Church could defect because a defection is precisely what their position would have to entail. The bottom line is that the first school of Sedevacantists, along with all heretics and schismatics throughout the history of the Church, lost a valid claim to apostolicity and unity of the Church when they severed communion with Rome. Additionally, proponents of school one further divisions with each and every priestly or episcopal ordination they illicitly confer.

School two erroneously proposes:

- The Church lost its apostolic hierarchy and cannot find it anywhere in the free world.
- The Church lost its sacraments by which sanctifying grace is made available to men.
- Unity of the Church does not necessitate having an identifiable hierarchy.

School two mutilates the indefectibility of the Church by having the apostolic hierarchy disappearing off the face of the Earth. Proponents of school two attempt to justify their position by claiming the disappearance of the apostolic hierarchy and sacraments is only temporary, and the Church will gloriously resurrect at the end of the Great Apostasy. Nevertheless they are again confounded by the doctrine of indefectibility: "Indefectibility—2. This is a property by which the Church cannot fail; it is that by which *she cannot either lose or have diminished any of her divine qualities or gifts even for a short time.*"[116]

---

116 Devine, *The Creed Explained*, 289.

Both schools erroneously propose:

- The Roman Catholic Church exists without its divinely laid foundation.
- The visible Church exists wherever faithful are found (Protestantism's invisible Church ecclesiology).[117]

We will address these faults again in subsequent chapters, especially in objection fifteen. All that is necessary to know for now with respect to indefectibility of the hierarchy and sacraments is that the hierarchy and the sacraments both belong to the essential constitution of the Church because Jesus Christ instituted them from the foundation of the Church, and the Sedevacantists lost them when they lost Rome.

Remnant Church Heresy

Having addressed some of which the Catholic Church is principally composed, this is an appropriate place to dispel another myth the Sedevacantists promote. The myth in many Sedevacantist circles is that *they* are the "remnant Church" in fulfillment of certain prophecies that predicted a greatly reduced Church in the end-times. Earlier we saw Dimond employ the Sedevacantist-remnant Church theory twice (emphasis added):

> …indefectibility of the Church requires that at least *a remnant* of the Church will exist until the end of the world…[118]

> There is not one teaching of the Catholic Church that can be quoted which is contrary to the fact that there is presently a counterfeit sect *which has reduced the true Catholic Church to a remnant* in the days of the

---

117 This ecclesiology denies the necessity of visible hierarchical unity.
118 Dimond, *The Truth*, 298.

Great Apostasy, which is presided over by antipopes who have falsely posed as popes.[119]

Indefectibility guarantees that the Church must remain unchanged in all of her essential constitutional components listed thus far, even if this Church is reduced to a handful of members. Accordingly, a "remnant Church" could only mean a Church reduced in its quantitative size while remaining unaffected in its composition. But note that this is *not* how Sedevacantists such as Dimond employ it. When Dimond and other Sedevacantists speak of the "remnant Church," they imply not only a small Church but also a Church that is incomplete or compromised in one or more essential areas. Therefore the remnant Church theory that today's Sedevacantists promote contravenes indefectibility and is a heresy.

In conclusion to objection one, it has been demonstrated that the Sedevacantist thesis is completely incompatible with the Church's doctrine of indefectibility. All Sedevacantist theories fail because they are based on the heretical premise that a defection of the Roman Church has occurred. Consequently all Sedevacantists are forced into the absurd position of denying the *possibility* of defection of the Church while simultaneously proposing that a defection has occurred *in fact*. Their confusion is a consequence of recognizing a defection in reality while knowing it could never happen. What this all boils down to is that the Sedevacantists have assumed the Church's contradictions in an attempt to save its infallibility. We end part III with the following charts depicting how Dimond's "remnant church" stacks up against the Catholic Church.

---

119   Ibid., 299.

On Indefectibility

Essential Constitutions Compared

Foundation*	Remnant Church	Catholic Church
Blessed Apostle Peter		√
Apostolic primacy		√
Rome		√
Roman Pontiff as successor to Peter	√	

Member/Component		
Apostolic hierarchy		√
Valid and licit sacraments		√

Characteristic, attribute, property		
Unity		√
Visibility		√
Authority		√
Immutability		√

* The four foundational components are mutually dependent, so one cannot exist in isolation from the other three.

Sedevacantist Heresies	School 1*	School 2**
The whole Church can fail entirely for a time		√
The visible Church can fail but not the invisible Church		√

50

The Church can fail in part for a time	√	√
The Church can lose attributes or perfections	√	√
The Church can retain maimed and vitiated attributes	√	√
Formal and material elements of apostolic succession are inessential to apostolicity		√
Apostolic succession is not severed when the Church must supply deficiencies in human transmission		√
Authority is not an indefectible property of the Church's essential constitution		√
Visibility of a Sedevacantist bishop, priest, chapel, or congregation suffices for visible, hierarchical unity of the Roman Church		√
The Church did not defect if a crisis warrants a self-constituted apostolic hierarchy		√
The Church did not defect if a crisis warrants no apostolic hierarchy		√
The Church lost its apostolic hierarchy and cannot locate it anywhere in the free world		√
The Church lost the sacraments by which sanctifying grace is made available to men		√
Unity of the Church does not necessitate a visibly unified, identifiable hierarchy	√	√
The Roman Catholic Church exists without a foundation	√	√
Visibility of the Church is only where faithful are found	√	√
A defection involving the Roman See occurred in some capacity	√	√

On Indefectibility

* School one is comprised of all Sedevacantists who propose that the apostolic hierarchy and sacraments continued after Vatican II by way of self-constituted men.
* School two is comprised of all Sedevacantists who propose that the apostolic hierarchy and sacraments have been lost indefinitely.

Summary

Non-Sedevacantists object to Sedevacantism because "The Gates of Hell cannot prevail against the Church; Christ said He would be with his Church all days until the end of the world; and that what all Sedevacantists are saying is contrary to the promises of Christ."[120] My position is agreement with this objection; the Sedevacantists contradict the Church's indefectibility in numerous ways. The first principal heresy of the Sedevacantists is that a defection of the Roman See occurred in fact. Dimond responds by contending that the Sedevacantist thesis does not involve a defection of the Church, and he relies on an abbreviated definition of indefectibility for support. I compared three definitions of the doctrine of indefectibility with Dimond's definition in order to demonstrate the Sedevacantists' shortcomings.

The Creed Explained by Rev. Arthur Devine describes indefectibility as pertaining to the Church's being or existence; its authority, perpetuity, visibility and immutability; the Apostolic See specifically; the Church's essential constitutional properties and attributes; and that indefectibility precludes deception. Devine also identified heresies pertaining to indefectibility, such as: the whole Church can fail entirely for a time; the visible Church can fail but not the invisible Church; and the Church can fail in part, at least for a time and even always, by losing this or that attribute or perfection or retaining it but maimed and vitiated.[121]

---

120 Dimond, *The Truth*, 298.
121 Devine, *The Creed Explained*, 289–292.

Christian Apologetics by Rev. W. Devivier defines the Church's indefectibility in the perpetuation of its interior constitution and exterior form and in the preservation of all of its properties and prerogatives. Devivier says the Church will never be deprived of its constituent elements, including its members, chiefs, and organization. The Church's essential properties and divine prerogatives are also indefectible, and they include its unity, sanctity, catholicity, authority, and infallibility. Devivier points out that indefectibility applies to the Church as a whole, not to each of its parts or particular churches. Lastly, Devivier identifies the following heresy: the invisible Church cannot fail, but the visible Church can fail even for short durations.[122]

The Catholic Encyclopedia describes the Church's indefectibility as its ability to preserve its essential characteristics unimpaired, the impossibility of constitutional change, its incorruptibility in faith or morals, its inability to lose its apostolic hierarchy or sacraments, its incapacity to suffer substantial change, and that the Church cannot err in defining the truths of revelation. Additionally *The Catholic Encyclopedia* states that indefectibility does not guarantee each part of the Church against heresy or apostasy, only the corporate body. Only to one particular Church is indefectibility assured—*the Roman See*.[123]

Dimond's definition of indefectibility is incomplete and leaves out numerous distinctions that would reveal deficiencies of Sedevacantism. Indefectibility is more than a continuance of believers sharing the same faith until the end of time. Indefectibility tells us that for any Church to be considered Roman Catholic, it must be identifiable by all of her essential components, attributes, and properties, even if she were reduced to a remnant of faithful. The "remnant Church" theory that the Sedevacantists promote is false and misleading because it teaches that a diminished Church in one or more essential areas is all that has survived the Second Vatican Council. By definition a diminished Church in any of its essential areas constitutes a defection.

---

122 Devivier, *Christian Apologetics*, 393–393.
123 Joyce, *The Catholic Encyclopedia*, 756.

Essence has been defined as a set of attributes that make an entity or substance what it is, that it has by necessity, and without which it would lose its identity.[124] In the analogy of the Church to the Barque of Peter, *Barque* signifies *Church* and *of Peter* signifies *of Rome* so that if her crew and passengers left the ship, they could no longer be identified as members of the Roman Catholic Church. Sedevacantists err in considering the barque itself as inessential to the existence and perpetuation of the Church and in believing its passengers can sever connection to it without losing their own identities. All Sedevacantists lost their Roman Catholic identities when they severed connection with the foundation of the Catholic Church.

The papacy is the foundation of Roman Catholicism; remove it or divide it and the whole institution crumbles to the earth. If the Church's foundation were articles of faith, such as are found in the Creeds of Catholic Faith, Sedevacantism would carry weight. Like the Eastern Orthodox Church, the Sedevacantists would then be able to condemn the Roman Church for falling into heresy or apostasy without contravening indefectibility of the entire Catholic Church.

The papacy consists of the following constituent components: the Apostle Peter, the sacred primacy (authority), Rome (the Holy See), and the Roman Pontiff. These constituent parts are mutually dependent; they cannot be divided without frustrating the end for which they exist—unity of the Church. The Sedevacantists do not have each of these components and must divide and redefine the papacy in order to make Sedevacantism *appear* to work.

According to the doctrine of indefectibility, individual parts of the Catholic Church as a whole can defect or apostatize but never the main stem, which is essentially comprised in the Roman Church. Because the Church founded by Christ is essentially juridical, the Roman Church is comprised of not only the Roman Pontiff but also the whole ensemble of departments or ministries that assist him with the government of the

---

124 "Essence."

Church. These include the Roman congregations, tribunals, and the offices of Curia.[125]

Two prevailing Sedevacantist theories attempt to explain the Roman Church's defection:

1. The Roman Church, Vicar of Christ, central government, and episcopal body defected from the Catholic faith and formally espoused heresy at some arbitrary point in time.
2. Non-Catholic infiltrators overthrew the Roman Church and replaced her visible head, central government, episcopal body, and seven sacraments with counterfeits at some arbitrary point in time.

For Sedevacantism to be true by either theory, a defection of the Church had to come first. Any defection of the Church, whether active or passive, is still a defection.

Indefectibility guarantees that the Church will never lose her apostolic hierarchy or sacraments. The Church is comprised of a visible head and an adjoined body comprised of the episcopacy; together they form the Church's essential hierarchical structure. The body of the Church militant is comprised of two parts, the *ecclesia docens* and the *ecclesia audiens*. Many Sedevacantists err in believing that the ecclesia audiens can perpetuate the Roman Catholic Church, but only the ecclesia docens belongs to the Church's indefectible constitution.

Concerning the indefectibility of the apostolic hierarchy and sacraments, two schools of Sedevacantism exist and are at odds with each other. The first school believes the apostolic hierarchy and sacraments are perpetuated after Vatican II by way of self-constituted individuals. The first school contradicts indefectibility because a self-constituted apostolic hierarchy does not exist in the Church founded by Jesus Christ, nor could the Church ever experience a crisis that could warrant such a thing unless the Church first defected according to its own terms. All

---

125 Ojetti, *The Catholic Encyclopedia*, 147.

Sedevacantist clergy, along with all heretics and schismatics throughout the history of the Church, lost a valid claim to apostolicity and the unity of the Church when they severed communion with Rome.

The second school of Sedevacantism consists of those who believe the apostolic hierarchy and sacraments have been lost indefinitely. Both schools contradict indefectibility by proposing that the Roman Catholic Church exists without Rome and that the visible Church exists wherever faithful are found (similar to Protestantism's invisible Church ecclesiology).

All Sedevacantists deny the *possibility* of a defection of the Church while simultaneously proposing that a defection has occurred *in fact*. Their confusion is a consequence of recognizing a defection in reality while knowing it could never happen. The Sedevacantists have assumed the Church's contradictions in an attempt to save its infallibility.

The Sedevacantists err in believing they can have both a great apostasy involving the Roman Church and the doctrine of indefectibility. The truth is that either the Roman Church is in a period of *sede vacante* because of a defection or else the present Roman Church headed by Pope Francis is still the Roman Catholic Church because indefectibility guarantees it.

Objections

~~~

Objection: You are confusing the city of Rome with the Diocese of Rome. The Holy See can relocate anywhere in the world. For example, for nearly seventy years preceding the Western Schism, the Holy See was located in Avignon. There were also various other periods when the Holy See and the Curia were in places other than Rome, sometimes separated from each other.[126] This proves that the Sedevacantist thesis does not contradict the First Vatican Council or the doctrine of indefectibility.

Answer: If the Holy See relocates to a satellite location in another geographical territory and governs from that territory, then there is neither a defection of Rome nor a contradiction with the First Vatican Council. If the Sedevacantists would like to claim that this is what happened in our time, let them prove the claim by showing their opponents the "real" Holy See and proving its legitimacy. If, however, the Holy See is taken over by a non-Catholic sect, if it has

---

126 *The Catholic Encyclopedia* states: "The papal reservations of benefices, customary in the Middle Ages, made necessary a more exact knowledge of the location of the 'Holy See,' e.g., when the incumbent of a benefice happened to die 'apud sanctam sedem.' Where was the 'Holy See,' when the pope lived apart from the ordinary central administration? From the thirteenth to the fifteenth century we find no satisfactory solution of this question, and can only observe the decisions of the Curia in individual cases." [Paul Maria Baumgarten, *The Catholic Encyclopedia*, Vol. 7 (New York: Robert Appleton Company, 1910).]

disappeared, if its constituent parts and members cannot be known, all of which various Sedevacantist sects claim, then a defection took place.

Objection: The Holy See could have been driven out of Rome and into exile. This would not contradict the First Vatican Council or the indefectibility of the Church.

Answer: 1. If the Holy See was driven from Rome then it must be visible and known or else the Roman Church defected. In that case let the Sedevacantists unveil the "real" Holy See. **2.** If the Holy See was driven from Rome then we should know the identities of the pope and the members of the other administrative offices of the "real" Church at the time of the purported takeover and subsequent exile, since they would have been in office at that critical time. Lists that show the names of successors of popes and important administrative government offices are readily available from that time. Let the Sedevacantists produce the names of these important people to prove that a defection did not take place.

Objection: The Church endured great persecutions during the first centuries, often existing only in the catacombs. If the Church did not defect in those times, then what the Sedevacantists are proposing also would not constitute a defection. The first centuries prove that your understanding of the Church's indefectibility is wrong.

Answer: 1. If the Sedevacantists would like to propose that the essential components of the Church's indefectible constitution (e.g., Holy See, visibility, unity, apostolicity, hierarchy, sacraments, etc.) ceased to exist in the first three centuries then let them support the claim. **2.** Even if they could do so, that would support Sedevacantism only insofar as both situations would contradict indefectibility. **3.** Whatever happened to the universal Church during the first centuries and several subsequent centuries would have little to do with the doctrine of indefectibility because neither the papal doctrines nor indefectibility's exclusivity to the Roman Church existed yet; these were later innovations.

Objection: The three sources you used to define the Church's indefectibility are fallible and could contain errors.

Answer: If someone can produce teachings with approbation from Church authority that contradict any of the referenced sources describing the Church's indefectibility or a legitimate historical precedence to the Sedevacantist thesis in contradiction to the provided definitions…congratulations to that person for helping support one of my premises in this work.

Objection: St. Athanasius wrote, "Even if Catholics faithful to tradition are reduced to a handful, they are the ones who are the true Church of Jesus Christ."[127] This proves that even great saints believed Sedevacantism was at least theoretically possible.

Answer: 1. For Roman Catholics a basic assumption must accompany the reading of this quote, or else St. Athanasius would be joining Dimond in denying Roman doctrines that should have been well known since the foundation of the Church. The basic assumption is that Athanasius's understanding of "the true Church of Jesus Christ" is congruent with the Church's indefectibility as well as the other points of doctrine that I will address in objections five, six, and fifteen. **2.** Athanasius lived when East and West were one Church. At that time, if the concept of losing the Church of Rome, its bishop, and a large percentage of the episcopal body under the Roman Pontiff was not considered contradictory to the Church's indefectibility, the

---

127 Francisco Radecki and Dominic Radecki, *Tumultuos Times: The Twenty General Councils of the Catholic Church and Vatican II and its Aftermath* (Wayne, MI: Saint Joseph's Media, 2004), 573-574.

reason is that it was not. Contrary to later Roman Catholic teaching, indefectibility of the Church was not a concept exclusive for Rome. **3.** In this historic example of the spread of Arianism, "the rock" of the Catholic Church was not the papacy, as it ought to have been according to Roman Catholic teaching on the papacy. Athanasius the Great, doctor of the Church and champion of orthodoxy, was the patriarch of Alexandria and from several accounts is on record condemning the Roman pope for not upholding the faith. If the Roman pretensions of the papacy were true, one would expect the roles of the Roman pope and Athanasius during the spread of Arianism to have been reversed or at least congruent. History reveals that there were times that Rome preserved the faith when other apostolic sees lost it and other times that other apostolic sees preserved the faith when Rome lost it.

Objection: Our Lady of La Sallette predicted, "Rome will lose the faith and become the seat of the Anti-Christ…the Church will be in eclipse."[128] That is exactly what has happened to the Roman Catholic Church! Anybody who can't see this is being punished by God with spiritual blindness because he or she doesn't love the truth.

Answer: Apparently the lady of La Salette was also unaware that the concept of Rome losing the faith contradicts the doctrine of indefectibility. The lady was also unaware that her prophecy would be officially dispelled just twenty-four years later, in the First Vatican Council's Dogmatic Constitution on the Church of Christ. Embarrassingly for this "prophet," dogmas are true retroactively. Moreover, if Sedevacantists insist on using this quote from La Salette, they ought to quote the passages that contradict Sedevacantism.[129]

---

128 "Modern History Sourcebook: The Apparitions at La Sallette, 1846," Fordham University, accessed May 17, 2015, http://legacy.fordham.edu/halsall/mod/1846sallette.asp.
129 The following links shed additional light on the purported visions and messages of La Salette: http://www.unitypublishing.com/prophecy/fake-salette.htm, http://www.romehasspoken.com/uploads/Dimond_and_La_Salette-1.pdf.

On Indefectibility

Objection: Indefectibility does not exclude antipopes posing as popes (as we have had numerous times in the past, even in Rome) or a counterfeit sect that reduces the adherents of the true Catholic Church to a remnant in the last days. This is precisely what is predicted to occur in the last days and what happened during the Arian crisis.[130]

Answer: The Roman Catholic doctrine of indefectibility excludes the possibility of Sedevacantism, as proven in objection one.

Objection: Heretics are the gates of hell and could never have authority over the Church of Christ. Heretics are not members of the Church. That's why a heretic could never be a pope. The fact that heretics currently rule from Rome proves that Sedevacantism is the only explanation for the current crisis.[131]

Answer: If heretics rule the Catholic Church right now, it does not prove that Sedevacantism is correct, but it would prove that the Church could contradict itself and remain the Church.

Objection: The Vatican II Church is manifestly heretical, so this proves that it is not the Roman Catholic Church.

Answer: Examining the evidence for the Sedevacantist claims against the post–Conciliar Church is not the objective of this work; holding Sedevacantists accountable to Roman Catholic doctrines is.

Objection: It is not Sedevacantists who expose the heretical Vatican II antipopes who are asserting that the gates of hell have prevailed against the Church; it is those who obstinately defend them as popes even though they can clearly be proven manifest heretics.[132]

---

130 Dimond, *The Truth*, 298.
131 Ibid., 299.
132 Ibid.

Answer: As proven in objection one, Sedevacantists contradict indefectibility of the Church. If the Vatican II Church also contradicts indefectibility, then Sedevacantists need to reconsider their beliefs about the Catholic Church.

Objection: If the Church did not consider Sedevacantism possible, true popes would not have authored documents such as *Cum Ex Apostolatus Officio*. Neither would the Church implement canon laws that remove heretics from office. Even theologians speculated about popes becoming heretics.

Answer: 1. Sedevacantism as a Vatican II countermovement contradicts indefectibility and is a heresy. **2.** With regard to the aforementioned documents and laws, it is my position that any given living magisterium remains at liberty to contradict its own teachings and history (e.g., adding the filioque, condemning and then approving heliocentrism, condemning and then approving religious liberty and ecumenism, etc.). **3.** Sedevacantism is not the same thing as the Church losing a man who falsely claims to be the pope. Sedevacantism is a theory of defection of the Church that attempts to disguise the fact by calling it a papal interregnum.

Objection: St. Ignatius of Antioch said, "Wherever the bishop appears, there let the people be; as wherever Jesus Christ is, there is the Catholic Church."[133] This proves that not all of the components of the Church have to be present in a remnant Church to be compatible with indefectibility.

Answer: More likely it proves that Ignatius was ignorant of the modern pretensions of the papacy, which contradicts the Catholic Church's claim that the papacy was instituted by Christ as a matter of divine law

---

133 "The Epistle of Ignatius to the Smyrnaeans," New Advent, accessed May 17, 2015. http://www.newadvent.org/fathers/0109.htm.

from the foundation of the Church. Ignatius was from Antioch, another Church of the East. From the perspective of Eastern Orthodoxy, the episcopacy was the highest authority in the Church, and all episcopal sees were considered the chairs of Peter, or apostolic sees. Indefectibility, as later taught by the Roman Church and covered in objection one, would not have been a recognized doctrine during the time of Ignatius.

Objection: During the Arian heresy, St. Athanasius wrote to his flock: "It is a fact that they have the premises—but you have the apostolic faith. They can occupy our churches, but they are outside the true faith."[134] This proves that your interpretation of indefectibility is wrong. It is the faith of its members that perpetuates the Church.

Answer: My understanding of the doctrine of indefectibility is correct. As with the Ignatius quote above, Athanasius of Alexandria would not have understood the Roman Church as being the only apostolic see nor that membership in the Church was contingent upon submission and obedience solely to Rome, as would later become a mandatory requirement for Roman Catholics and a principal cause of the thousand-year schism with Eastern Catholics.

Objection: The Gospel of Matthew makes it clear that the deception would be so great in the end-times that even the elect would be deceived: "For there shall arise false Christs and false prophets, and shall shew great signs and wonders, insomuch as to deceive (if possible) even the elect."[135] This is an obvious prophecy for our times and perfectly supports Sedevacantism.

Answer: This prophecy can support the Sedevacantists only if sacred scripture can contradict infallible Catholic doctrines. Therefore

---

134 Radecki, *Tumultuos Times*, 573-574.
135 Matt. 24:24.

either of two things can be concluded about Matthew 24:24: **1.** The Roman Church is neither infallible nor indefectible, which means the Eastern Orthodox Church has been justified in its stance against Rome since the schism. **2.** The Sedevacantists are essentially thinly disguised Protestants for ascribing a heretical interpretation of Matthew 24:24 against the Catholic Church.

Objection: St. Paul warns the faithful not to listen to anyone, even an angel from heaven, who preaches a new gospel.[136] The Vatican II popes have brought a new ecumenical gospel, so Sedevacantists are justified in not following these innovators.

Answer: The Catholic Church can contradict scripture and remain the Catholic Church, but the Sedevacantists cannot contradict the Catholic Church and remain Roman Catholics. Furthermore, scripture preceded the later version of the papacy.

Objection: You are wrong in your understanding of the indefectibility of the Roman See. All it means is that the pope will never officially teach heresy to the whole Church.

Answer: A pope's divine protection from teaching heresy to the whole Church describes his infallibility, which is not the same thing as the doctrine of indefectibility. Sedevacantists have the Roman See in the hands of non-Catholics; Dimond has it in the hands of the Antichrist. Irrespective of how, when, or why these are claimed to have occurred, they necessitate that a defection of the Church preceded it.

---

136 Galatians 1:8.

CHAPTER 2

On the Vicoration of Christ

...much assemblies have only take place in times of great constitutional disturbances, when either there was no pope or the rightful pope was indistinguishable from antipopes. In such abnormal times the safety of the Church becomes the supreme law, and the first duty of the abandoned flock is to find a new shepherd, under whose direction the existing evils may be remedied.[137]

OBJECTION FIVE CONTINUES THE IMPORTANT subject begun in objection one regarding the essential constitution of the Church. In objection one we saw how the Roman Pontiff is an essential component of the Church's foundation: the papacy. Here we find that opponents of Sedevacantism object to the possibility of a vacancy of the papacy for forty or more years.

My position is agreement with this objection, but only from a Roman Catholic perspective. The reason is that Catholic ecclesiology makes the Roman Pontiff indispensable to the Church. In fact fundamental characteristics of the Church are so entirely dependent upon the Vicar of Christ that the Sedevacantists must respond to this objection with an

---

137 J. Wilhelm, *The Catholic Encyclopedia*, (New York: Robert Appleton Co., 1908), Vol. IV, 426.

answer that must be identified as the Sedevacantists' second principal heresy—the Vicar of Christ is accidental to the Church.

Nevertheless, the Sedevacantists' defense based on papal interregnums[138] is excellent. The truth is the Sedevacantists are correct—papal interregnums do occur, and the Church continues to exist. Moreover it is probably true that the Church could exist for forty or more years without a Vicar of Christ. But contrary to what the Sedevacantists think, this does not support their position; it only undermines the papacy.

Throughout this work I make it clear that I do not believe in the divine prerogatives of the papacy, and I am grateful for Vatican II's clash with Sedevacantism for helping me arrive at my conclusions. The Sedevacantists' response to objection five concerning papal interregnums lends considerable support to my own conclusions as well as to the validity of the claims of the Eastern Orthodox Church, and I attempt to impart these to the reader as an alternative and far better explanation for all that has ensued in the Catholic Church since Vatican II.

The ongoing debate between the Sedevacantists and their opponents takes on new meaning when one begins to understand that Catholic ecclesiology does not necessarily have to coincide with how the Church exists and functions in reality. Contradictions between what can be and what should never be is the reason Sedevacantists and non-Sedevacantists are both wrong and right simultaneously. Unfortunately, in a doctrinal stalemate with the Holy See there is no contest; scattered, headless Sedevacantists lose every time, and so once again the Sedevacantists find themselves being punished by the same system they are attempting to defend.

---

138 Also called *Sede Vacante*. The period during which an episcopal see or diocese is vacant, that is, without a bishop. Generally applied to the See of Rome. (Hardon, *Modern Catholic Dictionary*, 496–497.)

Objection Five

❦

The Church cannot exist without a pope, or at least it cannot exist for 40 years without a pope, as Sedevacantists say...[139]

---
139 Dimond, *The Truth*, 308.

Part I

Interregnums

❧

Defection in Disguise

Sedevacantism rests entirely on the myth that the Catholic Church is presently enduring a papal interregnum that began approximately in 1958.[140] The Sedevacantists will argue that since there is nothing contradictory or abnormal about papal interregnums, which began and continued since the death of the first Roman pope, Sedevacantism is tenable—in fact the only tenable position. This is a clever strategy because the Sedevacantists are somewhat correct; there is nothing contradictory about papal interregnums, historically speaking. If the Church were truly enduring a papal interregnum at present, even an extraordinarily long one, it is unlikely that the fact could be contested, especially without a serious rival contender to the office of Peter. Therefore Sedevacantists such as Dimond attempt to convince their opponents that Sedevacantism is essentially the same thing as a papal interregnum.

But here is the catch: The Sedevacantists are not really proposing that the Church is experiencing a papal interregnum; they just deceptively call it one. This strategy has been quite successful in winning converts to Sedevacantism because there is much truth in what Sedevacantists

---

140 The various Sedevacantist factions do not agree on the actual date the purported papal vacancy began.

teach about papal vacancies. Let us look at how Dimond sells this concept in his opening reply to objection five:

> The Church has existed for years without a pope, and does so every time a pope dies. The Church has experienced a papal interregnum (i.e., period without a pope) over 200 different times in Church history. The longest papal interregnum (before Vatican II apostasy) was between Pope St. Marcellinus (296-304) and Pope St. Marcellus (308–309). It lasted for more than three and a half years. Further, theologians teach that the Church can exist for even decades without a pope."[141,142]

Here we are seeing how a shrewd manipulator works. Dimond is correct about all of the above since they are historical facts. The manipulation involved, however, is to convince readers that one thing is the same as another thing when in reality they are two very different things. In fact Sedevacantism appears to work only because it misrepresents itself. You see, what the Sedevacantists are really proposing is by no stretch of the imagination a papal interregnum, and most Sedevacantists know it. Sedevacantism, in all of its shapes, sizes, and colors, is essentially a movement of traditional Catholics that recognizes the defection of the Church while attempting to hide the fact. In other words Sedevacantism is essentially a theory of defection, not a theory of papal interregnum.

Let the reader be advised of the clever manipulation on the part of Dimond and other Sedevacantists who attempt to pass heresy off as a legitimate theory of an extraordinarily long papal interregnum. For those who may be confused, or for those who may have skipped chapter one, it would be beneficial to go back and read that chapter before proceeding here in order to understand the ways Sedevacantism necessarily entails a

---

141 Dimond, *The Truth*, 308.
142 In his book Dimond begins his response to objection six by returning to the subject of objection five—papal interregnums. I have combined that portion of objection six into objection five.

defection of the Church. Proposing that the Mystical Body of Christ has mutated into the end-times, apostate Church of the Antichrist cannot possibly be mistaken for a papal interregnum, but this has not stopped Sedevacantists from attempting to falsify this connection. Whatever else one might choose to call it, the Church is not enduring a papal interregnum.

For the sake of argument, let us ignore the fact that the Sedevacantists misrepresent themselves and pretend that the Roman See has been vacant for the past fifty-seven years. That hypothetical scenario, as imagined by the Sedevacantists today, always involves a defection of the Church. For instance a real interregnum does not disintegrate the hierarchical structure of the Church, as does Sedevacantism. One of many critical functions that must always remain in the Church is the capacity to elect the next pope. We know this because there must always be shepherds in Christ's Church until the end of the world (de fide).

However, according to the Sedevacantists, the headless Church, wherever they imagine it to exist, is incapable of electing a pope; well, at least a real one. We know *that* because the history of the Sedevacantist movement records numerous failed attempts at electing popes, some of whom still dwell among us. There is no way around the fact that Sedevacantism is essentially a theory of defection, yet it has still served a valuable purpose in the grand scheme of things. This should become clearer as we progress and reach the end of this work.

Still, Dimond and the Sedevacantists have defined their position clearly—the Catholic Church does not always need a Roman Pontiff. But now consider this: If the Catholic Church did not need a Roman Pontiff for the past fifty-seven years, then what could possibly make a Roman Pontiff necessary in the fifty-eighth year? The logical conclusion of the Sedevacantist position reveals what I have identified as the Sedevacantists' second principal heresy: The Vicar of Christ is accidental to the Roman Catholic Church.

Next Dimond makes an interesting point about what the Church does *not* teach about papal interregnums:

> Since there is no teaching which puts a limit on such a papal interregnum (a period without a pope), and since the definitions of Vatican I on the perpetuity of Papal Office make absolutely no mention of papal vacancies or how long they can last, if the definitions of Vatican I disprove the sedevacantist position (as some claim), then they also disprove the indefectibility of the Catholic Church—every single time the Church finds itself without a pope. But this is impossible and ridiculous, of course.[143]

Granting that Dimond's assertion is true and no teaching exists that limits papal interregnums, it follows that he and the Sedevacantists must also believe that a papal interregnum can go on longer than fifty-seven years. But what would happen if we were to spin Dimond's statement around and propose it as a question to the Sedevacantists? For instance if it is true that there are no limitations on how long papal interregnums can last, how long would Dimond and the Sedevacantists be willing to say a papal interregnum can last? For example can a papal interregnum last one hundred years? How about two hundred years? How about five hundred years? What about eight hundred years? If eight hundred years were possible then what would preclude one thousand or more years?

If Dimond were to stop me at any of these arbitrarily selected durations for any reason whatsoever, he would have to be able to say why that duration would be untenable. Remember Dimond's own words: "There is no teaching that puts a limit on papal interregnums."[144] Therefore he must agree that it is theoretically possible for a papal interregnum to last indefinitely. Furthermore, if Dimond were to stop me at any duration, his reason would have to be something other than "because that would be absurd" or "our Lord would never allow it to go on that long" because these are the same objections raised by non-Sedevacantists today, which Dimond won't hear of.

---

143 Dimond, *The Truth*, 310.
144 Ibid.

Finally, if Dimond were to answer "an interregnum can last as long as God permits," then let such a nonanswer serve as an indirect admission that a papal interregnum could last indefinitely, perhaps one thousand or more years, because, as Sedevacantists are wont to say, no one can predict what God would or would not permit—oddly enough even when it contradicts infallible teachings of his Church.

Notwithstanding certain contradictions all papal interregnums pose to the papacy and that we will explore in part II, how could one determine that any given duration of papal vacancy is compatible with the doctrine of indefectibility of the Church? I am unaware of a teaching that answers this question, but it is reasonable to assume that if a papal interregnum has already persisted beyond the point where the structured means of electing a Roman Pontiff is incapacitated (e.g., if the College of Cardinals or the entire episcopacy defected or vanished from the face of the Earth), then indefectibility of the Church has been violated. If that is true, then it must be said that Sedevacantism was viable only *before* the defection but not after. In other words today's Sedevacantist movement came too late. Though reluctant to admit this, I think many Sedevacantists realize it, which is why some have abandoned hope for the restoration of the papacy or "resurrection of the Church" and direct their efforts toward promoting the end of the world instead.[145]

In theory Sedevacantists must accept that there is nothing incompatible between the doctrine of indefectibility of the Church and a papal vacancy that lasts for one thousand or more years. The obvious implication is that the Vicar of Christ is nonessential to the existence and the perpetuation of the Roman Catholic Church; he is only an accessory. But if the Sedevacantists are right, and the Vicar of Christ *is* only an accessory, it must be explained why the Church made him the visible foundation of the unities of faith and communion. Would not Christ have known better than to make the unity of the Church contingent on an

---

145 The end-of-world mentality is seen repeatedly throughout the history of Christianity. For the Sedevacantists it can be attributed to despair and desperation in holding a dead-end position.

object that comes and goes, at times for three, fifty, one hundred, or perhaps one thousand years?[146] Surely the Sedevacantists must agree that essential characteristics of the Church, such as visibility, unity, authority, infallibility, etc., are much too indispensable to rest upon a person who essentially amounts to an ornament.

So which is it? Is the Vicar of Christ accidental to the Church, as the Sedevacantist theory necessitates and in which case the papacy becomes suspect of an innovated doctrine? Alternatively, is the Vicar of Christ, as the Vatican Council states, "the perpetual principle and visible foundation of both unities (faith and communion...),"[147] in which case the Vicar of Christ belongs to the essential constitution of the Church and therefore cannot be absent for fifty-seven years?

Let us now return to our earlier definition of essence, which was described as "an attribute or set of attributes that make an entity or substance what it fundamentally is, which it has by necessity, and without which it loses its identity."[148] In the following excerpts from "Christ Founded a Visible Church," Catholic apologists Bryan Cross and Thomas Brown explain why the Roman Pontiff belongs to the essence of the Church (emphasis added):

> *The Catholic position, on the other hand, is that visible hierarchical unity belongs to the essence of Christ's Mystical Body.* For that reason, according to Catholic doctrine, hierarchical unity cannot be lost unless the Mystical Body ceases to exist...*For there to be a visible hierarchy, it is not enough for each member to be ordered to an invisible Head. Merely being ordered to an invisible Head is fully compatible with having no visible hierarchy.* Yet for there to be a visible hierarchy, some visible human persons need to have an ecclesial authority that others do not. According to Catholic doctrine, the authority Christ gave to His Apostles and their successors is threefold: the authority to teach, the authority to lead men to holiness by

---

[146] Remember, the Sedevacantists must agree that papal interregnums could be indefinite.
[147] Denzinger, *The Sources of Catholic Dogma*, 1821.
[148] "Essence."

way of the sacraments, and the authority to govern the Church. These also correspond to Christ's threefold office of prophet, priest, and king. *Furthermore, for a visible hierarchy to be one, it must have a visible head. Only if each member of a visible hierarchy is ordered to one visible head can the visible hierarchy itself be one. And only if the visible head is essentially one can the visible hierarchy be essentially one. If the visible head of the hierarchy were plural, then the visible hierarchy would not be essentially unified, but at most only accidentally unified.*

Since Christ, having ascended into Heaven, is no longer visible to us ("and a cloud received Him out of their sight," Acts 1:9), therefore He appointed a visible steward (or "vicar") before His ascension, to be the visible head of His visible Body. The single visible head of the visible hierarchy is implied when Jesus says, "there shall be one fold..."[149]

Here Cross and Brown insert Pope Pius XII's encyclical *Mystici Corporis Christi* #40, which I will reference later, and Pope Leo XIII's encyclical *Satis Cognitum* #10, and then continues:

We see here that grace does not destroy nature, but builds on it and perfects it. This is why villages and cities have mayors, and even why our country has a president. Just as in a natural society there needs to be a unified hierarchy and a visible head, *so in the society of the faithful there must be a unified hierarchy and a visible head. For the same reason that virtually every Protestant congregation has a head pastor, the entire visible Church also requires a visible head. The Church as a visible organism preserves the visible head established by Christ, and thus retains all three marks of unity. Without a visible head, the Mystical Body would be reduced to the ontological equivalent of visible pins invisibly connected to an invisible pin-cushion. That is because without a visible head, a visible hierarchy is only accidentally one, because intrinsically it is potentially many separate hierarchies. Many separate*

---

149 "Christ Founded a Visible Church," last modified Monday, December 1, 2014, http://www.calledtocommunion.com/2009/06/christ-founded-a-visible-Church/.

hierarchies are not a visible unity; they are ontologically equivalent to many separate individuals. They are a mere plurality, not an actual unity.

A "visible Church" made up of separate visible hierarchies would be equivalent in its disunity to a merely invisible Church having some visible members. *Therefore a visible head belongs to the essence of the Mystical Body, since a body cannot have mere accidental unity, but must have unity essentially. In other words, an ecclesiology that is analogous to visible pins invisibly connected to an invisible pin-cushion is equivalent to a denial of the visibility of Christ's Mystical Body because such an ecclesiology denies the essentially unified hierarchy necessary for a body to be a body. It makes no difference whether the pins are individual Christians or individual congregations. Without an essentially unified visible hierarchy, a composite whole cannot be a body, let alone a visible body. And when hierarchical unity is abandoned, nothing preserves unity of faith or unity of sacraments. In this way each one of the three "bonds of unity" depends on the other two.*[150]

We will revisit Cross and Brown's excellent article more than once in this work. What is most relevant to objection five is that Cross confirms that the Roman Pontiff belongs to the Church's essential constitution. If the Church's teachings coincided with reality, it would be impossible for the Church to exist for forty or fifty-seven years without the Vicar of Christ. Thus the Sedevacantists face another dilemma. The teachings on the papacy are either false, in which case something or someone other than the pope is responsible for the Roman Pontiff's functions during the past half century, or else Sedevacantists are mistaken in their conviction that Francis is not the real Roman Pontiff. Assuming the Sedevacantists will not concede the second proposition, they are forced to rework the dogmatic teachings on the papacy. Later we will see how Dimond attempts this feat by ascribing visible unity of the Church to an *unmanned* and *free-floating* office of the papacy instead of to the Roman Pontiff.

---

150 Ibid.

The reader is forewarned of Dimond's error, which will confound the First Vatican Council's teachings, that the primacy is the underlying basis for unity with the same council's unmistakable teaching that the Roman Pontiff realizes actual unity of the Church by exercising the primacy. We will explore this in more detail in objection six. The point is that if the Vicar of Christ were only accidental to the existence and perpetuation of the Roman Catholic Church, which belief is shared by most Sedevacantists whether or not they realize it, then the Roman Pontiff is nothing more than a bishop or patriarch. This is worth serious consideration for all who hold the Sedevacantist position because it is unlikely that Sedevacantists have fully understood their theory's implications. In fact the Sedevacantists are more in agreement with Eastern Orthodox Christians, whom they consider schismatics, than they realize.

The problem that arises for Sedevacantists is that the Church's dogmatic teachings have made the Vicar of Christ necessary to the existence and perpetuation of the Church. Apparently the only Sedevacantists who understand this correctly are those who have attempted to elect their own popes.[151] As ludicrous or perhaps funny as it may seem that some Sedevacantists have attempted to elect their own popes, those who have attempted this feat should actually be commended for correctly understanding the relationship of Christ's Vicar to his Church. Their correct understanding is what compels them to elect one, albeit uncanonically, whereas most Sedevacantists remain imperviously oblivious to the fact that not having a Vicar of Christ in order to maintain at least a semblance of unity is a principal reason why they have failed to mount a formidable resistance to the Vatican II revolutionaries. Moreover, that the Sedevacantists have failed to produce a credible contender to the papacy in more than five decades is a solid piece of evidence that the Sedevacantist thesis is untenable, for as is proven in this work, a Vicar of Christ belongs to the essential constitution of the Church—*he is not accidental.* Hence there must be a Vicar of Christ. The question must

---

151 These Sedevacantists are often referred to as *Conclavists*.

be asked: Why haven't the Sedevacantists elected him?[152] The answer is simple: They cannot.

Unfortunately the window of opportunity for Sedevacantists to elect a pope has long since passed, as a rival claimant to the Roman See was required *before* the Church defected, not after. Again, once a defection has been proven, there is nothing anyone can do to change the fact. No modernist conversions back to tradition, no prophecies, no miracle workers, no Sedevacantist bishops, and no Sedevacantist-elected popes can save the Church because the very fact of Rome's defection means that the Church failed to save itself when it was supposed to. Regardless of what happens to the Catholic Church in the future, real history has been recorded with much help from the Sedevacantists.

Let us for a moment consider the implications of the Sedevacantists' failure to elect a pope during the period where it was still possible to do so. What should we make of the fact that a *legitimate* papal contender did not materialize before Rome's defection? I believe this tells us two important things. First it tells us that the traditional Catholic movement was never to be trusted. Instigators of revolutions and wars know that the most serious threat to their success is an organized, unified resistance. They also understand that the best way to deal with the anticipated opposition force is to lead it.[153] This would explain why championed traditional Catholic leaders who burst onto the scene, ostensibly to oppose Vatican II, adamantly refused to initiate the most obvious and obligatory action for the safety of the Church and the salvation of souls—elect a Roman Catholic to the chair of Peter without delay. Instead these

---

152 Interestingly the Vatican II revolutionaries understood something that today's Sedevacantists do not—Roman ecclesiology made the Roman Pontiff essential to the existence and perpetual unity of the Church. Despite its numerous problems, the modern Church is at least nominally united under a visible head in Rome while headless Sedevacantists continue to splinter into sects at rates rivaling only the Protestants following the Reformation.

153 No one had a better feel for this than the late W. F. Strojie (1912–1987). Strojie was a retired chief aerographer of twenty years in the US Navy, a Roman Catholic layman, a husband, and a father. He wrote brilliantly on Vatican II, the post-Conciliar popes, and the traditional Catholic resistance, which includes ninety-three letters, several pamphlets, and books.

so-called heroes led the faithful on two very different paths that each ended with the same results: confusion, disunity, and impotency. Both paths effectively rendered Sedevacantism dead on arrival. Consequently today's generation of Sedevacantists have all the knowledge and information required to save the Church and not a shred of apostolic authority to use it. With hindsight it appears the revolutionaries' plan worked to perfection.

The second and far more important lesson we can learn from the Sedevacantist movement's failure to elect a Roman Pontiff is this: Francis is he. If this were not so, divine providence would have arranged for a Vicar of Christ to preserve the unity and indefectibility of the Church. We know this because the foundation of the Church is the Roman papacy, of which the Roman Pontiff is its essential human component.

In concluding part I, we can now reasonably understand why Dimond lists objection five as a most common objection against the Sedevacantists. The belief that the Church can exist for forty years without a Vicar of Christ is certainly incongruent with Roman Catholicism.

Part II:

Glitches in the System

<hr>

Let us now turn our attention to some of the problems the papacy creates when we compare it to what we know about how the Church functions in reality. To begin with, the perpetuation of the Catholic Church during periods without a Roman Pontiff would seem to make the Roman Pontiff just a bishop like any other, as opposed to a Vicar of Christ. We can infer this because an organic organism cannot survive the loss of a vital organ. Notice the language used in reference to the Church:

> 17. One must not think, however, that this ordered or "organic" structure of the body of the Church...[154]

> 53. The organic constitution of the Church is not immutable. Like human society, Christian society is subject to a perpetual evolution.[155]

As we know, the teachings on the papacy are such that the Roman Pontiff is indispensable to the existence and continuance of the Roman Church. In reality, however, the Sedevacantists are correct; the Church

---

154 "Mystici Corporis Christi," Papal Encyclicals Online, accessed May 2, 2015, http://www.papalencyclicals.net/Pius12/P12MYSTI.HTM.
155 "Lamentabili Sane," Papal Encyclicals Online, accessed May 2, 2015, http://www.papalencyclicals.net/Pius10/p10lamen.htm.

could probably exist indefinitely without a Roman Pontiff. Interestingly the Church is designed to function in the absence of a Roman Pontiff and does so quite efficiently each time the Holy See becomes vacant. Not to be misunderstood as a miraculous property of indefectibility at work, it would appear that the Church continues to exist without a pope for essentially the same reason the Eastern Orthodox Church continues to exist in the absence of a patriarch: routine vacancies of apostolic sees preceded the first *serious* claims to the divine prerogatives ascribed to the papacy.

The Eastern Orthodox Church has always argued that in early centuries, bishops of *all* apostolic sees (i.e., those of the Churches of the East and West) shared authority as brother bishops governing sister churches, and collectively they comprised the one holy catholic and apostolic Church of Christ. Under this arrangement the loss of any apostolic see would not mean death of the Church because the Church would not have been identified exclusively in any one see, as it is in Roman Catholicism. Had Jesus Christ instituted the papacy, the Roman Church could not sustain the loss of the Vicar of Christ because the Church's own dogmatic teachings made certain essential properties and attributes of the Church rest entirely upon his person alone. The loss of the Church's visible head should be akin to the loss of any person's head (i.e., fatal).

If the Church were not an organic organism then it would really be a corporation or an artificial person. As a corporation the Church could exist indefinitely but not actually live in an organic sense. Though a Roman Pontiff could head an inorganic church, it would not be dependent upon him to exist. A corporation would continue to exist independently of its designated head, which is what we know to be true about the Church because of papal interregnums. This reality contradicts Catholic ecclesiology and lends support to the Eastern Orthodox Church's understanding of the Church's form of government. After all, the Catholic Church has never been understood as being the *artificial* Body of Christ but rather the *Mystical* Body of Christ whose members truly constitute one living organism in Christ.

II. The Union of the Faithful with Christ

67. ...Fathers from the earliest times teaches that *the Divine Redeemer and the Society which is His Body form but one mystical person*, that is to say, to quote Augustine, *the whole Christ*.[156]

Cross and Brown explain how the Church is a living body in the following excerpts (emphasis added):

> At the top of the hierarchy is Christ, the Head of the Body. The Head and members together form one Body, *with one shared divine life*. The life of a body is its soul, in which *all the members of the body are made to be alive and to share in the same life of the body*. So likewise, the Life of the Body of Christ is the Holy Spirit, who is the Soul of the Church. This is why St. Paul says that by one Spirit the Corinthian believers were baptized into one Body and all made to drink of that one Spirit. This incorporation into Christ's Mystical Body is what is meant by union with Christ. When St. Paul says, "It is no longer I who live, but Christ lives in me," (Gal. 2:20) this should not be understood in an individualistic "me-and-Jesus" sense, but as referring to our union with Christ in His Mystical Body, the Church. *Our union with Christ is accomplished through our incorporation into His Mystical Body, the Church, which is composed of many members*. Likewise, when St. Paul says in Galatians 3:27–28 that those who have been baptized into Christ are all one in Christ, he is referring to believers being incorporated into the unity of Christ's Mystical Body, the Church. Concerning that union, St. Augustine wrote:
>
> > Let us rejoice and give thanks that we have become not only Christians, but Christ. Do you understand, brothers, the grace of Christ our Head? Wonder at it, rejoice: we have become Christ. For if He is the Head, we are the members; He and

---

156 Pius XII, "*Mystici Corporis Christi*," 51.

we form the whole man…the fullness of Christ, therefore; the head and the members. What is the head and the members? Christ and the Church.

Notice the strong language that St. Augustine uses. Because of our union with Christ the Head in His Mystical Body, we are not only Christians, but, in a true sense, Christ. How is that possible? Because the members and Head form one "whole man." Of that "whole man" St. Thomas Aquinas wrote:

> The Head and members are as one mystical person [*quasi una persona mystica*] and therefore Christ's satisfaction belongs to all the faithful as being His members.[157]

The continuation of the Church during papal vacancies actually runs contrary to the principle of all organic life, which dies if it loses a vital organ. Following this principle we can understand why, if the divine prerogatives ascribed to the papacy were true, it would be impossible for the Church to exist without a pope for *any* duration, let alone for fifty-seven years. The fact that Catholic teachings on the papacy must allow for the continuance of the living organism without a vital organ is a contradiction. A logical explanation for this contradiction is that the papacy is not the real foundation of Christ's Church; the Catholic Church must have preceded it. This would explain why some fathers and doctors of the early Church were quite confused on the meaning of Matthew 16:18. For example how could it be possible that Augustine did not know with absolute certitude that *rock* meant Peter and not Christ five centuries after the foundation of the Catholic Church?[158]

---

157 "Christ Founded a Visible Church."
158 The early Church fathers waivered on this doctrine in various writings. For example Guettée cites Augustine's 18th Sermon, 124th Tract, and his Book 1 of Retractions, which mention "the rock" as being Christ, not Peter (pp. 174–175). Contrarily Guettée quotes Ambrose's teaching that the truth confessed by St. Peter is the foundation of the Church and that no promise was made to his person or to his subjective faith (171–172).

But what about the fact that the Church's teachings clearly emphasize that *Christ himself is the head of the Church*? Would that not explain why the Church can exist without a pope, who is merely his vicar? The answer is no. The Church made essential characteristics entirely dependent upon the Roman Pontiff, *not Christ*.[159] The Catholic Church cannot have it both ways. Either the Roman Pontiff or Jesus Christ is responsible for these characteristics, but not both, otherwise there would be no need for a Vicar of Christ. Again, in objection six we shall examine how dogma defines that Peter *and his successors* are commissioned by Christ to bring the Church together and to sustain it.

Passing the Torch

Most Catholics, including Sedevacantists, do not think to ask questions about the papal system, such as, "Why do papal vacancies or interregnums even occur?" The obvious answer to this question is that popes are mortal and must eventually die, but that is not what I am driving at. If Jesus Christ truly granted Peter's successors special prerogatives as expressed in Vatican Council I, there should never have been a single interregnum in the Church from Peter all the way to Francis.

Two ways the Church could be organic and simultaneously perpetual are as follows: The first way would be if the Church had no *single* visible head whose death or absence would render the body headless. An example could be if a unified episcopacy functioned as a visible head. Because the episcopacy is not singular, as is a pope, the death or absence of any one bishop or patriarch would not conflict with the Church's organic composition. The second way would be if Christ had arranged that the Church could never incur interregnums. But wouldn't a total absence of all interregnums require immortality of Roman Pontiffs? No. In his treatise "The Vatican Dogma," Sergius Bulgakov wrote that Christ could have perpetuated the papacy without personal immortality of the

---

159 This is another area where the Church appears to contradict itself, sometimes even within the same body of work.

Roman Pontiffs as such: "...the pope ought in his life-time to consecrate his successor."[160]

When we are considering what the papacy is supposed to be, we see that Christ could not have implemented a more important law. But, as we know, the Catholic Church does not meet either of these two conditions. Bulgakov wrote (emphasis added):

> Indeed, if the Vatican dogma is consistently thought out, the interruptions of Papacy naturally brought about by the death of a pope must cause dogmatic perplexity: if a *vicarius Christi* can exist at all, how can he be mortal? How can the actual order of Papacy be interrupted, as undoubtedly happens through death? *A patriarchate may become vacant when a patriarch dies or is removed, but then patriarchy is not a special holy order, which Papacy is supposed to be. Patriarchy is an ecclesiastical office with exalted rank and special jurisdiction attached to it, but as far as holy orders are concerned a patriarch is a bishop—and the order of episcopacy, like that of priesthood, is not interrupted by the death of its individual representatives, and will go on till the end of time. With Papacy the case is different: a break is caused by the death of its representatives, since a pope exists only in the singular.*
>
> *If it be said that Papacy is not a special order but only an office, since the pope is in bishop's orders, that will be quite in keeping with the view of the universal Church before the schism, but it will be contrary to the Vatican doctrine.* According to it, there is a special grace *(charisma)* given to Peter and his successors—*veritatis et fidei nunquam deficientis*—which constitutes the order of Papacy. Roman Catholic theology has gradually raised St. Peter so high above the other Apostles that he is no longer regarded as one of them but as a prince of Apostles. In addition to the general apostolic charisma he has his own, personal one, similarly to the way in which episcopacy includes priesthood. A bishop celebrates the liturgy like a priest, and does not differ from him in this respect, but it does

---

160 "The Vatican Dogma," OrthodoxChristianity.net, accessed December 2, 2014, http://www.orthodoxchristianity.net/articles/39-the-vatican-dogma.

not follow that they are of equal rank. *The same considerations apply to the Catholic conception of the pope, for whom a fourth and highest degree of holy orders has been created.* True, Catholic literature contains no direct expression of the idea that Papacy is the highest of holy orders—that of *episcopus episcoporum* or *episcopus universalis*, but this is either evasiveness or inconsistency; *the special and exceptional place assigned to the "primate" in Catholic canonical writings can have no other meaning.*

But if Papacy be understood as a special order of St. Peter (*Tu es Petrus* is sung when the newly elected pope is carried in procession), the difficulties which have already been mentioned stand out all the more clearly...The dogmatic teaching about the pope must certainly be made less presumptuous and confine itself to regarding the pope as simply a patriarch but that, of course, means the fall of the whole Vatican fortress. In any case, as has been said already, *the mere fact of the death of a pope has dogmatic implications which have not yet been satisfactorily dealt with by the Roman theologians.*

Still greater dogmatic importance for the problem of Papacy attaches to intentional and artificial interruptions in papal succession, due to the papal court's desire to manage by themselves for a time, without the vicarius Christi. What becomes meanwhile of the fullness and infallibility of ecclesiastical power? If the answer be that it remains with the Church, this means that the Church can do without a pope, being "widowed" for a time like a diocese without a bishop. This clearly proves, one would have thought, not that the Church is a function of Papacy, but Papacy is a function of the Church which can, in certain circumstances, make up for the absence of the pope.

The problem which the death of a pope raises indirectly, comes openly to the fore in the case or ecclesiastical schism when there is more than one pope in existence. *When this happened the Church itself, through its highest organ—the council, settled matters, judged the popes, deposed some and appointed others. The superiority of the council to the pope, dogmatically laid down at the Councils of Constance and Basel, had been exercised* by them before this dogmatic proclamation was made. Those councils rejected the claim that the pope is not subject to any ecclesiastical jurisdiction, "*prima sedes a nemine judicatur.*" They judged and deposed the popes, and neither the Church, nor Pope Martin V appointed by the Council of Constance, nor his successors, objected to this. To object would have meant questioning their own legitimacy and admitting that they were usurpers.[161]

WHY INHERITANCE WORKS

The Catholic Church considers itself Christ's kingdom of heaven on Earth. Cross and Brown explain:

> Many Christians do not realize that the Catholic Church is and claims to be the Kingdom of Heaven on earth, in the Kingdom's nascent stage. They mistakenly think of the Kingdom as either entirely invisible, entirely spiritual, or entirely future. Lumen Gentium specifically affirms that the Church is Christ's Kingdom:
>
>> The Church, or, in other words, the kingdom of Christ now present in mystery, grows visibly through the power of God in the world.
>
> By "present in mystery" the Council meant that the Catholic Church is the Kingdom of Heaven in its beginning or seminal stage, i.e., the stage prior to the return of Christ. We do not now see the fullness of the Kingdom. But the Catholic Church is the present rule of Christ on the earth. Jesus did not say to Peter, "I give you the keys of the Church, but I retain the keys of the Kingdom." Rather, Jesus said to Peter, "I will give to you [*singular*] the keys of the Kingdom of Heaven." The keys of the Kingdom of Heaven are the apostolic authority over the Church. That is why the Catechism says, "The Church is the seed and beginning of this kingdom. Her keys are entrusted to Peter." To fulfill the Father's

---

161 Ibid.

will, Christ ushered in the Kingdom of heaven on earth. The Church is the Reign of Christ already present in mystery…When would God set up this Kingdom that will never be destroyed? At the time of the fourth kingdom of men, namely the kingdom of Rome. This was fulfilled at the time of Christ. A Protestant who conceives of Christ's Kingdom as something invisible or spiritual may agree that Christ introduced His Kingdom two-thousand years ago, but not see that this Kingdom is the Catholic Church.[162]

The traditional means of becoming king was by inheritance. At least up until the Church's version of the French Revolution (i.e., Vatican II), popes were considered kings.[163] According to the divine prerogatives ascribed to the papacy, it would have made far more sense if popes were required to choose their own successors, as Bulgakov suggested earlier. By way of inheritance, even a temporary break in papal succession would never occur, as an heir to the chair of Peter would preexist the death of the Roman Pontiff, thus assuring that the divine prerogatives ascribed to the papacy would never be wanting in the Church, not even for a moment. Only in that way would the divine office of the Vicar of Christ be truly perpetual.

Bulgakov also alluded to the historical problems heresy and the superiority of councils presents to the papacy. Heresy on the part of the Roman Pontiff undoubtedly breaks the line of papal succession. One notorious example is the case of Pope Honorius I. Forty years after

---

162 "Christ Founded a Visible Church."

163 Pope Paul VI was the last pope to wear the papal tiara and the last pope to receive a true coronation ceremony, in 1963. ("Tiara of Pope Paul VI," *Wikipedia*, accessed December 13, 2014, http://en.wikipedia.org/w/index.php?title=Tiara_of_Pope_Paul_VI&oldid=633550992.

Honorius reigned as pope, he was anathematized[164] for heresy by the Third Council of Constantinople. Notwithstanding the problems that an excommunicated pope poses to the dogmatic decrees of the First Vatican Council, who will honestly say the line of papal succession was not broken somewhere between AD 625 and 638, while Honorius reigned as Roman Pontiff? If it were true that a heretic could never be a pope, and if it were true that the papacy remains an unbroken line of succession all the way back to Peter, this historical case is a problem that will linger indefinitely because Honorius was a heretic whose excommunication severed papal succession.

Ascension of Power

Bulgakov's observations go deeper yet. Consider that in the Roman hierarchical system of authority that claims to emanate from God, it does not make sense that those of lesser ecclesiastical positions should appoint one to a higher position. On this point Bulgakov wrote: "…bearers of lower hierarchical orders cannot ordain to higher orders, so that the consecration of a pope by bishops (cardinals) is canonically and sacramentally unmeaning…"[165]

Bulgakov's point is excellent. The Church is a kingdom ruled by an earthly king endowed with divine powers, and divine power must *descend* not *ascend*. In a hierarchical Church, laymen do not confer orders on deacons; deacons do not confer ordinations to the priesthood; and priests do not confer episcopal consecrations. How did it ever come about that any of the aforementioned should possess the power to appoint one to the highest ecclesiastical office if it is true that no one

---

164 The familiar anathema sit (let him be anathema, or excommunicated) appears to have been first applied to heretics at the Council of Elvira (Spain) in 300–6 and became the standard formula in all the general councils of the Church, as against Arius (256–336) at I Nicea in 787. (Etym. Greek *anathema*, thing devoted to evil, curse; an accursed thing or person; from *anatithenai*, to set up, dedicate.) (Hardon, *Modern Catholic Dictionary*, 24.)

165 "The Vatican Dogma."

can give what he does not have—*nemo dat quod non habet*? After all the Roman Catholic Church does not derive its power from the faithful in the same way a democracy derives its power from its people.

From a Roman Catholic perspective, Peter was appointed the first Vicar of Christ directly by Jesus Christ himself, not the apostolic college, so this *ascending* power conferred in subsequent papal elections definitely did not originate in AD 33.[166] If Jesus endowed Peter's successors with special divine prerogatives, then it only makes sense that these should be passed on directly from the one who possesses them, which would provide for a more authentic and proper meaning to *apostolic succession*, especially concerning a divine appointment of Vicar of Christ.

VICAR OF PETER

From the absence of a scriptural connection between the papacy and the city of Rome to Peter's continuous action through the Roman Pontiffs, the doctrine of the papacy comes across as shifty. In fact if the Vicar of Christ were renamed Vicar of Peter, nothing would be lost in meaning. Consider how the First Vatican Council teaches that *Peter* acts through the Roman Pontiffs (emphasis added): "And he (Peter) up to this time and always lives and presides and exercises judgment in his successors, the bishops of the holy see of Rome…"[167]

Rather than assert that *Jesus Christ* does not abandon the guidance of the Church, which would have been consistent with the doctrine of indefectibility and the direct words of Christ in sacred scripture—"behold I am with you all days, even to the consummation of the world"[168]—the First Vatican Council makes this assertion of Peter: "Therefore the disposition of truth remains, and blessed Peter persevering in the accepted

---

166 In objection six we will see how the First Vatican Council explicitly states that the primacy was instituted in Peter directly from Christ and that the primacy was not given to the Church in order to transmit it to Peter. We will also explore the likely reason the Church had to reverse this policy for Peter's successors.

167 Denzinger, *The Sources of Catholic Dogma*, 1824.

168 Matthew 28:20.

fortitude of the rock does not abandon the guidance of the Church which he has received."[169]

Incredibly, just seventy-three years after the First Vatican Council, Pope Pius XII misconstrued the Church's dogmatic teaching on who guides and rules the Church through the Roman Pontiffs. Rather than reiterate the Council's unambiguous teaching that it is Peter who does not abandon the guidance of the Church and that it is Peter who lives, presides, and exercises judgment *in the Roman Pontiffs*, Pope Pius XII wrote something quite different (emphasis added):

Visibly and Ordinarily

40. But we must not think that He rules only in a hidden or extraordinary manner. On the contrary, *our Divine Redeemer also governs His Mystical Body in a visible and normal way through His Vicar on earth.* You know, Venerable Brethren, that after He had ruled the "little flock" Himself during His mortal pilgrimage, Christ our Lord, when about to leave this world and return to the Father, entrusted to the Chief of the Apostles the visible government of the entire community He had founded. Since He was all wise He could not leave the body of the Church He had founded as a human society without a visible head. Nor against this may one argue that the primacy of jurisdiction established in the Church gives such a Mystical Body two heads. For Peter in virtue of his primacy is only Christ's Vicar; so that there is only one chief Head of this Body, *namely Christ, who never ceases Himself to guide the Church invisible, though at the same time He rules it visibly, through him who is His representative on earth.* After His glorious Ascension into heaven this Church rested not on Him alone, but on Peter too, its visible foundation stone. That Christ and His Vicar constitute one only Head is the solemn teaching of Our predecessor of immortal memory Boniface VIII in the Apostolic Letter

---

[169] Denzinger, *The Sources of Catholic Dogma*, 1824.

Unam Sanctam; and his successors have never ceased to repeat the same.[170]

53. As Bellarmine notes with acumen and accuracy, this appellation of the Body of Christ is not to be explained solely by the fact that Christ must be called the Head of His Mystical Body, but also *by the fact that He so sustains the Church…*[171]

As we can see, Peter and Jesus Christ are used interchangeably in various Catholic teachings, yet obviously they are not the same person. So who really guides, governs, and sustains the Catholic Church—Jesus or Peter? If it were said that Jesus guides, governs, and sustains the Church *through* Peter, very well, but such an arrangement makes sense only while Peter was still alive, not after his death. Besides, Pius XII was quite clear that Christ rules the Church through "him who is his representative on earth," which is obviously not Peter. Obviously Pope Pius XII blatantly contradicted the First Vatican Council.

Moreover, because pre–Vatican II contradictions do not evade the Sedevacantists, it would be interesting to know which position they hold on who guides, governs, and sustains the Church. If it is Peter who operates through the Roman Pontiffs, then let the Sedevacantists explain how blessed Peter "does not abandon the guidance of the Church which he has received"[172] if there has been no Roman Pontiff in whom he "always lives and presides and exercises judgment"[173] for the past fifty-seven years. If Sedevacantists claim that Jesus steps in when Peter's ghost steps out, then let them explain why the Lord has failed to maintain visible unity among the Sedevacantists and furthermore why Peter should even be necessary.

---

170   Pius XII, "*Mystici Corporis Christi*," 44.
171   Ibid., 47.
172   Denzinger, *The Sources of Catholic Dogma*, 1824.
173   Ibid.

Although contradictions such as the aforementioned may seem trivial to most Roman Catholics, I believe they are important pieces of a much larger picture. Rather than excuse such contradictions and inconsistencies in a fundamental doctrine as human error, they ought to be recognized also as a natural progression of a doctrine's human origin. Sergius Bulgakov wrote:

> I repeat, these facts have a dogmatic significance; Roman Catholics are fond of saying that Providence has preserved the see of Rome from dogmatic errors, but in this case it may with equal justice be said that Providence allowed certain facts, the dogmatic significance of which was to preserve the Roman See from making false claims and to give clear indications of the right course.[174]

In conclusion, Dimond's answer to objection five essentially boils down to two points:

1. Papal interregnums prove the Church can exist without a pope.
2. Father Edmund James O'Reilly speculated that the Church could last thirty-nine years without a pope; therefore, *theologians*[175] taught that the Church could exist without a pope for an indefinite period without violating indefectibility.[176]

With respect to the first point, papal interregnums do indeed prove the Church can exist without a pope, but that fact certainly does not support today's Sedevacantist movement because Sedevacantism does

---

174 "The Vatican Dogma."

175 I am unaware of more than one theologian who thought the Church could be without a pope for thirty-nine or more years, yet Dimond states there is more than one.

176 Dimond lends great weight to O'Reilly's statement despite the fact that it is merely an opinion of a fallible man—an observation he is usually fast to make against others when they contradict his positions. Dimond would be the first person to point out that in the case of a theologian contradicting Catholic dogma, there is no contest; the theologian must be dismissed.

not really entail a papal interregnum; it entails a defection of the Church. Furthermore any papal interregnum, especially one lasting thirty-nine years, as Fr. O'Reilly thought possible, *does* contradict the First Vatican Council's dogmatic teachings on the papacy.[177] The explanation for this is that if the Church has contradicted itself, so must its theologians.

With respect to point two, most Sedevacantists make a very big deal about Father Edmund O'Reilly's speculation about a thirty-nine-year papal interregnum. Being that Father O'Reilly wrote about this after Vatican I, does not this prove there is no contradiction between Sedevacantism and Vatican I's papal dogmas? More likely it proves that theologians contradict dogmatic councils whenever dogmatic councils contradict history.[178]

Finally, while it is contradictory to propose that the Church can be without a Roman Pontiff for thirty-nine or fifty-seven years, in reality the Church could probably exist indefinitely without him. The fact that the Church continues to function at times without a pope does not support the Sedevacantist thesis; it weakens the papacy. In the next objection, objection six, we will look more closely at how Dimond attempts to divide and conquer the Papacy in order to save the Church.

---

[177] Father O'Reilly's opinion is obviously contradictory to Vatican Council I, and Dimond is forced to draw attention to it in his book (Dimond, *The Truth*, 310).

[178] Like Vatican II, the First Vatican Council saw great internal turmoil when several members of the hierarchy cited numerous historical contradictions to the papal dogmas. Vatican I's papal dogmas eventually caused a schism.

Summary

NON-SEDEVACANTISTS OBJECT TO SEDEVACANTISM BECAUSE *the Church cannot exist without a pope, or at least it cannot exist for forty years without a pope, as Sedevacantists say.*[179] My position is in agreement with this objection because Catholic ecclesiology makes the Roman Pontiff indispensable to the Church. The Sedevacantists respond to this objection by contending that the Roman Pontiff is not always necessary to the Church and presenting papal interregnums or routine vacancies of the papacy as evidence.

The Sedevacantist position rests on the fallacious argument that the Roman Catholic Church is presently enduring a papal interregnum that began approximately in 1958. Sedevacantists such as Dimond attempt to manipulate others into accepting that Sedevacantism is essentially the same thing as a papal interregnum by disguising the theory's real implications, but this attempted connection is a misrepresentation. Sedevacantists are not really proposing that the Church is experiencing a papal interregnum, but they deceptively call it one.

Sedevacantism is essentially a movement within traditional Catholicism that theorizes that the indefectible Catholic Church has defected. Examples of some of the tenets of Sedevacantism that prove this include that the Church's hierarchical structure has disintegrated; that the Church's capacity to elect a Roman Pontiff has been incapacitated; and that the Mystical Body of Christ has mutated into the end-times,

---

179 Dimond, *The Truth*, 308.

apostate Church of the Antichrist. None of these things, as well as numerous others addressed in objection one, can be misconstrued as a papal interregnum.

Dimond correctly points out that the Church does not have a teaching that limits how long a papal interregnum can last. It follows that the Sedevacantists must also accept that a papal interregnum could last one thousand or more years. The logical sequence of Sedevacantism is that the Vicar of Christ is accidental to the Catholic Church. This I identified as the second principal heresy of the Sedevacantists.

Roman Catholic apologists Bryan Cross and Thomas Brown explain why visible hierarchical unity belongs to the essence of the Church and why a visible hierarchy must have a visible head to be essentially one. Cross says that a visible head belongs to the essence of the Mystical Body of Christ because a body must have unity essentially, not merely accidentally.[180]

The dogmatic teachings of the Church make the Roman Pontiff essential, not accidental. Consequently Dimond attempts to rework the dogmatic teachings of the papacy. The reader was forewarned of Dimond's error that confounds the First Vatican Council's teaching that the apostolic primacy is the underlying basis for unity, with the same council's teaching that the Roman Pontiff must exercise the primacy for the actual realization of unity.

Because Sedevacantism necessarily entails that a defection of the Church occurred, Sedevacantism was only a viable position *before* the defection but not after. Sedevacantism arrived too late and is now impotent thanks to the leadership of the traditional Catholic movement, which essentially stranded the Catholic faithful in dead-end positions.

The Sedevacantists' failure to elect a legitimate Roman Pontiff in fifty-seven years confirms that the leadership within traditional Catholicism was never to be trusted and that today's Sedevacantist movement is untenable. If these were not true, divine providence would have arranged for a valid pope at the time of the revolutionary Second Vatican Council to uphold the deposit of faith and maintain unity of the

---

180 "Christ Founded a Visible Church."

Church. That God provided no such pope supports one of the premises of this work—that Francis is the true pope. Any future Sedevacantist-initiated pope is automatically disqualified.

The perpetuation of the Church during papal vacancies runs contrary to the principles of all organic life, which must die if it loses a vital organ. That the Church continues to exist and function without its visible head and source of unity is an indication that the papacy is not the original foundation of Christ's Church. The real foundation of the Catholic Church preceded the Roman claims on the papacy.

If the divine prerogatives ascribed to the papacy were true, the Church would collapse without its visible head; popes would appoint their successors; there could never be a break in papal succession; divine authority would never ascend from inferiors who never possessed it; and authoritative papal encyclicals defining the Church of Christ would never confound the *Vicar of Christ* as the *Vicar of Peter*.

Father O'Reilly's theological opinion is contradictory to the teachings of the First Vatican Council. The best explanation is that theologians contradict dogmatic councils when dogmatic councils contradict history.

Finally, while it is contradictory to propose that the Church can be without a Roman Pontiff for thirty-nine or fifty-seven years, in reality the Church could probably exist indefinitely without him. The fact that the Church can function without a pope does not support the Sedevacantist thesis; it weakens the mythological claims on the papacy.

Objections

❦

Objection: You said that a true pope was necessary before the defection but not after a defection. You also said that once a defection occurred, it would be too late to elect a pope. Your premise is wrong. A defection of the Church did not occur as you say because the Sedevacantists have been the continuation of the true Church all along. Furthermore the Sedevacantist bishops can unite and elect a true pope and end the great apostasy.

Answer: 1. As proven in chapter one, if Sedevacantism were true then the Church would have defected. Once the Church provably defects, that fact cannot change. Hence any attempted fixes or corrections later are meaningless, and that includes the election of a "true" pope. **2.** Because the Sedevacantists have in fact proven the defection of the Catholic Church, they automatically disqualify themselves along with every single group or movement that comes along and makes claims of being or perpetuating the "true" Church. That is precisely why Sedevacantism is so devastating to Roman Catholicism and at the same time supportive of Eastern Orthodoxy. This also explains why most Catholics dismiss or ignore the Sedevacantists. Sedevacantism taken to its logical conclusion throws the baby out with the bathwater.

Objection: There is nothing contrary to indefectibility in saying that we have not had a pope since the death of Pope Pius XII in 1958.[181]

---
181 Dimond, *The Truth*, 309.

Answer: 1. Objection one addresses the Sedevacantists' numerous contradictions with the doctrine of indefectibility. **2.** The Sedevacantists are not really proposing that the Church has been without a "true" pope since Pius XII (i.e., a routine papal interregnum); they are proposing that a defection of the Catholic Church occurred. The so-called "papal interregnum" is a smokescreen the Sedevacantists use to disguise their theory of the Catholic Church's defection.

Objection: If the Church has been without a pope at least two hundred times, and sometimes even for the length of nearly three years, then all but obstinate heretics understand that the Catholic Church does not cease to exist just because of a long papal interregnum.

Answer: If the Church presently has existed without a "true" pope and a Holy See since 1958, then Sedevacantists should be the first people to realize that the papacy is not the real foundation of Christ's Church.

Objection: You said Sedevacantists believe the Roman Pontiff is accidental to the Church, but that is not true. Sedevacantists do not believe the Roman Pontiff is accidental; they say only that the Church can continue to exist and function at times without him. This is proven every time there is an interregnum.

Answer: Sedevacantists are confused about what they believe. If the Church can exist indefinitely without a pope then by definition he is not necessary. That being said, the Sedevacantists' confusion is not entirely their fault because in order to defend the papal system, it is necessary to espouse some contradictions in order to avoid other contradictions. In this example the Sedevacantists make a verbal attempt to uphold the teachings on the papacy, which makes the Roman Pontiff the foundation stone and source of unity of the Church while the Church itself is permitted to contradict its own teachings in reality. That the Church can survive the lapse of a vital component is contradictory to the principles of all organic life, which makes the doctrine on the papacy spurious. If anyone doubts this, let him conduct a public experiment: Let the doubter lop off his own head and report back with the results in thirty-nine years. This experiment should conclusively demonstrate whether a living organism could live thirty-nine years without its head.

Objection: The Mystical Body of Christ is both material and spiritual. Therefore it doesn't have to follow the laws of an organic organism such as that of a human person. The Church can suffer the loss of its visible head because the Catholic teaching is that the real head is Christ, and the pope is just his vicar.

Answer: Human persons are also material and spiritual; nevertheless they die without a *vital* organ. The Church cannot have it both ways. If it wishes to claim for itself a Vicar of Christ with divine prerogatives in the person of the Roman Pontiff and in whom essential characteristics of the Church are solely dependent, then he must be vital to the life of the Church.

Objection: You said you didn't believe Vatican I's papal dogmas, yet you seem to defend the council's teaching that unity of the Church hinges on the Roman Pontiff rather than the office of the papacy. You contradicted yourself.

Answer: I believe that the divine prerogatives ascribed to the papacy are false, not that a pope could not serve as the Church's visible head and source of cohesion for the Church in the same way that a CEO or president serves a human organization. There is nothing miraculous about this; it works naturally.

Objection: The fact is that interregnums have occurred, some for long durations, and the unity of the Church has been maintained. So to what or to whom do we ascribe the unity of the Catholic Church during past papal interregnums?

Answer: The Roman Church, which includes the Church's administrative government (i.e., the Curia).

Objection: The fact that a pope was always elected after an interregnum proves that unity was maintained during all past papal interregnums.

Answer: Probably true. However, one can also argue that unity of the Church is deferred during interregnums and is not restored until a pope is elected.

Objection: What proofs exist to support that argument?

Answer: The Sedevacantist movement supports that argument. Unity has never existed among the Sedevacantists. Every contested papal election in the history of the Church also supports the argument. For example the Great Western Schism began because of a papal interregnum and a contested election of the next pope. Had Pope Gregory XI selected his own successor, *an interregnum that produced a contested election* and a three-way schism in the Western Church would not have been possible. Unity of the Western Church was severely compromised and not restored until the competing sides unanimously agreed upon a pope four decades later.

Objection: You said unity of the Church ceased to exist during the Great Western Schism, but that is false. At all times the true Church remained unified in the Roman line of popes.

Answer: This is not a fact; it is only a popular opinion, and it remains contested to this day. But since Sedevacantists frequently cite the Great Western Schism as a precedent for our times, I think it is worth stating that it catches them in another quagmire. If the Roman line of popes maintained unity of the Church during the schism, this would support the teaching of the First Vatican Council that the Roman Pontiff is the source of the visible unity of the Church, as opposed to Dimond's "papacy of desire" (to be addressed in objection six). On the other hand, if the Roman line of popes did not maintain unity of the Church then it is a blow to both Sedevacantists and the Roman claims about the papacy. None other than Pope Gregory XII provided the strongest evidence supporting the latter opinion by voluntarily abdicating the office of the papacy for the sake of ending the Great Western Schism and *restoring unity of the Church.*

Objection: St. Nicholas of Fluh (1417–1487) gave this prophecy:

> The Church will be punished because the majority of her members, high and low, will become so perverted. The Church will sink deeper and deeper until she will at last seem to be extinguished, and the succession of Peter and the other Apostles to have expired. But, after this, she will be victoriously exalted in the sight of all doubters.[182]

Answer: Roman Catholics must dismiss any prophecies or interpretations of prophecies that contradict Catholic doctrines. In this example Sedevacantists often interpret this prophecy in a way that is contradictory to other doctrines of the faith.

---

182 This quotation is attributed to Nicholas of Fluh in error. Apparently Cardinal Nicholas of Cusa made this prophecy. ("Dr. J.J.I. Von D Döllinger's Fables Respecting the Popes in the Middle Ages," Google Books, accessed May 17, 2015, https://books.google.com/books?vid=0o5gZXZPy84SyfDX7wo&id=JucQAAAAIAAJ&pg=PA337&dq=%252522other+Apostles+to+have+expired%252522&as_brr=1&hl=en#v=onepage&q&f=false.)

CHAPTER 3

The First Vatican Council (1869–1870)

❧

> To be right in everything, we ought always to hold that the white which I see, is black if the hierarchical Church so decides it, believing that between Christ our Lord, the bridegroom, and the Church, His bride, there is the same spirit, which governs and directs us for the salvation of our souls. Because by the same spirit and our Lord who gave the Ten Commandments, our holy mother the Church is directed and governed.
>
> — St. Ignatius[183]

The subject of objection five, the necessity of the Vicar of Christ, continues in objection six as we explore the First Vatican Council, Session Four—First Dogmatic Constitution of the Church of Christ *(Pastor Aeternus)*. Opponents of Sedevacantism claim that the theory contradicts specific teachings in the dogmatic constitution. My position is agreement with this objection; the First Vatican Council absolutely contradicts the claims of the Sedevacantists. This chapter comprises my rebuttal to Dimond's defense of the Sedevacantist position.

---

183 David L. Fleming, *The Spiritual Exercises of St. Ignatius: A Literal Translation and a Contemporary Reading* (St. Louis: The Institute of Jesuit Sources, 1978), 234.

Dimond addresses three passages from the dogmatic constitution and attempts to prove why they do not contradict the claims of the Sedevacantists. In turn I will address Dimond's answers and explain how he distorts and twists the meanings of the three passages in order to match a new ecclesiology, which I have come to regard as the "papacy of desire."[184]

Dimond's papacy of desire is an attempt to circumvent the Sedevacantists' failures, such as their inability to account for the Holy See and their impotency to reproduce one. The reason for these failures is that the Sedevacantist movement cut off its nose to spite its face by endeavoring to prove the defection of Rome.

Although it is possible for something other than a living person to serve as the source of visible unity in an organization, ascribing this function to something invisible or intangible would undermine the papacy and lend support to the Eastern Orthodox Church. The Eastern Churches do not consider the foundation of the Church as the person of Peter per se but rather as Christ himself, whom Peter's confession of faith—"Thou Art the Christ, the Son of the Living God"—revealed. In contrast the Catholic Church teaches dogmatically that it is Peter and subsequently his successors who are the foundation of the Church as well as its principle of visible unity, not merely an immaterial entity such as Dimond's papacy of desire. Thus in this chapter we encounter the third principal heresy of the Sedevacantists—papacy of desire is sufficient for membership in and visible unity of the Church.

---

184 Similar to Father Leonard Feeney, Dimond adamantly rejects the Church's teachings of "baptism of desire" and "baptism of blood," which allow unbaptized souls to attain eternal salvation provided the sacrament of baptism is so *desired* before death. According to Dimond, the effect of the sacrament of baptism (justification) cannot be attained without the material sacrament itself. Ironically, Dimond proposes a new ecclesiology, which essentially allows one to receive the effects of the Holy See (e.g., visible unity, sanctity, Catholicity, apostolicity, etc.) without its material existence provided only that it is *desired*. The hypocrisy in rejecting the Church's long-standing doctrine of baptism of desire while simultaneously adopting a novel doctrine that allows papacy of desire is extraordinary.

In response to objection six, Dimond attempts to divide the papacy in order to claim some portion of its effects and alleged powers. But, as proven in objection one, the Sedevacantists have no claim to any portion of the papacy. No further proof is needed than to recall Christ's purpose for instituting the papacy—unity of the Church—and then to observe the Sedevacantists.

Finally we will explore additional holes in the papacy's armor and draw some conclusions that are most reasonable as well as favorable to the Eastern Orthodox Church.

Objection Six

Vatican I's definition on the perpetuity of the Papal Office contradicts the claims of the Sedevacantists.[185]

---

[185] Dimond, *The Truth*, 310.

Part I

Pastor Aeternus: First Dogmatic Constitution on the Church of Christ

OVERVIEW

DIMOND CITES JUST THREE PASSAGES from the First Vatican Council's dogmatic constitution *Pastor Aeternus*. However, the constitution covers many important things about the papacy and its relationship to Sedevacantism. Although we will not examine the entire session in detail, I direct the reader's attention to the following points that stand out from just a cursory reading of the dogmatic constitution:

- The purpose of the Church is the permanent duration of the work of redemption.
- The papacy is the foundation of the Catholic Church.
- The papacy's primary function is unity.
- Rome is the foundation of the papacy.
- Rome identifies the Vicar of Christ.
- Roman Pontiffs realize unity of the Church.
- Visible unity of the Catholic Church is permanent.
- Unity with the Holy See identifies the hierarchy and the faithful.

The First Vatican Council (1869–1870)

- Unity with the Roman Pontiff is compulsory.
- The Holy See cannot fail or defect.

The reader should observe how each of the salient points is interconnected in some way. The reader should also have gained an understanding of how Sedevacantism attempts to divide, alter, or omit these various points in such a way that their symbiotic relationships are dissolved, leaving gaps in what *should be* the Church's permanent attributes and properties that always distinguish it as being the true Church of Christ. For example, a typical Sedevacantist will claim that the Church must have unity while disclaiming the necessity of a visibly unified hierarchy. For another example a typical Sedevacantist will claim that while the office of the papacy is permanent, neither the Holy See nor a Roman Pontiff is required to access and utilize it. The result of rendering these points is always a mutilated conception of the Church. I will briefly support these summary points with excerpts from the dogmatic constitution.

- The purpose of the Church is for the permanent duration of the work of redemption:

  > The eternal Pastor and Bishop of our souls, in order to render the saving work of redemption perennial, willed to build a holy Church…[186]

- The Papacy is the foundation of the Church:

  > …placing the blessed Peter over the other apostles He established in him the perpetual principle and visible foundation of both unities, upon whose strength the eternal temple might be erected…[187]

---

186 Denzinger, *The Sources of Catholic Dogma*, 1821.
187 Ibid.

Comment: In objection one we saw how Peter is only one of four constituent parts of this foundation, the others being his primacy, Rome, and the Roman Pontiff.

- The Papacy's principal function is unity of the Church:

  > ...that the episcopacy itself might be one and undivided, and that the entire multitude of the faithful through priests closely connected with one another might be preserved in the unity of faith and communion...[188]

Comment: The primacy's efficacy depends on a Roman Pontiff. In order for unity to remain a permanent characteristic of the Church, perpetual papal succession is required. I will address the constitution's meaning of "perpetual successors" in part II.

- Rome is the foundation of the papacy:

  > ...all ages have known that the holy and most blessed Peter, chief and head of the apostles and pillar of faith and foundation of the Catholic Church, received the keys of the kingdom from our Lord Jesus Christ, the Savior and Redeemer of the human race; and he up to this time and always lives and presides and exercises judgment in his successors, the bishops of the holy see of Rome...[189]

Comment: Here we are concerned with Rome, the Holy See or Roman diocese where the Vicar of Christ and the central government of the Catholic Church are located. We must remember a critical point: that *Peter's primacy is permanently bound to Rome, not a successor person.* This essentially makes the Roman See the foundation of the papacy. Also

---
[188] Ibid.
[189] Ibid., 1824.

recall from chapter one that the Sedevacantists do not have Rome in any capacity and cannot therefore have Peter or the primacy (i.e., all Sedevacantists are missing the correct foundation of the Catholic Church).

- Rome identifies the Vicar of Christ:

> Therefore, whoever succeeds Peter in this chair, he according to the institution of Christ himself, holds the primacy of Peter over the whole Church.[190]

Comment: The identity of the Vicar of Christ is a matter of eternal salvation. So that nobody should ever suffer doubt or confusion as to who the Vicar of Christ is, Vatican I made his identity easily recognizable by permanently binding him to Rome. The faithful will know who the Vicar of Christ is by his occupancy of the Roman See, not the orthodoxy of his teaching.

- Roman Pontiffs realize the unity of the Church:

> For this reason "it has always been necessary because of mightier pre-eminence for every Church to come to the Church of Rome, that is those who are the faithful everywhere," so that in this See, from which the laws of "venerable communion" emanate over all, they as members associated in one head, coalesce into one bodily structure.[191]

Comment: I will address the necessity of the Roman Pontiff in part II.

- Visible unity is permanent:

---

190 Ibid.
191 Ibid.

> Moreover, what the Chief of pastors and the Great Pastor of sheep, our Lord Jesus, established in the blessed Apostle Peter for the perpetual salvation and perennial good of the Church, this by the same Author must endure always in the Church which was founded upon a rock and will endure firm until the end of the ages. [192]

Comment: Visibility of the Church will be addressed in Chapter 4.

- Unity with the Holy See identifies the hierarchy and the faithful:

> Furthermore We teach and declare that the Roman Church, by the disposition of the Lord, holds the sovereignty of ordinary power over all others, and that this power of jurisdiction on the part of the Roman Pontiff, which is truly episcopal, is immediate; and with respect to this the pastors and the faithful of whatever rite and dignity, both as separate individuals and all together, are bound by the duty of hierarchical subordination and true obedience, not only in things which pertain to faith and morals, but also in those which pertain to the discipline and government of the Church [which is] spread over the whole world, so that the Church of Christ, protected not only by the Roman Pontiff, but by the unity of communion as well as of the profession of the same faith is one flock under the one highest shepherd. This is the doctrine of Catholic truth from which no one can deviate and keep his faith and salvation.[193]

- Unity with the Roman Pontiff is compulsory:

---

[192] Ibid.
[193] Ibid., 1827.

> If anyone thus speaks, that the Roman Pontiff has only the office of inspection or direction, but not the full and supreme power of jurisdiction over the universal Church, not only in things which pertain to faith and morals, but also in those which pertain to the discipline and government of the Church spread over the whole world; or, that he possesses only the more important parts, but the whole plentitude of this supreme power; or that this power of his is not ordinary and immediate, or over the Churches altogether and individually, and over the pastors and the faithful altogether and individually: let him be anathema.[194]

Comment: One of the most important duties of the faithful is to maintain unity with the Roman Pontiff, not to scrutinize or judge him for orthodoxy in doctrine. The reason for this is evident in the final point.

- The Holy See cannot defect or fail.

> And, since the gates of hell, to overthrow the Church, if this were possible, arise from all sides with ever greater hatred against its divinely established foundation, We judge it to be necessary for the protection, safety, and increase of the Catholic flock, with the approbation of the Council, to set forth the doctrine on the institution, perpetuity, and nature of the Sacred Apostolic Primacy, in which the strength and solidarity of the whole Church consist…[195]

Comment: Recall that the Roman Church is indefectible: "Only to One particular Church is indefectibility assured, viz. to the See of Rome…"[196]

---

194 Ibid., 1831.
195 Ibid., 1821.
196 Joyce, *The Catholic Encyclopedia*, 756.

Remember, indefectibility extends not only to the Roman Pontiff in his official teaching office[197] but also to the Roman Church in general, which includes a central government. There should never be a reason for the faithful to sever communion with the Holy See, even if Anthony Quinn were its occupant, because they have been assured that error, infidelity, heresy, and defection of the Holy See are impossible.

DIMOND'S ARK

An ecumenical council purportedly speaks for Jesus Christ, and Vatican Council I's teaching is simple and unambiguous: The bishop of Rome is Vicar of Jesus Christ—follow, obey, or suffer eternal damnation.[198] But would God ever punish those who remain faithful to this precept? According to the Sedevacantists, he has. Let us hear from Dimond: "Leaving the Church without a pope for an extended period of the Great Apostasy is the punishment inflicted by God on our generation for the wickedness of the world."[199]

I will cast aside Dimond's attempt to pass off a theory of defection as a papal interregnum again and focus instead on the implication of Dimond's statement toward God. According to Dimond God used his Church to imbed a simple, dogmatic formula into the minds and hearts of Catholics—*maintain unity with Roman See for salvation*—and then switched the formula in order to inflict a massive punishment on the Church because he became angry. How does God switch the formula? He sets a trap that will ensnare all but the elect by first commanding

---

197 Closely related to and yet understood as distinct from his infallibility.

198 Though not explicitly stated, one of the constitution's most important themes was not new; it had existed since at least AD 1302, when Pope Boniface VIII dogmatically declared: "With faith urging us we are forced to believe and to hold the one, holy, Catholic Church and that, apostolic, and we firmly believe and simply confess this (Church) outside of which there is no salvation nor remission of sin...*Furthermore, we declare, say, define, and proclaim to every human creature that they by necessity for salvation are entirely subject to the Roman Pontiff.*" [Italics added]. (Denzinger, *The Sources of Catholic Dogma*, 468–469.)

199 Dimond, *The Truth*, 309.

the faithful to maintain unity with the Holy Roman See and then subsequently allowing it to defect (see objection one) and become the seat of the Antichrist. Dimond's theory can be considered blasphemous, for God is not a deceiver.

> God is not a man, that he should lie, nor as the son of man, that he should be changed. Hath he said then, and will he not do? hath he spoken, and will he not fulfill? [200]

> Let no man, when he is tempted, say that he is tempted by God. For God is not a tempter of evils, and he tempteth no man. [201]

In the book of Genesis, God destroys the world in a great flood. Many Sedevacantists refer to the story of Noe as a proof that the Sedevacantist thesis is not outside the limitations of what God will permit. After all if God could destroy the whole Earth, he certainly could allow a great deception to take place in order to test the faith of his elect. But comparing Noe's ark to Sedevacantism is comparing apples and oranges. While God once did punish the world for its wickedness, he did not do so by way of trickery or deceit. Moreover, God mercifully provided the elect with the ark (a precursor to the Catholic Church) as the means of salvation. In the story of Dimond's ark, however, God punishes the Church for the world's wickedness and provides the elect with Dimond. The reader may inquire, "What does the wickedness of the world have to do with God altering the plan of salvation so the Holy See is destroyed and salvation is rerouted to Dimond?" The answer, of course, is nothing. Dimond portrays God as a deceiver who punishes fidelity and obedience to one of his Church's most important precepts.

If the teachings of Vatican I's dogmatic constitution were true, even an extraordinary, end-times deception allowed by God to test the fidelity of his elect could be understood only as the forces of evil (i.e.,

---

200 Numbers 23:19.
201 James 1:13.

the Antichrist) luring the faithful *away from* the Roman See, which was purportedly established by the institution of Christ himself (de fide). According to Dimond, however, if God gets mad enough, he just might punish the faithful for doing what he commanded them to do in the first place. The moral of the story of Dimond's ark is that the Catholic faithful should not be in communion with the Holy See and the Roman Pontiff because they are no longer the Holy See and Roman Pontiff; God set a trap in order to test them, and Dimond exposed it. Consequently all who wish to be saved must be in communion with Dimond.

Part II

The Papacy of Desire

❦

WE WILL NOW ADDRESS THE three specific passages from the dogmatic constitution to which Dimond responds in his book. As I make important distinctions, readers will understand how the doctrines on the papacy contradict the Sedevacantists. Additionally we will see how the doctrines on the papacy contradict other doctrines on the papacy. Lastly we will see how doctrines on the papacy contradict the actual papacy.

The very first thing that stands out about Dimond's opening answer to objection six is that he addresses a different objection than the one to which he is supposed to respond. We will begin there.

Objection six in Dimond's book reads: "Objection 6: Vatican I's definition on the perpetuity of the Papal Office contradicts the claims of the Sedevacantists."[202]

Dimond responds (emphasis original): "Answer: **Vatican I's dogmas don't contradict a vacancy of the Papal See**; in fact, it's only those who reject the Vatican II antipopes who can consistently accept these papal dogmas, since Benedict XVI utterly rejects them."[203]

The reader should immediately notice that Dimond is responding to an objection that was never made. Obviously there is a significant

---
202 Dimond, *The Truth*, 310.
203 Ibid.

difference between Vatican I contradicting *the claims of the Sedevacantists* and Vatican I contradicting *a vacancy of the Papal See*. The rejection of Sedevacantism is based on the former, not the latter. It is a blatant falsification of the non-Sedevacantist position to say that they claim Vatican I's dogmas contradict a vacancy of the Papal See. Furthermore it is also a falsification of the Sedevacantists' position to say that Sedevacantism is merely a vacancy of the Papal See. As previously addressed in objection five, there is a world of difference between a legitimate papal vacancy and Sedevacantism. Once again the reader is cautioned not to fall for Dimond's attempt to disguise Sedevacantism's theory of the defection of the Catholic Church as a routine papal interregnum.

Passage One

The first passage from the First Dogmatic Constitution on the Church of Christ that Dimond addresses is found in the introduction. Dimond begins (emphasis original):

> Vatican I declares that the Papacy is the Perpetual Principle and Visible Foundation of Unity.
>> Vatican I, Dogmatic Constitution on the Church of Christ, Sess. 4, July 18, 1870: "But, that the episcopacy itself might be one and undivided, and that the entire multitude of the faithful through priests closely connected with one another might be preserved in the unity of faith and communion, **placing Peter over the other apostles He established in him the perpetual principle and visible foundation of both unities**, upon whose strength the eternal temple might be erected, and the sublimity of the Church might rise in the firmness of this faith."
>
> That what Christ instituted in St. Peter (THE OFFICE OF PETER) remains the perpetual principle and visible foundation of unity EVEN TODAY, AND WHEN THERE IS NO POPE, is proven every time a Catholic who is a sedevacantist converts an Eastern "Orthodox"

Schismatic to the Catholic Faith. The Catholic (who is a sedevacantist) charitably informs the Eastern Schismatic that <u>he (the Eastern Schismatic) is not in the unity of the Church</u> because he doesn't accept what Christ instituted in St. Peter (the office of the Papacy), in addition to not accepting what the successors of St. Peter have bindingly taught in history (the Council of Trent, etc.). **This is a clear example of how the Office of the Papacy still serves—and will always serve—as the perpetual principle of visible unity, distinguishing the true faithful from the false (and the true Church from the false)**. This is true when there is no pope, and for the sedevacantist today. This dogmatic teaching of Vatican I doesn't exclude periods without a pope and it is not contrary to the sedevacantist thesis in any way.[204]

Dimond's example of converting members of the Eastern Orthodox Church to Sedevacantism is *not* an example of how the "Office of the Papacy still serves...as the perpetual principle of visible unity," but it is an excellent example of why it is so dangerous to ascribe visible unity of the Church to something or someone other than the Roman Pontiff, especially if his last name is Dimond. According to Dimond visible unity is not only attainable without the Roman Pontiff, but some Sedevacantists (presumably himself) are actually in possession of it. Let us see how he does this.

The Vatican Council's teaching on visible unity of the Church as embodied in the Roman Pontiff is undeniable.[205] This is problematic for the Sedevacantists because they require visible unity to be considered the Roman Catholic Church, but they do not have a Roman Pontiff. To

---

204 Ibid., 311.
205 Note: Vatican II appears to override Vatican I's dogmatic teaching that the Roman Pontiff is the principle of the Church's unity by ascribing the Roman Pontiff's function to the Holy Spirit: *"It is the Holy Spirit,* dwelling in those who believe and pervading and ruling over the entire Church, who brings about that wonderful communion of the faithful and joins them together so intimately in Christ *that he is the principle of the Church's unity."* [Italics added]. (Vatican Council II, "*Unitatis Redintegratio*," 501.) Ascribing unity of the Church to the Holy Spirit as opposed to the Roman Pontiff squares nicely with Vatican II's ecumenical theme and novel teaching on partial communion with the Church. This way heretics and schismatics can now be in the unity of the Church even if they reject the papacy.

get around this problem, Dimond transfers the Roman Pontiff's functions to another agent. The unifying agent in Dimond's Church? The "Office of the Papacy." Let us have a look at how Dimond explains this. He wrote (emphasis original):

> The Office of the Papacy is the office of St. Peter which is occupied by every true and lawful Bishop of Rome. This means and guarantees that every time there is a true and valid occupant of the office he is endowed by Christ with infallibility (in his authoritative and binding teaching capacity), he is endowed with supreme jurisdiction over the universal Church, and he is the visible head of the Church. **That remains true for every true and lawful occupant of the Papal Office until the end of time. This doesn't mean that the Church will always have such an occupant, as Church history and more than 200 papal vacancies prove,** nor does it mean that antipopes reigning from Rome are an impossibility (such as Antipope Anacletus II, who reigned in Rome from 1130–1138).[206]

Although Dimond correctly describes characteristics that accompany the office of the papacy, he leaves out something important. In addition to being the Church's visible head, the Roman Pontiff is also the source of the Church's unities of faith and communion. Because visible unity is what Dimond is supposed to be addressing, his failure to mention this critical function is especially conspicuous. Nevertheless, Dimond is correct when he says that every time there is an occupant of the office, the aforementioned prerogatives accompany him.

What Dimond does not mention is that the opposite is also true: Every time there is not a true and valid holder of that office, the powers that accompany a holder of this office must remain arrested. In other words when there is no occupant of the office then there is no person who speaks infallibly, no person who has supreme jurisdiction over the universal Church, no visible head of the Church, and, most importantly

---

206 Dimond, *The Truth*, 312–313.

for purposes of this discussion, no source of visible unity of the Church. This could explain why Dimond does not mention the connection between the Roman Pontiff and the visible unity of the Church.

OFFICE OF THE PAPACY—SOME CLARIFICATIONS

Let us be clear on Dimond's position. We recall that Dimond is attempting to claim that Sedevacantists such as himself have visible unity of the Church because of the permanence of the office of the papacy. To understand why Dimond is wrong, some important clarifications on the office of the papacy are necessary. An *office* is a position with authority. In this case this authority is the same originally held by Peter in virtue of having received the sacred primacy. We recall how Ott described the primacy in chapter one as follows: "Primacy means first in rank. A primacy may be one of honour, of control, of direction (primatus directionis), or of jurisdiction, that is, of government. A primacy of jurisdiction consists in the possession of full and supreme legislative, juridical and punitive power."[207]

Because the primacy is permanently bound to the Roman See, the office itself is the position of bishop of the Diocese of Rome.

The primacy itself functions through an interdependent system comprised of the Apostle Peter, the Roman See, and the Roman Pontiff. In this system each component is interdependent, so dividing them would not fulfill the divine will. For example the Apostle Peter died two thousand years ago; the primacy itself is inorganic and immaterial; and only a designated successor bishop to the Roman See is authorized to wield the powers of the primacy. Because Christ did not will for his Church to be governed by an invisible, inorganic, intangible, or illegitimate power, all of the components of the papacy work together to achieve the end for which the papacy exists—unity of the Church. How do we know this? First because the Vatican Council says Christ instituted the primacy *in the person* of the Apostle Peter: "So we teach and declare that according to the testimonies of the Gospel the primacy of jurisdiction over the

---

207 Ott, *Fundamentals of Catholic Dogma*, 279.

entire Church of God was promised and was conferred immediately and directly upon the blessed Apostle Peter by Christ the Lord."[208]

Second because Christ instituted *human successors* to Peter in his primacy and *permanently bound them to Rome*: "If anyone then says that it is not by the institution of Christ the Lord Himself, or by divine right that the blessed Peter should has perpetual successors in the primacy over the universal Church, or that the Roman Pontiff is not the successor of blessed Peter in the same Primacy, let him be anathema."[209]

Third because the Vatican Council repeats the words of Christ: "… that all might be one, just as the Son Himself and the Father are one."[210]

Lastly these passages:

> But, that the episcopacy itself might be one and undivided, and that the entire multitude of the faithful through priests closely connected with one another might be preserved in the unity of faith and communion, placing the blessed Peter over the other apostles He established in him the perpetual principle and visible foundation of both unities, upon whose strength the eternal temple might be erected…[211]

> …so that the Church of Christ, protected not only by the Roman Pontiff, but by the unity of communion as well as of the profession of the same faith is one flock under the one highest shepherd.[212]

Notice that the First Vatican Council does not say *by unity with the Blessed Apostle Peter* or *by unity with the apostolic primacy* the Church becomes one flock. Vatican I specifically teaches *that by unity with the Roman Pontiff, the Church becomes one flock*. Human succession is mandatory.

Referencing Leo XIII's encyclical letter *Satis Cognitum*, Ott wrote: "The unity both of faith and of communion is guaranteed by the Primacy

---

208 Denzinger, *The Sources of Catholic Dogma*, 1822.
209 Ibid., 1825.
210 Ibid., 1821.
211 Ibid.
212 Ibid., 1827.

of the Pope, the Supreme Teacher and Pastor of the Church (centrum unitatis: D 1960)."[213]

Notice again that Ott does not write that the unities of faith and communion are guaranteed by the primacy but rather *the person* who is supreme teacher and pastor of the Church.

The Catholic Encyclopedia states:

> The Church's doctrine as to the pope was authoritatively declared in the Vatican Council in the Constitution "Pastor Aeternus." The four chapters of that Constitution deal respectively with the office of Supreme Head conferred on St. Peter, *the perpetuity of this office in the person of the Roman pontiff,* the pope's jurisdiction over the faithful, and his supreme authority to define in all questions of faith and morals.[214]

Again, notice the explicit language in the emphasized clause above. The perpetuity of the office is not ascribed to Peter nor to the primacy that is bound to the Roman See. *The perpetuity of Peter's office is ascribed to the person of the Roman Pontiff.*

While it is true that the primacy still exists during papal interregnums, Dimond is wrong when he claims that the end for which the primacy exists is attained in and of itself. Not so. As just explained, the primacy of Peter is an inoperative power without the Roman Pontiff, the living person through whom Peter purportedly exercises it. The primacy merely entitles its occupant to exercise certain powers in virtue of the Apostle Peter. If this were not true, there would have been no need for Christ to establish the primacy in a human or to establish human succession. So although the primacy itself does not cease to exist during vacancies of the Roman See, the same cannot be said for the Church's visible unity of faith and communion, neither of which *should be able* to exist without the Vicar of Christ, who is commissioned to bring it all together.

---

213 Ott, *Fundamentals of Catholic Dogma*, 303.
214 Joyce, *The Catholic Encyclopedia*, 260-261.

The First Vatican Council (1869–1870)

The Church's visible unities of faith and communion, each of which is a permanent and unchangeable characteristic of the Catholic Church, are contingent on the existence of the Roman Pontiff or his expedient election and not the permanence of Peter's primacy. In other words the underlying basis for the Church's visible unity may be said to rest in the Blessed Apostle Peter's primacy, but its manifestation is forever embodied in the Roman Pontiff. The primacy remains an arrested power without a Roman Pontiff to exercise it.

So far we have established five key points about the papacy:

1. Peter's primacy is the *underlying basis* for unity.
2. The primacy is permanently bound to Rome.
3. The office of the papacy is the position of the primacy.
4. A Roman Pontiff must fill/exercise the office.
5. These points are symbiotic in order to realize the end for which Christ instituted the papacy: unity of the Church.

The reader will recall from objection one that the foundation of the Church is the papacy and that its material and human components belong to the Church's essential constitution. Consequently it is useless to argue that a material foundation is optional. In describing the constitution of the Church as both material and spiritual, Pope Leo XIII wrote:

The Church Always Visible

The connection and union of both elements is as *absolutely necessary* to the true Church as the intimate union of the soul and body is to human nature.[215]

Nevertheless, the Sedevacantists will insist that they have not severed connection to the foundation of the faith. As we read above, Dimond

---
215 Leo XIII, *Satis Cognitum*, 388.

claims he still possesses unity of the Church by the office of the papacy, of which the Sedevacantists claim to be in possession. Other Sedevacantists claim that their particular sect is in communion with what amounts to a variation of Dimond's unmanned office, which they refer to as "eternal Rome,"[216] as if an invisible Rome can suffice for material Rome and its living members. Let us recall a point I previously made concerning the relationship of the primacy to Rome: If the Papacy is the foundation of the Roman Catholic Church, Rome is the foundation of the papacy. The point is that the Sedevacantists have neither.

As we can see, Dimond understands the office of the papacy as being a free-floating, invisible entity without a material foundation, which can function on its own accord without authorized human representation. This is what allows some Sedevacantists to imagine that the office of the papacy now dwells in makeshift chapels and seminaries around the world. The only thing Dimond *may* have correct is that the office of the papacy is invisible, and even that would be contingent upon his agreement that the office is the position of Peter's primacy.

However, "the office" (i.e., the primacy) is not free-floating, without material foundation, or capable of functioning without authorized human representation. Again, the primacy is one part of a four-part, symbiotic system comprised of both material and immaterial components. Dimond not only attempts to divide the system, but he is missing all four components, which automatically debunks his claim of possessing the office of the papacy.

---

216 "ARE WE WITH ROME? YES. We are, as the Rule states, bound to obey two authorities: the valid and legitimate successors of a valid and true Pope AND the Roman Church. This implies that there can be situations where a Pope MAY NOT BE a valid and legitimate Pope. Therefore, in such circumstances, one obeys the Roman Church. This is the 'Eternal Rome'—at once, seat and symbol of the One, Holy, Catholic and Apostolic Church founded by Jesus Christ." ("The Franciscans: Who Are We?," last modified Wednesday, January 6, 1999, http://friarsminor.org/whoarf2.html#ROME.)

The First Vatican Council (1869–1870)

THE PAPACY OF DESIRE VERSUS THE HOLY SEE

According to the Sedevacantists, the Holy Roman See is gone. This is how we are able to identify the third principal heresy of the Sedevacantists: The papacy of desire is sufficient for membership in and visible unity of the true Church of Christ.

Dimond's papacy of desire is essentially a heretical ecclesiology that errs in two ways. First it attempts to divide the mutually dependent components of the papacy in order to claim some portion of its powers and purpose. One example is ascribing the Church's visible unity to the primacy but omitting that the primacy must be exercised by a human successor to Peter. Second the heretical ecclesiology is based on the complete absence of any traceable, material foundation of the Church. In other words this ecclesiology teaches that it is not necessary that the Holy See exists materially; it need exist only spiritually. Thus membership in and unity of the Church are attained merely by one's desire to be united to what is essentially an invisible Church.

I will revisit this Sedevacantist myth in chapter four, concerning the visibility of the Church, but for our purposes in support of objection six, it is paramount to understand that the constituent components of the foundation of the Catholic Church, *both spiritual and material*, cannot be divided without destroying it. Dimond's papacy of desire divides that which cannot be divided and is overtly heretical.

Papacy of desire is the logical sequence to Sedevacantist thesis, which is essentially a theory of the defection of the Holy See. Because the Sedevacantists are forbidden to admit the fact, a new ecclesiology was proposed that is remarkably similar to Protestantism's invisible Church ecclesiology except that the Sedevacantists ostensibly recognize the authority of the Holy See. Unfortunately they have not been able to locate it for fifty-seven years, and they lack the power to reproduce it. Again, if the Holy See cannot be accounted for, a defection occurred.

The Sedevacantist Delusion

CONVERSIONS TO DIMOND'S ARK

Earlier we read Dimond's explanation for how his papacy of desire works. Let us look at it again (emphasis original):

> That what Christ instituted in St. Peter (THE OFFICE OF PETER) remains the perpetual principle and visible foundation of unity <u>EVEN TODAY, AND WHEN THERE IS NO POPE</u>, is proven every time a Catholic who is a sedevacantist converts an Eastern "Orthodox" Schismatic to the Catholic Faith.
>
> The Catholic (who is a sedevacantist) charitably informs the Eastern Schismatic that <u>he (the Eastern Schismatic) is not in the unity of the Church</u> because he doesn't accept what Christ instituted in St. Peter (the office of the Papacy), in addition to not accepting what the successors of St. Peter have bindingly taught in history (the Council of Trent, etc.). **This is a clear example of how the Office of the Papacy still serves—and will always serve—as the perpetual principle of visible unity, distinguishing the true faithful from the false (and the true Church from the false)**. This is true when there is no pope, and for the sedevacantist today. This dogmatic teaching of Vatican I doesn't exclude periods without a pope and it is not contrary to the sedevacantist thesis in any way.[217]

Dimond attempts to demonstrate how the office of Peter is responsible for visible unity of the Church with an example of conversions from Eastern Orthodoxy to Sedevacantism. However, because Dimond is wrong about how the Church realizes unity and of what unity of the Church consists, his example of Eastern Orthodox conversions is also wrong. The first problem is that Sedevacantists are not in the Church;

---

217 Dimond, *The Truth*, 311.

they are in schism with the Holy See, which makes it impossible for converts to Sedevacantism to come into the Church. For example it is anybody's guess which Sedevacantist sect an Eastern Orthodox convert could wind up in, demonstrating once again that Sedevacantists do not have unity of the Church. Moreover, since Dimond considers all Sedevacantists who disagree with him to be outside the *true* Church, it would be more appropriate to say that Dimond believes the unity of the Church consists in himself (see "Dimond's ark" in a previous segment).[218]

Papacy of Desire Ends in Schism

Dimond's example of Eastern Orthodox conversions to the Sedevacantist position will always end in schism. To illustrate this we can compare the Old Catholics,[219] who came into existence at the time of the First Vatican Council (1869–1870), with the Sedevacantists, who came into existence near the time of the Second Vatican Council (1962–1965). At the First Vatican Council, some theologians and bishops adamantly opposed the dogmas on the Papacy. Namely, they objected to the pope's infallibility and cited examples of historical teaching errors in the papal office. When Pius IX pushed the papal dogmas through, a schism ensued. Today the Church considers the Old Catholic Church schismatic.

Fast forward to the time of Vatican II, and we find that Sedevacantists came into existence for essentially the same reasons. Like their predecessors the Old Catholics, Sedevacantists reject conciliar doctrines because they see them as contradictory. According to

---

218 In the cutthroat Sedevacantist world, there is no possibility for unity because there is no Holy See. For example, influential Sedevacantists such as bishops, priests, writers, and editors usually end up on Dimond's heretic list.

219 Old Catholics: "The sect organised in German-speaking countries to combat the dogma of Papal Infallibility. Filled with ideas of ecclesiastical Liberalism and rejecting the Christian spirit of submission to the teachings of the Church, nearly 1400 Germans issued, in September, 1870, a declaration in which they repudiated the dogma of Infallibility 'as an innovation contrary to the traditional faith of the Church.'" ("Old Catholics," New Advent, accessed May 3, 2015, http://www.newadvent.org/cathen/11235b.htm.)

Dimond's reasoning, the Old Catholics should also be considered the *true* Roman Catholic Church because they meet his criteria for possessing the office of the papacy. We recall Dimond's criterion is that one accepts what Peter's successors bindingly taught in history (e.g., Council of Trent, etc.). Using Dimond's reasoning, anyone who converts to the Old Catholic Church has as valid a claim to being a member of the true Church of Christ, as does a Sedevacantist. According to Dimond, possessing the Holy See where the primacy is permanently bound is not a requirement for any group to be considered the true Church; it is only necessary to desire it. This illustrates why Dimond's criteria for what constitutes visible unity of the Church is subjective and immaterial and always ends in schism.

In conclusion to the first passage from *Pastor Aeternus* cited by Dimond, we have seen that he claims that the Church's first mark, visible unity, is realized without all of the constituent parts to the papacy. The reader will now understand how and why the doctrines of the Church refute him, as does the disunity of the various Sedevacantist sects in existence today. Because the Vatican Council is clear that the Vicar of Christ is essential to visible unity of the Church, non-Sedevacantists who cite this particular passage from the dogmatic constitution in refutation of the Sedevacantists are correct. As much as I do not accept the Vatican Council's dogmas as divinely revealed truths, Dimond certainly does, and the first one he addresses backfires on him with a shell that effectively blows up the core of his theory. The undeniable truth is that according to Roman Catholic ecclesiology, the Vicar of Christ brings it all together. Unfortunately Dimond has neither a Vicar of Christ nor a legitimate way to get one, and Rome itself is out of the question.

Passage Two

Dimond addresses the second passage from *Pastor Aeternus* as follows (emphasis original):

The First Vatican Council (1869-1870)

2: The Papacy will endure forever

> Vatican I, Dogmatic Constitution on the Church of Christ, Sess. 4, Chap. Moreover, **what the Chief of pastors and the Great Pastor of sheep, the Lord Jesus, established in the blessed Apostle Peter** for the perpetual salvation and perennial good of the Church, this by the same Author **must endure always in the Church which was founded upon a rock and will endure firm until the end of ages.**

Yes, what Christ instituted in St. Peter (i.e., THE OFFICE OF THE PAPACY) must endure always until the end of ages. What is the Office of the Papacy? The Office of the Papacy is the office of St. Peter which is occupied by every true and lawful Bishop of Rome. This means and guarantees that every time there is a true and valid occupant of the office he is endowed by Christ with infallibility (in his authoritative and binding teaching capacity), he is endowed with supreme jurisdiction over the universal Church, and he is the visible head of the Church. **That remains true for every true and lawful occupant of the Papal Office until the end of time. This doesn't mean that the Church will always have such an occupant, as Church history and more than 200 papal vacancies prove**, nor does it mean that antipopes reigning from Rome are an impossibility (such as Antipope Anacletus II, who reigned in Rome from 1130-1138). This definition proves nothing for the non-sedevacantist, so let's move on.[220]

There is no question that *Pastor Aeternus* teaches that the office of the papacy will endure forever and continue to function in the purpose for which it exists. However, as established in the first passage, the primacy can do nothing in and of itself; it must be exercised by the living successor of Peter. Accordingly, for visible unity to remain permanent in the Church, the Roman Pontiff is necessary by way of *uninterrupted*

---

220 Dimond, *The Truth*, 312-13.

succession, so let us now move on to address the third passage from the dogmatic constitution. As we proceed, we will see how a transfer of Peter's primacy to Rome is without foundation but necessary for the Roman Church if it intended to maintain a claim of superiority over Eastern Christianity. To secure the Western Church's ambitions, binding Peter's primacy to human successors would not be sufficient; a permanent connection to Rome had to be established.

Passage Three
Dimond addresses the third and final passage from *Pastor Aeternus* as follows (emphasis original):

> 3. "Peter will have perpetual successors in the Primacy over the Universal Church"
>
>   Pope Pius IX, *First Vatican Council*, Sess. 4, Chap. 2, [Canon]. "<u>If anyone then says that it is not</u> from the institution of Christ the Lord Himself, or <u>by divine right that the blessed Peter has perpetual successors in the primacy over the universal Church, or that the Roman Pontiff is not the successor of blessed Peter in the same primacy</u>, let him be anathema."

This is the favorite canon of those who argue against the sedevacantist "thesis"; but, as we will see, it also proves nothing for their position. Words and distinctions are very important. Understanding distinctions and words can often be the very difference between Protestantism and Catholicism.

The canon from Vatican I condemns those who deny *"that Peter has <u>perpetual successors in the primacy</u> over the universal Church."* Notice the phrase "perpetual successors **IN THE PRIMACY**." This, as we have seen, does not mean and cannot mean that we will always have a pope. That is why it doesn't say that "we will always have a pope." It's a fact

The First Vatican Council (1869–1870)

that there have been periods without a pope. So what does the canon mean?[221]

Dimond correctly interprets this canon as being a condemnation of a heresy held by schismatics: "This heresy—which denies that a pope is the successor of St. Peter <u>in the same primacy perpetually</u> (that is, *every time there is a pope until the end of time, he is a successor in the same primacy*, with the same authority St. Peter possessed)—is precisely what this canon condemns."[222]

Passage three is a "favorite canon of those who argue against the Sedevacantist 'thesis'" because most people can recognize the difference between a *successor* and a *primacy*. In the English translation of this passage, *perpetual* is the adjective defining *successors*, not p*rimacy*. So the question is, does the above passage mean that Peter will have *perpetual successors* who share in the same primacy? Or does it mean that Peter will have sporadic successors who share in his *perpetual primacy*?

Dimond's interpretation is the latter, but as already established, this interpretation creates contradictions with Roman ecclesiology (i.e., visible unity as well as the purported uninterrupted papal succession).[223] Because visible unity of the Church is contingent on a Vicar of Christ, the answer can only be that perpetual successors *and* perpetual primacy are both correct. Yes, the primacy is perpetual, but that Peter will have *perpetual successors* is also correct because the first mark of the Church is dependent on the person of the Roman Pontiff, not the primacy, so that without him the unity of the Church should be neither attainable nor sustainable.

This interpretation seems to be most consistent with the other teachings of the dogmatic constitution. However, do any other proofs exist that confirm my understanding of the First Vatican Council's teaching

---

221 Ibid., 313.
222 Ibid.
223 The Sedevacantists are forced to hold a contradictory position that the papacy is an *unbroken succession* dating to Peter except when antipopes and heretics rule the Holy See.

on the necessity of the perpetual presence of Roman Pontiffs for visible unity of the Church? Yes, and I will cite two (emphasis added):

> *That the Primacy is to be perpetuated in the successors of Peter* is, indeed, not expressly stated in the words of the promise and conferring of the Primacy by Our Lord, but if flows as an inference from the nature and purpose of the primacy itself. As the function of the Primacy is to preserve the unity and solidarity of the Church; and as the Church, according to the will of her Divine Founder, is to continue substantially unchanged until the end of time for the perpetuation of the work of salvation, the Primacy also must be perpetuated. *But Peter, like every other human being, was subject to death (John 21, 19), consequently his office must be transmitted to others. The structure of the Church cannot continue without the foundation which supports it (Mt. 16, 18): Christ's flock cannot exist without shepherds (John 21, 15–17).*[224]

What is most interesting about Ott's passage is that it reaffirms the fact that the Roman Pontiff belongs to the Church's foundation. The structure of the Church rests on human successors in the Roman Pontiffs so that without successors, the primacy cannot be perpetuated. Obviously if the primacy cannot be perpetuated, neither can the unity and solidarity of the Church.

The second confirmation comes from the Second Vatican Council: "The Roman Pontiff, as the successor of Peter, is the perpetual and visible source and foundation of the unity both of the bishops and of the whole company of the faithful."[225,226]

Obviously if Christ really instituted the papacy, he did not intend for his Vicar to be a sporadic presence in the Church, as Dimond falsely implies, nor did he intend for his vicar to be redundant to the apostolic primacy. Christ intended for his vicar to remain a perpetual presence

---

224 Ott, *Fundamentals of Catholic Dogma*, 282.
225 Vatican Council II, *"Lumen Gentium,"* 31.
226 The quoted passage from *"Lumen Gentium"* uses endnote 30: "See Vatican Council I, Dogmatic Constitution Pastor Aeternus: Denz. 1821 (3050 f.)."

The First Vatican Council (1869–1870)

in the Church because only *he* is appointed to wield the power of the primacy "...that the episcopacy itself might be one and undivided, and that the entire multitude of the faithful through priests closely connected with one another might be preserved in the unity of faith and communion..."[227]

Again we need only to observe the perpetual disunity of the Sedevacantist movement despite Dimond's claim that "the Office of the Papacy still serves—and will always serve as the perpetual principle of visible unity" to prove that his interpretation is wrong. If the Vicar of Christ were not necessary to maintain the visible unity of the Church, perhaps Dimond would like to explain why the office of the papacy has failed to preserve visible unity among Sedevacantists.

Next Dimond attacks a straw man by claiming that the non-Sedevacantist understanding of "perpetual successors" is that the Church must *literally always* have a pope (emphasis original): "**Thus, in order to be consistent**, non-sedevacantists who quote Vatican I against the sedevacantist 'thesis' must argue that the Church can never be without a pope, not even for a moment (a patent absurdity)."[228]

Dimond's argument is inapplicable to the majority of Catholics who reject Sedevacantism. Most non-Sedevacantists do not understand *perpetual successors* to mean that the Church cannot be without a pope "not even for a moment." Dimond sets up this straw man and proceeds to knock him down in the person of Christopher Ferrara as though it means something, but the Church did not intend for *perpetual successors* to mean that the Church must never have a single vacancy, even due to death.[229] *Perpetual successors* means the Church will have a continuous, uninterrupted succession of popes, even during those times when rival antipopes coexist.

In "The Creed Explained" from objection one, Devine provided the Church's understanding of *perpetuity* as meaning "continuation without

---

227 Denzinger, *The Sources of Catholic Dogma*, 1821.
228 Dimond, *The Truth*, 311.
229 Ibid.

interruption."[230] In other words Sedevacantism's string of six successive antipopes ruling the Roman See for the past fifty-seven years interrupts papal succession and violates this canon. The only way Sedevacantism would not contradict *perpetual successors* would be if the Sedevacantists could prove that legitimate Roman Pontiffs have simultaneously existed since the first Antipope[231] conquered Rome. This would entail proving that the Holy See moved to a satellite location, which the Sedevacantists cannot do. Despite the fact that some Sedevacantists theorize that a true line of popes exists somewhere since Vatican II, Sedevacantism still fails for a whole host of reasons, not the least of which is that this alleged pope has failed to exercise the primacy and maintain unity of the Church for the past half century.

VICAR WITHOUT A SEE

Having established what the Church means by *perpetual*, I will now change modes to that of critic of the Roman papacy, as we turn our attention to the meaning of *successors* in this canon. According to the introduction and entire first chapter of the dogmatic constitution, Christ instituted the primacy *in* Peter. There can be no mistaking that this office was bestowed immediately and directly upon his person: "He established *in him* the perpetual principle and visible foundation of both unities…"[232]

The distinction of the institution in Peter is important because, as was covered previously, the Church is a living organism comprised of living members. According to the scripture passages used to support the institution of the papacy, Christ did not establish a *see* as the foundation

---

230 Devine, *The Creed Explained*, 290.
231 Antipope: "A false claimant of the Holy See in opposition to a pontiff canonically elected. At various times in the history of the Church illegal pretenders to the Papal Chair have arisen, and frequently exercised pontifical functions in defiance of the true occupant." [Elisabeth Christitch, *The Catholic Encyclopedia* (New York: Robert Appleton Company, 1907), Vol. 1, 582.]
232 Denzinger, *The Sources of Catholic Dogma*, 1821.

of the Church, although he easily could have done so. In fact a connection of the institution of the papacy to Rome is entirely absent from sacred scripture. According to the scripture passages cited to prove the institution of the papacy as well as the first chapter of the dogmatic constitution, Christ specifically chose a man without a see as his vicar. In my opinion this is where the papacy reveals itself as the work of human hands.

Subsequent chapters of the dogmatic constitution define several additional characteristics of the office of the papacy. The primary characteristic of interest for our purposes in objective six is the apostolic primacy's inseparable link to Rome. Although among Roman Catholics the legitimacy of a Roman connection has always been assumed, I think it is important to ask, "Why the connection to Rome at all?"

When understanding the scriptural basis for the institution of the office of the papacy, one must ask how it ever came to be a dogma that the successors of Peter are exclusively Roman Pontiffs. Remember, Christ's conferral of the primacy in Peter[233] is complete in sacred scripture long before Peter travels to Rome, yet Vatican I inseparably links Peter's primacy with the See of Rome as though this see, *yet to exist* at the time of this revelation, had something to do with it. In fact the foundation of the Roman Catholic Church essentially shifts from being the primacy of Peter in chapter one to the primacy of Rome in chapters two and three. But what in the world does the office originally bestowed upon Peter have to do with a city?

It is important to understand that Peter would have been endowed with the office of the papacy before he founded a see, the first of which was reportedly Antioch, where "the disciples were first called Christians."[234] If Peter possessed his office at any time prior to his journey to Rome, and it is certain that he would have, then how could the First Vatican Council permanently bind the primacy to Rome and claim it was by the institution of Christ?

---

233 John 21:15–17.
234 Acts 11:26.

Let us have a closer look at the canon in question: "If anyone then says that it is not from the institution of Christ the Lord Himself, or by divine right that the blessed Peter has perpetual successors in the primacy over the universal Church, or that the Roman Pontiff is not the successor of blessed Peter in the same primacy, let him be anathema."[235]

The first problem that arises when breaking down the meaning of this canon is determining whether the clause "from the institution of Christ the Lord Himself, or by divine right" is also applicable to the second part of the canon. If this clause applies only to the first part of the canon then there would be no *immediate* problem. However, we can easily infer that *Pastor Aeternus* did in fact connect the clause "from the institution of Christ the Lord Himself, or by divine right" to the second part of this canon: "…the Roman Pontiff is the successor of blessed Peter in the same primacy." In fact just prior to this canon we read: "Therefore, whoever succeeds Peter in this chair, he according to the institution of Christ himself, holds the primacy of Peter over the whole Church."[236]

Again, there can be no misunderstanding that the dogmatic constitution attributes the primacy of Rome directly to the institution of Christ himself. The very words "in this chair" unmistakably refers to the Roman See. This warrants further inquiry.

According to *Pastor Aeternus*'s precise teaching on the institution of the primacy, the primacy was conferred on Peter; this much is clear. Yet no basis exists for connecting the primacy to Rome *by the institution of Christ*. Peter's subsequent connection to Rome many years after the institution of the primacy, as important as it was, cannot change the institution of the primacy one iota. Although there is no scriptural basis even for the first part of the canon, which states that Peter will have perpetual successors, we can at least argue that it was an unwritten facet of this divine revelation, whereas a connection between the institution of the primacy and Rome makes very little sense. If that were Christ's intention, it would have been most fitting

---

235 Denzinger, *The Sources of Catholic Dogma*, 1825.
236 Ibid., 1824.

for him to have founded the Roman See and installed Peter as its bishop as opposed to instituting the primacy in a man who was not yet bishop of a see.

How the theologians of the First Vatican Council claimed it is by the institution of Christ that the Roman Pontiff is the successor to Peter in the primacy certainly seems to be more of a self-serving innovation than divine revelation. For the sake of argument, let us assume the Roman theologians meant that only the first part of the canon is to be understood as instituted directly by Christ despite the fact that the contrary is said to be held as the favored opinion.[237] In that case we might infer that they intended *perpetual successors* to include Rome only by extension of the divine law mandating that Peter should have (yet to be determined) successors. Thus the Roman connection would not be considered *fide divini* but rather *fide infallibili*.

Still this does not solve the problem. If Christ instituted *something* in Peter and intended for *it* to be passed on to his successors, it cannot be said that He only partially instituted it. Again, what Christ allegedly instituted is explicitly stated in the dogmatic constitution—the primacy; and we know when this action was completed—John 21:15–17.[238] In any

---

237 The dogma merely states that the Pontiff of Rome at any time is, in fact, the holder of the Primacy. On what legal title the association of the Roman Pontiff's Chair with the Primacy rests, is not defined. The more usual theological viewpoint is that it rests not on the historical fact that Peter worked and died as Bishop of Rome, but on positive ordinance of Christ or that of the Holy Ghost—that it is, therefore, of Divine origin. If the connection of the Primacy with the See of Rome were of Church Law only, then a separation of the Primacy from the Roman Bishop's Chair by the Pope, or by the General Council would be possible: but since it is of Divine Law, a separation is impossible. (Ott, *Fundamentals of Catholic Dogma*, 283.)

238 John 21: 15–17 reads: "When therefore they had dined, Jesus saith to Simon Peter: Simon son of John, lovest thou me more than these? He saith to him: Yea, Lord, thou knowest that I love thee. He saith to him: Feed my lambs. He saith to him again: Simon, son of John, lovest thou me? He saith to him: Yea, Lord, thou knowest that I love thee. He saith to him: Feed my lambs. He said to him the third time: Simon, son of John, lovest thou me? Peter was grieved, because he had said to him the third time: Lovest thou me? And he said to him: Lord, thou knowest all things: thou knowest that I love thee. He said to him: Feed my sheep."

case the question that needs to be asked is, "Who are the *real* successors of Peter?"

PETER'S REAL SUCCESSORS

The answer to this question is not as straightforward as Roman Catholics believe, despite the fact that the First Vatican Council made the answer a dogma. In order to determine who Peter's successors are, it is first necessary to determine exactly what Peter received from Christ, because whatever *it* was is all that can reasonably be claimed was Christ's intention to remain in his Church by succession. In other words Peter's successors need not become anything other than what Peter became upon receiving it; otherwise Christ's conferral of the primacy to Peter would have been deficient. In order to answer the question, we turn to the words of *Pastor Aeternus* to ascertain all that Peter received *immediately* and *directly* from Christ the Lord Himself: "If anyone then says that the blessed Apostle Peter was not established by the Lord Christ as the chief of all the apostles, and the visible head of the whole militant Church, or, that the same received great honor but did not receive from the same our Lord Jesus Christ directly and immediately the primacy in true and proper jurisdiction: let him be anathema."[239]

According to the above passage, the following items are what Peter received from Christ in the institution of the primacy:

1. An appointment of chief of the apostles.
2. An appointment of the visible head of the Church.
3. Supreme authority (jurisdiction) over the whole Church of God.

According to the First Dogmatic Constitution on the Church of Christ, these are the three things conferred directly on Peter by Jesus Christ. However, because the Vatican Council also made it a dogma that

---
239 Denzinger, *The Sources of Catholic Dogma*, 1823.

the *Roman* Pontiff is the exclusive successor to Peter's primacy, it is reasonable to look to find where Christ founded the Roman See and instituted Peter as the first bishop of Rome because that is the only way Rome *should have* exclusive claim to a primacy instituted by Christ. Do we find this appointment conferred in either sacred scripture or sacred tradition? No. Nowhere do we find that Peter was made bishop of Rome by the institution of Christ or that Christ even founded a see. In fact Peter did not immediately found the Roman See, as would be expected if his primacy were inseparably linked to Rome by the institution of Christ, for he went on to govern as bishop of Antioch. Therefore all that Christ instituted—a visible head of his Church, who held a primacy of jurisdiction over the whole Church of God—is all that should be claimed by succession.

Remember, according to the dogmatic constitution, Christ entrusted the primacy to a man without a see, and that man did not receive a see because of the conferral. If the prince of the apostles and visible head of the Church held a primacy of jurisdiction over the whole Church of God without any connection whatsoever to Rome or any other see, and if it is true that his successors inherit that same primacy as instituted by Christ, which the Vatican Council makes exceptionally clear, then there is no basis for Rome's exclusive claim to the apostolic primacy. And so the answer to the question "who are the real successors of Peter?" has emerged.

So then, who are Peter's successors? Can a successor of Peter in the primacy be a Roman Pontiff? Certainly Peter's successor *could* be a Roman Pontiff. Then again his successor could just as well be the patriarch of Constantinople or the archbishop of New York. Why? Because a successor in the primacy, if such an office really existed, was not originally linked to a see but only to a man. Ideally, then, and much more consistent with the papal dogmas on the institution of the primacy, a successor to Peter in the truest sense would hold no particular see at all, at least not as a condition of being the Vicar of Christ.

According to the Vatican Council's teachings on the institution of the primacy and the scriptures used to support it, all that is necessary to become Peter's successor is that he receive universal jurisdiction and become the visible head of the whole Church of God. In short the answer to the question "who are Peter's successors?" is that they *should be anyone* who receives what Christ instituted—no more, no less. Accordingly an exclusive claim to the rights of the primacy should belong to no see but only to a person. After all why would the universal pastor identify exclusively with any see if he were truly appointed visible shepherd of them all? That the *Roman* Pontiff is the successor of Peter in his same primacy is definitely not by the institution of Christ, for according to the First Vatican Council's dogmatic teachings, it is certain that Rome had no portion in its institution. Rome would not come into play until Peter's arrival there long after the primacy had been instituted.

THE REVERSAL

In conclusion of passage 3, there are just two additional points I would like to make. First, at some point the primacy conferred on Peter had to be *regifted* to the Church for future use in papal elections. Yet the First Vatican Council stated:

> To this teaching of the Sacred Scriptures, so manifest as it has been always understood by the Catholic Church, are opposed openly the vicious opinions of those who perversely deny that the form of government in his Church was established by Christ the Lord; that to Peter alone, before the other apostles, whether individually or all together, was confided the true and proper primacy of jurisdiction by Christ; or, of those who affirm that the same primacy was not immediately and directly bestowed upon the blessed Peter himself, but upon the Church, and through this Church upon him as the minister of the Church herself.[240]

---

240 Ibid., 1822.

The First Vatican Council (1869–1870)

And so we see that what had been given to Peter exclusively and entirely *separate* from the Church would later become the exclusive possession of Rome so that after Peter's martyrdom, *the Church* would forever transmit the primacy to Roman Pontiffs. This reversal of the original arrangement instituted by the Lord is very interesting. Consider the following excerpt from a description of the Holy See: "The primacy of Rome makes its bishop, commonly known as the Pope, the worldwide leader of the Church."[241]

Why would the Church make such a big deal about how the primacy was conferred on Peter directly and completely distinct from the Church and then reverse policy for his successors? If Christ's institution of the papacy were true, should not the primacy of his vicar give primacy to the see over which he *chooses* to preside, being that a successor to Peter is a person as opposed to a diocese of a city or territory?

The answers to the above questions are not difficult to discern, and I do not believe they have anything to do with the fact that Jesus would not be physically present to confer the primacy on His future vicars. As discussed in objection five, Christ's physical presence would not have been necessary to transfer the primacy to Peter's successors, as it easily could have been arranged for popes to consecrate their own successors. Although historically some popes did consecrate their successors, this was never established as a practice pertaining to divine law, as would be expected if the divine prerogatives ascribed to the papacy really existed since the foundation of the Church. Therefore, the theologians of the First Vatican Council were limited in how they could formally establish Peter's primacy in Rome, which is what they really wanted all along.

For example the Vatican Council could not decree that the primacy was conferred on the Roman See directly because, as previously

---

[241] "Holy See," last modified December 1, 2014, http://en.wikipedia.org/w/index.php?title=Holy_See&oldid=601690896.

discussed, that see had not existed yet. Neither could the Vatican Council decree that the primacy was conferred on the Church in general because that would be self-defeating to Rome's exclusive claim to the primacy. God forbid that after Peter's death, this power of the primacy should return to the Church *in general* for future transmittance to the next Vicar of Christ and wind up in Constantinople or Antioch. The truth is that the Roman Church had long desired to be the *first* Church among all the Churches, and to realize its ambitions it used the scriptural accounts of Peter as the pretext to establish an exclusive primacy in Rome. That is why the First Vatican Council made a special emphasis on how the primacy was conferred directly on the person of Peter instead of on the Church. Through Peter's valiant finale in Rome, it could then be claimed that his successors in the primacy remain adjoined forever to the glorious see of Rome. The First Vatican Council's dogmatic teaching of the primacy of the Roman Pontiffs was motivated by a prevailing insecurity of losing its power during the tumultuous political times of the First Vatican Council as well as its longstanding competition for superiority with the Churches of the East.

Finally, in AD 1870, Rome elevated the primacy of Rome and its Pontiffs to the highest status—dogma—and in so doing made Rome's universal supremacy binding on the faithful as a condition for salvation. Following Vatican I the faithful could never again entertain alternative explanations for the schism between the East and West in AD 1054—God had spoken. Interestingly God changed his mind again at Vatican II.

New Classification of Heretic—Honest
This brings me to my final point. Sedevacantists often criticize Vatican II and the post–Vatican II hierarchy for undermining and at times rejecting the dogmas on the papacy. Dimond wrote (emphasis original):

The First Vatican Council (1869–1870)

BENEDICT XVI COMPLETELY REJECTS THIS CANON AND VATICAN I

Benedict XVI, *Principles of Catholic Theology* (1982), p. 198: "**Nor is it possible, on the other hand, for him to regard as the only possible form and, consequently, as binding on all Christians the form this primacy has taken in the nineteenth and twentieth centuries** *[ed.—This means the schismatics don't have to accept Vatican I]*. **The symbolic gestures of Pope Paul VI and, in particular, his kneeling before the representative of the Ecumenical Patriarch [the schismatic Patriarch Athenagoras] were an attempt to express precisely this** and, by such signs, to point the way out of the historical impasse… **In other words, Rome must not require more from the East with respect to the doctrine of the primacy than had been formulated and was lived in the first millennium**. When the Patriarch Athenagoras [the non-Catholic, schismatic Patriarch], on July 25, 1967, on the occasion of the Pope's visit to Phanar, **designated him as the successor of St. Peter, as the most esteemed among us, as one who presides in charity, this great Church leader was expressing the ecclesial content of the doctrine of the primacy as it was known in the first millennium. Rome need not ask for more.**"

This means, once again, that **according to Benedict XVI all Christians are not bound to believe in the Papacy as defined by Vatican I in 1870. This means that the "Orthodox" schismatics are free to reject the Papacy.** This is a blatant denial of Vatican Council I and the necessity of accepting the primacy by the man who claims to be "the pope." Who will cry out against this abominable madness?[242]

---

242 Dimond, *The Truth*, 314.

For his part Dimond lands on the mark. Cardinal Ratzinger's writings certainly undermine the papacy, which has even greater significance when one considers that he would later become pope. According to the dogmatic teachings of the Roman Catholic Church, such statements coming from any member of the Church would be heretical. Yet a remarkable irony resounds about Cardinal Ratzinger's controversial writings on the papacy in relation to Eastern Orthodoxy: while his undermining of the papacy may very well show the Cardinal to have been a heretic, it can also be said that it showed him to have been an honest one.

In concluding objection six on the three passages from the First Vatican Council's First Dogmatic Constitution on the Church of Christ, it is incontrovertible that the sacred and apostolic primacy is permanently bound to the Roman See and that the Sedevacantists lost Rome to the Vatican II revolutionaries. Whether or not the Sedevacantists agree that a string of six antipopes interrupts perpetual successors ruling the Roman See or that the Roman Pontiff realizes visible unity of the Church is immaterial, being that the Sedevacantists lost any claim to the sacred and apostolic primacy when they lost Rome. As the First Vatican Council dogmatically teaches, the primacy is an indispensable component to the Church's first mark—unity. Hence, without the Holy See in a material capacity, there cannot be even a mistaken claim of visible unity of the Church; the Sedevacantists' perpetual disunity proves the fact. There is more to follow on the Church's visible unity in objection fifteen.

Summary

Non-Sedevacantists claim "Vatican I's definition on the perpetuity of the Papal Office contradicts the claims of the Sedevacantists."[243] My position is agreement with this objection; Vatican I does contradict Sedevacantism. Although Dimond addresses only three specific passages from the First Vatican Council in his defense of the Sedevacantists, we began this chapter with an overview of *Pastor Aeternus*—The First Dogmatic Constitution on the Church of Christ.

A cursory reading of *Pastor Aeternus* reveals the following noteworthy points:

- The purpose of the Church is the permanent duration of the work of redemption.
- The papacy is the foundation of the Church.
- The papacy's principal function is unity.
- The papacy's foundation is Rome.
- Rome identifies the Vicar of Christ.
- Roman Pontiffs realize unity of the Church.
- Visible unity is permanent.
- Unity with the Holy See identifies the hierarchy and the faithful.
- Unity with the Roman Pontiff is compulsory.
- The Holy See cannot fail or defect.

---

243 Ibid., 310.

The above points are interconnected and flow harmoniously together. The Sedevacantists attempt to divide them in such a way that their symbiotic relationship is dissolved, leaving gaps in what *should be* the Church's permanent attributes and properties that always identify it as being the true Church of Christ.

One of the most important duties of the faithful is to maintain unity with the Holy See. The faithful will know who the Vicar of Christ is by his occupancy of the Roman See, not the orthodoxy of his teaching because the Holy See cannot fail, defect, or deceive them.

Following an overview of the dogmatic constitution, we explored the story of "Dimond's ark." In this story Dimond paints a picture of God as *the deceiver* who essentially punishes the faithful for obeying one of his Church's most important precepts. Paradoxically, instead of providing the faithful with the ark (i.e., Church) to avoid the chastisement, as in the story of Noe, God takes away the Church and leaves them with Dimond. The moral of the story is that the Catholic faithful should not be in communion with the Holy See because God used it to set a deadly trap in order to test them.

We began part II by exposing Dimond's argumentative fallacy in answering an objection that was not made. The reader was again cautioned about falling for Dimond's repeated attempts to disguise Sedevacantism's theory of the defection of the Church as a routine papal interregnum.

The first passage Dimond addressed from the dogmatic constitution is a declaration that "the Papacy is the Perpetual Principle and Visible Foundation of Unity." Because Dimond and the Sedevacantists do not possess the papacy, they must attempt to rework (divide and omit) its key components in order to claim portions of it. In this example Dimond attempted to separate the "Office of the Papacy" (presumably he means the primacy) from Rome, where it is permanently bound. However, because the sacred and apostolic primacy functions through an interdependent system comprised of the Apostle Peter, the Roman See, and the Roman Pontiff, these components cannot be divided without frustrating the end for which they exist—unity of the Church. Dimond is missing each of the aforementioned components to the papacy and teaches a new doctrine I have appropriately titled the "papacy of desire."

Dimond's papacy of desire is essentially a heretical ecclesiology that errs in two ways. First it attempts to divide the constituent components of the papacy in order to claim some portion of its powers and purpose. One example is ascribing the Church's visible unity to the primacy but omitting how the primacy must be exercised by a human successor to Peter. Second, the papacy of desire teaches that the Holy See need not exist materially, only spiritually. Thus membership in and unity of the Church are attained merely by one's desire to be united to what is essentially an invisible Church.

The third principal Sedevacantist heresy was identified: Papacy of desire is sufficient for membership in and visible unity of the Church. Papacy of desire is the logical sequence to Sedevacantist thesis, which is essentially a theory of the defection of the Church. Because the Sedevacantists are forbidden to admit the fact, they concocted a new ecclesiology remarkably similar to Protestantism's invisible Church theory.

Examples of why Dimond's papacy of desire ends in schism are the Old Catholic Church, which was a recent forerunner to today's Sedevacantists, and Eastern Orthodox conversions to Dimond's ark. Both examples illustrate why ascribing unity of the Church to someone or something other than the Roman Pontiff ends in schism.

The second passage Dimond addresses from the dogmatic constitution *Pastor Aeternus* states that "the sacred and apostolic primacy will endure in perpetuity." Again Dimond attempts to divide the components of the papacy in order to claim some portion of its powers. However, as explained in the first passage, the primacy can do nothing in and of itself; it must be exercised by the human successor of Peter.

The third passage Dimond addresses from the dogmatic constitution *Pastor Aeternus* states that "by the institution of Christ the Lord, Peter will have perpetual successors in the primacy over the universal Church and that the Roman Pontiffs are the successors to Peter in the same primacy." Dimond's interpretation of this canon is that Peter will have sporadic successors who share in his perpetual primacy. However, this cannot be so, as the Church's permanent mark of unity is embodied in the Vicar of Christ. Therefore the correct interpretation must be that perpetual successors *and* perpetual primacy are both correct. "Perpetual successors" is understood to mean a continuous, uninterrupted succession of popes. The Sedevacantists' string of six consecutive antipopes ruling the Roman See violates this canon.

Lastly I presented some criticisms of the papal system. First, there is no basis for connecting Peter's primacy to the Roman See by the institution of Christ in scripture or in the dogmatic constitution's account of the institution. The institution of the primacy was complete in the Gospel of John.[244] According to the dogmatic constitution, Christ chose a man *without a see* as his vicar. Furthermore Peter did not receive a see because of having received the primacy. Therefore Peter's successors should be anyone who receives what Christ instituted—no more, no less. All that Christ instituted—an appointment of universal jurisdiction and a visible head of his Church—is all that should be legitimately claimed by papal succession, for Peter purportedly held these two powers before he founded a see. Furthermore the primacy should belong to a see only insofar as that see is presided over by the Vicar of Christ.

Another criticism is the constitution's reversal in the mode of transmission of the primacy. The dogmatic constitution teaches that Christ conferred the primacy directly on Peter, and it condemns an opinion that *the primacy was conferred on the Church, which in turn transmitted it to Peter as the Church's minister*.[245] However, subsequent to Peter, the Church reversed this process by transferring the primacy to Rome, which then transmitted the primacy to Roman Pontiffs. I shared my opinion as to the real reason for this reversal as being the best way for the Roman Church to claim the primacy in perpetuity, for if the primacy was to be

---

244 John 21:15–17.
245 Denzinger, *The Sources of Catholic Dogma*, 1822.

conferred hand to hand, it could potentially wind up anywhere in the world—*other than Rome.*

Finally, Dimond cited Cardinal Ratzinger's writings that undermined the papacy. The former cardinal's writings show him to have been honest in his assessment of the historical relationship between Rome and the Eastern Orthodox Church.

Objections

Objection: You claimed that the primary duty of the faithful is to maintain communion with the Holy See, but that is false. The First Vatican Council states that the Holy Spirit was not promised to the successors of Peter "that by his revelation they might disclose new doctrine, but that by His help they might guard sacredly the revelation transmitted through the apostles and the deposit of faith, and might faithfully set it forth."[246] The Vatican II hierarchy has made new doctrines and has failed to religiously guard and faithfully expound the revelation or deposit of faith transmitted by the apostles. Therefore the primary duty of the faithful is to adhere to the true Catholic faith and expose usurpers, heretics, and apostates.

Answer: 1. This work is not about the Vatican II hierarchy; it is about holding Sedevacantists accountable to the Church's doctrines. As the above passage states, the duty of guarding and feeding the flock belongs to the magisterium, *not* the faithful. If guarding and expounding the deposit of faith were commissioned to the faithful then the faithful would be the magisterium. Notwithstanding the fact that most Sedevacantists have presumed that duty, the real duty of the faithful was explicitly stated elsewhere in the dogmatic constitution:

---

[246] Ibid., 1836.

The First Vatican Council (1869–1870)

> For this reason it has always been necessary because of mightier pre-eminence for every Church to come to the Church of Rome, that is those who are the faithful everywhere, so that in this See, from which the laws of venerable communion emanate over all, they as members associated in one head, coalesce into one bodily structure.[247]

Pope Pius X wrote: "The office divinely committed to Us of feeding the Lord's flock has especially this duty assigned to it by Christ, namely, to guard with the greatest vigilance the deposit of the faith delivered to the saints, rejecting the profane novelties of words and oppositions of knowledge falsely so called."[248]

Notice to whom the obligation is assigned: the teaching office of the Church (i.e., the magisterium), not the Sedevacantists. The Sedevacantists have only assumed the responsibilities of the magisterium because the real one defected. **2.** In reality the living magisterium interprets doctrines of the faith as well as how it will incorporate tradition; doctrines of the faith and sacred tradition do not determine who represents the living magisterium. **3.** In the event that one of the Church's chosen front men deviates from a chartered course, we might expect to see another case of SPDS, or *sudden pontifical death syndrome* (e.g., Pope John Paul I, 1978–1978).

Objection: As you say, the first duty of the faithful is to maintain unity with the Holy See—not an apostate or heretical sect that claims to be the Holy See.

Answer: The Holy See must be accounted for from the beginning of the purported vacancy up until this present moment or a.) Rome is it; b.) The Church defected.

---

247 Ibid., 1824.
248 Pius X, "*Pascendi Dominici Gregis* (On the Doctrine of the Modernists)," in *The Papal Encyclicals* (Raleigh: McGrath Publishing Company, 1981), 71.

Objection: There is no contradiction between Sedevacantism and the teachings of Vatican I. The First Vatican Council includes language that reads, "…in this See [Rome], from which the laws of venerable communion emanate over all, they as members associated in one head, coalesce into one bodily structure"[249]; "the apostolic see holds a worldwide primacy."[250] These imply that the Roman Church is responsible for visible unity of the Church, not necessarily the Roman Pontiff per se.

Answer: **1.** If the Catholic Church teaches anywhere that something other than the Roman Pontiff is responsible for the visible unity of the Church then it contradicts itself. **2.** Two or more entities (i.e., vacant Holy See and Roman Pontiff) sharing dual responsibility for the Church's visible unity means two visible heads, the latter head being superfluous since popes periodically die. **3.** The names *Holy See* and *Apostolic See* are terminology for the ordinary jurisdiction of the Bishop of Rome. **4.** The pope allegedly exercises his authority through the Roman Curia, not the other way around. If the Curia exercises its authority through the pope, then the pope is a figurehead, which would make Peter a figurehead according to Roman Catholic ecclesiology. **5.** The real reason the Vatican Council includes language about the primacy belonging to the Roman See was already addressed—either Roman enthusiasts transferred this alleged authority from a living person to the Roman See or they risked sharing it with every see in the universal Church.

Objection: What if the teachings emanating from the magisterium today contradict the teachings of a past magisterium? What you are saying leaves no recourse to Catholics who attempt to uphold Catholic dogma.

Answer: Notwithstanding the fact that this is supposed to be impossible and therefore never a concern for the faithful, it happens to be a very good question because in reality this occurs. When it happens that

---

249 Denzinger, *The Sources of Catholic Dogma*, 1824.
250 Ibid., 1826.

The First Vatican Council (1869–1870)

knowledgeable Catholics happen to notice contradictions in magisterial teachings, they must make a decision. One of the following is how most Catholics fared following Vatican II:

1. They convinced themselves that contradictory reforms are not contradictory and embraced them.
2. They convinced themselves that non-Catholics are Catholics and became schismatic.
3. They convinced themselves that the Roman Catholic Church is not the Roman Catholic Church and founded their own churches.

A minority of Catholics have chosen instead to detach intellectually and emotionally from a contradictory system because they realized that anything less is to bear the Church's contradictions.

Objection: The importance of Rome to the Church is that Peter, the first pope, founded the Roman See and suffered martyrdom in Rome. It makes perfect sense that the papal dogmas of Vatican I permanently connected the Roman Pontiff to Rome.

Answer: There is no dispute of the importance of Peter or the Roman See to the Catholic Church. Even the early Church recognized in the Roman See a *primacy of honor,* granted by Council.[251] Nevertheless,

---

[251] "If, as is affirmed, these are necessary to uphold the sovereign pontificate, it is but another reason for desiring its fall-because this pontificate is an usurpation. This we proceed to demonstrate in the present work. To reach this end we shall have recourse neither to questionable arguments nor to declamation. Facts drawn from original sources are summoned as witnesses. We take the Roman episcopate at the origin of Christianity, follow it through centuries, and are able to prove incontestably, that during eight centuries the spiritual Papacy, as we understand it at the present day, had no existence; that the bishop of Rome was during three centuries only a bishop, with the same rank as the others; that in the fourth century he received a primacy of honor without universal jurisdiction; that this honor has no other foundation than the decrees of the Church; that his restricted jurisdiction over certain neighboring Churches is supported only upon a custom legalized by Councils." (Guettée, *The Papacy*, 21–22.)

the prerogatives later ascribed to the Roman Pontiff did not exist in the early centuries of the Church. How the primacy of the Roman Pontiff became a dogma is dubious for reasons already explained. Notwithstanding the greatness of Peter, he was only an apostle. If any see should have a special primacy by the institution of Christ, it ought to have been the see representing the sacred grounds consecrated by his own blood as opposed to a see in another geographical territory consecrated by the blood of an apostle. The Holy Land of both Old and New Testaments, where the Son of the living God suffered, died, and rose from the dead, far exceeds the importance of an apostle's see irrespective of how great an apostle he may have been. In fact in the early centuries, the See of Jerusalem was acknowledged as the "mother of all the Churches"[252,253] for precisely these reasons. If one endeavors to explore the political climate of the early Church, a different picture emerges in the connection between Rome and the primacy.

Objection: Peter was bishop of Rome at the time of his martyrdom, which automatically makes his successors Roman Pontiffs.

Answer: The bishop who follows Peter in the Roman See should be Peter's successor as bishop of Rome but not necessarily in his primacy in the same way that a bishop of Antioch is a successor of Peter in that see but does not inherit Peter's primacy.

---

252 "The Church of Jerusalem is the 'Mother of all Churches' of all of Christendom, because it was in Jerusalem that the Church was established on the day of Pentecost with the descent of the Holy Spirit on the disciples of Jesus Christ. From Jerusalem the gospel of Christ was spread to the world." ("Church of Jerusalem," last modified Monday, March 19, 2012, http://orthodoxwiki.org/index.php?title=Church_of_Jerusalem&oldid=108084.)

253 In his letter to Pope Innocent, the patriarch of Constantinople, Photius wrote: "And what I do not further understand is, that you call the Church of Rome the mother of the other Churches. The mother of the Churches is that of Jerusalem, which surpasses them all in antiquity and dignity." (Guettée, *The Papacy*, 356.)

The First Vatican Council (1869–1870)

Objection: Divine revelation ended with the death of the last apostle, not after Peter received the office of the papacy. There is nothing controversial about the Vatican dogmas, which states that the Roman Pontiffs are successors to Peter in the primacy, because divine revelation had not yet ended at the time of his death.

Answer: The *totality* of divine revelation ended with the death of the last apostle but the *specific* divine revelation of the institution of the primacy ended the moment Peter received it (John 21:15–17). Otherwise Peter could not have possessed it prior to Rome. Another way to understand this is by answering the question: If Peter had died before he was bishop of Antioch, who would his successors in his primacy have been, and what would they have received?

Objection: In Vatican I's explanation of the institution of the primacy in Peter (*Dogmatic Constitution*, chapter one), only the first clause of the canon, which promises that Peter will have perpetual successors, is by the institution of Christ. The second clause does not say his successors must be Roman Pontiffs by the institution of Christ. Here is what *The Catholic Encyclopedia* has to say about this:

> A question may be raised as to the precise dogmatic value of the clause of the second canon in which it is asserted that the Roman pontiff is Peter's successor. The truth is infallibly defined. But the Church has authority to define not merely those truths which form part of the original deposit of revelation, but also such as are necessarily connected with this deposit. The former are held *fide divina*, the latter *fide infallibili*. Although Christ established the perpetual office of supreme head, Scripture does not tell us that He fixed the law according to which the headship should descend. Granting that He left this to Peter to determine, it is plain that the Apostle need not have attached the primacy to his own see: he might have attached it to another. Some have thought that the law establishing the succession in the Roman episcopate became known to the Apostolic

Church as an historic fact. In this case the dogma that the Roman pontiff is at all times the Church's chief pastor would be the conclusion from two premises—the revealed truth that the Church must ever have a supreme head, and the historic fact that St. Peter attached that office to the Roman See. This conclusion, while necessarily connected with revelation, is not part of revelation, and is accepted *fide infallibili*. According to other theologians the proposition in question is part of the deposit of faith itself. In this case the Apostles must have known the law determining the succession to the bishop of Rome, not merely on human testimony, but also by Divine revelation, and they must have taught it as a revealed truth to their disciples. It is this view which is commonly adopted. The definition of the Vatican to the effect that the successor of St. Peter is ever to be found in the Roman pontiff is almost universally held to be a truth revealed by the Holy Spirit to the Apostles, and by them transmitted to the Church.[254]

Answer: 1. According to this article, a question remains as to how the primacy of the Roman Pontiff became a dogma. However, the question certainly appears to have been answered just prior to the canon itself. The dogmatic constitution states: "Therefore, *whoever succeeds Peter in this chair*, he *according to the institution of Christ himself*, holds the primacy of Peter over the whole Church."[255]

Another translation reads: "Therefore *whoever succeeds to the chair of Peter obtains by the institution of Christ himself*, the primacy of Peter over the whole Church…"[256]

The First Vatican Council clearly attributes the primacy of the Roman See to the institution of Christ himself by the clause "in this chair" (i.e., the Roman See). Discussions on this subject should not even exist except for the fact that the dogmatic teaching happens

---

254 Joyce, *The Catholic Encyclopedia*, 263.
255 Denzinger, *The Sources of Catholic Dogma*, 1824.
256 "Decrees of the First Vatican Council," Papal Encyclicals Online, accessed May 3, 2015, http://www.papalencyclicals.net/Councils/ecum20.htm.

to be contradictory for reasons already explained (i.e., Rome was not established when Peter received the primacy). **2.** If it is maintained that Christ himself instituted this law (fide divina), evidently the apostles did not see an urgent need to act upon it, for instead of establishing an integral component of the foundation of the entire Catholic Church in Rome, Peter reigned as bishop of Antioch. **3.** If the Holy Ghost established this law later (fide divina), then Christ's conferral of the primacy in John 21:15–17 was incomplete, and Peter would have been only partially endowed with it. **4.** If it were said that Peter personally attached his office to the Roman See (fide infallibili), then Peter's successor was not a person per se but rather a diocese. This opinion undermines the significance of Christ's purported institution of the primacy in the person of Peter by shifting it to *a diocese that would forever make its bishop* the Vicar of Christ as opposed to the Vicar of Christ making the see he presides over the see of primacy. If Christ intended for the primacy to be contingent upon a see as opposed to a see being contingent upon his vicar, it is reasonable to expect that Christ would have founded a see and installed Peter as its bishop. **5.** Most importantly, that the office of the papacy can be shown as a nonentity in Christian antiquity makes the papal dogmas not believable. The truth is that neither Christ nor the Holy Ghost nor Peter himself attached a primacy to Rome; the primacy was an honorary designation granted by council several centuries after the foundation of the Catholic Church in order to pacify Rome. Much later the Western Church invented the divine prerogatives ascribed to the papacy, attached them to the Roman Church, and effectively severed itself from the Eastern Churches in AD 1054. By so doing the Western Church accomplished what it wanted—the reduction of five apostolic sees down to one: *Rome*. When one's ambition is to rule the Church of Christ, eliminating the competition is an effective way to accomplish it. Nobody should understand this better than the Sedevacantists, for that same ambition is alive and well among them.

Objection: Antipopes have reigned from Rome while posing as popes—something we saw in the case of Anacletus II during the Great Western Schism. There is also a theological axiom: "Plus or minus does not mutate the species, a change in degree does not affect the principle." If the Church did not defect or lose perpetual papal succession during a three-year-and-seven-month vacancy, then the Church will not defect or lose perpetual papal succession during a forty-year vacancy. The principle is the same unless one can cite a specific teaching of the Church that declares a limit to a papal interregnum.[257]

Answer: 1. Sedevacantism is not a position that posits a papal interregnum; it is just marketed as one. Sedevacantism is essentially a position that posits a defection and dissolution of the Holy See, a truth the Sedevacantists have yet to accept. **2.** *Perpetual successors* in the primacy means one pope will follow another without interruption, not that there will literally be a pope every moment. Sedevacantism's string of successive antipopes occupying the Roman See destroys papal succession. **3.** In order for Sedevacantists to make a true comparison between Sedevacantism and the Great Western Schism, they would need to show a credible claimant to the papacy as well as the satellite location of the Holy See—neither of which they can do or else they would have done it. **4.** If the Roman line of popes held the unity of the Church together during the Great Western Schism, this would support the necessity of the Roman Pontiff to the unity of the Church and would contradict the Sedevacantists, especially since, according to Dimond's criteria, all three rival claimants to the papacy during the Western Schism possessed the office of the papacy—two of them *by desire*. **5.** The Great Western Schism does more harm to the papal pretentions and to the Sedevacantist thesis than good. The schism involved a tearing asunder of the Roman See from *within*, which contradicts indefectibility. **5(a).** Additionally the interpretation that the

---

257 Dimond, *The Truth*, 310.

Roman line of popes held the unity of the Church together is merely an opinion that does not receive unanimous support. For example consider Broderick's commentary:

> ...doubts still shroud the validity of the 3 Rival lines of pontiffs during the 4 Decades subsequent to the still disputed papal election of 1378. This makes suspect the credentials of the cardinals created by the Roman, Avignon, and Pisan Claimants to the Apostolic See. Unity was finally restored without a definitive solution to this question; for the Council Of Constance succeeded in terminating the Western Schism, not by determining which of the 3 current claimants was the rightful one, but by eliminating all of them by forcing their abdication or deposition, and then setting up a novel arrangement for choosing a new pope acceptable to all sides. To this day the Church has never made any official, authoritative pronouncement about the papal line of succession for this confusing period; nor has Martin V or any of his successors. Modern scholars are not agreed in their solutions; although they tend to favor the Roman line.[258]

5(b). Broderick's commentary about the Great Western Schism severely undermines the credibility of the papacy in another far more important way—*the schism was not resolved by determining the rightful Vicar of Christ but instead by a council and all three claimants to the papacy abdicating their offices.* We should not overlook the importance of this. Because the Sedevacantists maintain that one of the three papal claimants during the Great Western Schism was the legitimate Roman Pontiff, the unanimous abdication by all three rival papal claimants shatters the meaning of a Vicar of Christ. If during the Western Schism Gregory XII was the legitimate Vicar of Christ, how could he possibly surrender his divine office in exchange for a peaceful resolution with

---

258 "The Sacred College of Cardinals: Size and Geographical Composition (1099–1986)," mgh-bibliothek.de, accessed May 3, 2015, http://www.mgh-bibliothek.de/dokumente/z/zsn2a045837.pdf.

schismatics? Are not the Sedevacantists the first people to criticize this type of behavior in the words, deeds, and omissions of the Vatican II hierarchy? Wrong or right, was this action very different from the actions of the post–Vatican II popes? **5(c).** Lastly a further undermining of the office of the papacy was demonstrated when some members of each of the two rival papacies broke away and elected a third pope in Pisa, knowing that one of the two rival popes they just left had to be the true Vicar of Jesus Christ on Earth. Did these cardinals and bishops not know that a third rival pope would necessarily have to be an antipope? This action conveys a mind-set that a manmade office (Vicar of Christ) could be negotiated and/or reestablished anywhere, anytime, with anybody, upon group consensus and with enough political support. In other words anybody could be Vicar of Christ, even when one already existed. Undoubtedly many of today's Sedevacantists would agree.

Objection: Upon the death of Pope Clement IV on November 29, 1268, the Church delayed naming a new Pope until choosing St. Gregory X on September 1, 1271.[259] According to what you have written about the necessity of a pope to the unity of the Church, there could not have been unity of the Church during the longest papal interregnum in history. Your interpretation of the Vatican Council's teachings on the necessity of the Roman Pontiff for the unity of the Church is proven wrong by this fact alone. If the office of the papacy (without a Roman Pontiff as its occupant) is not responsible for the visible unity of the Church then how do you explain the visible unity of the Church during more than two hundred papal interregnums in Church history?

Answer: It is dogmatically defined that unity of the Church is realized by the Roman Pontiff. If unity of the Church exists during papal

---

259 Dimond, *The Truth*, 310.

The First Vatican Council (1869–1870)

interregnums then something or someone else is responsible for it. In fact a special set of laws exists just for this purpose.[260]

Objection: You just affirmed Dimond's argument that the office of the papacy, with or without a visible Roman Pontiff, still serves as the visible foundation for unity of the Church.

Answer: 1. I did not agree that unity of the Church continues to exist during papal interregnums. Although it is probably true, an argument can also be made that unity is not always preserved. A contested papal election that results in a schism and the Sedevacantist movement supports that argument. **2.** Dimond's "papacy of desire" argument for unity is defeated in objections five and six. **3.** Dimond is wrong to attribute unity of the Church to a supernatural cause. If Dimond were not bound to uphold the myths of the papacy, he would have been closer to the truth had he ascribed unity of the Church to Rome, which is what the laws of sede vacante were intended to accomplish. Of course then Dimond would require Rome to make a claim of unity.

Objection: Again, you just affirmed Dimond's argument that the office of the papacy is the source of unity of the Church, even without a pope. The office of the papacy is really the same thing as Rome.

---

260 "The Holy See does not dissolve upon a Pope's death or resignation. It instead operates under a different set of laws *sede vacante*. During this interregnum, the heads of the dicasteries of the Roman Curia (such as the prefects of congregations) cease immediately to hold office, the only exceptions being the Major Penitentiary, who continues his important role regarding absolutions and dispensations, and the Camerlengo of the Holy Roman Church, who administers the temporalities (i.e., properties and finances) of the See of St. Peter during this period. The government of the See, and therefore of the Catholic Church, then falls to the College of Cardinals. Canon law prohibits the College and the Camerlengo from introducing any innovations or novelties in the government of the Church during this period." ("Holy See," Wikipedia, The Free Encyclopedia, last modified December 1, 2014, http://en.wikipedia.org/w/index.php?title=Holy_See&oldid=601690896.

Answer: 1. The office of the papacy is not Rome; it is bound to Rome. Again, the office of the papacy is the position of Peter's primacy. Because the primacy is permanently bound to the Roman See, the office itself is the position of bishop of Rome. If the unity of the Church is maintained during papal interregnums, it is not necessarily because of some mysterious power at work but more likely because of Rome, although certainly not in the way most of the Sedevacantists understand Rome (i.e., as a mystical entity). 2. Whether one chooses to ascribe the visible unity of the Church to the Roman Pontiff exercising his office as the Vatican Council dogmatically teaches or to a centralized government of the Roman See (e.g., the Roman Curia, the College of Cardinals, etc.), it does not make a difference for the Sedevacantists because they do not have either one. According to the Sedevacantist theory, the Holy See disappeared or dissolved, which constitutes a defection. 3. Because papal vacancies occurred long in advance of the papacy's purported powers, a system to maintain unity during vacancies was already in place. In reality there is no such thing as a Vicar of Christ or a divinely instituted primacy of supreme jurisdiction in the Roman See; the office of the papacy is a self-serving innovation of the Roman Church. Therefore the true foundation of the Roman Catholic Church is not a divinely instituted papacy; the "claimed" foundation is essentially a manmade papacy fronting a government headed chiefly by a body of men who comprise the Roman Curia, and it is through this governing body that the Church would be able to maintain visible unity with or without a bishop. However, see point number two above to recall why this does not help the Sedevacantists.

Objection: You first claimed that the disunity of the Sedevacantists is proof that the Roman Pontiff is the cause of unity of the Church, and then you said that the claims of the Roman papacy are myths. You contradict yourself.

Answer: The Roman claims of the papacy are myths, but I never said that unity could not exist in myths. Additionally it is problematic that

The First Vatican Council (1869–1870)

Sedevacantists do not have a Roman Pontiff because it is the cause of their disunity, but it is more problematic that they believe in the myths of the papacy (i.e., infallibility and indefectibility) because myths are the cause of their contradictions.

Objection: You said that unity of the Church cannot exist without a pope and then went on to ascribe unity to the Curia or College of Cardinals. You contradict yourself.

Answer: I remind the reader that throughout this work, I play two hands simultaneously. On one hand I show how Sedevacantism is contradictory and on the other how the Church is allowed to contradict itself and remain the Church. In answer to this objection, I showed how the Church teaches that visible unity is contingent on the Vicar of Christ but this does not mean the Church functions this way in reality. The Church can maintain unity during papal interregnums and the laws of sede vacante exist because the original foundation of the Roman Church was not the papacy. The later Roman Catholic rendition of "Vicar of Christ"[261] was superimposed over a previously established

---

[261] "The first record of the application of this title to a Bishop of Rome appears in a synod of 495 with reference to Pope Gelasius I. But at that time, and down to the 9th century, other bishops too referred to themselves as vicars of Christ, and for another four centuries this description was sometimes used of kings and even judges, as it had been used in the 5th and 6th centuries to refer to the Byzantine emperor. Earlier still, in the 3rd century, Tertullian used 'vicar of Christ' to refer to the Holy Spirit sent by Jesus. Its use specifically for the Pope appears in the 13th century in connection with the reforms of Pope Innocent III, as can be observed already in his 1199 letter to Leo I, King of Armenia. Other historians suggest that this title was already used in this way in association with the pontificate of Pope Eugene III (1145–1153). This title 'Vicar of Christ' is thus not used of the Pope alone and has been used of all bishops since the early centuries. The Second Vatican Council referred to all bishops as 'vicars and ambassadors of Christ,' and this description of the bishops was repeated by Pope John Paul II in his encyclical *Ut unum sint,* 95. The difference is that the other bishops are vicars of Christ for their own local churches, the Pope is vicar of Christ for the whole Church." ("Pope," *Wikipedia,* accessed March 14, 2015, http://en.wikipedia.org/w/index.php?title=Pope&oldid=646849753.

system of Church governance that is still in practice today in the Eastern Orthodox Church as well as the Oriental Orthodox Church.

Objection: If the Catholic Church was not originally founded on the papacy, as you say, then you are claiming the Church did not have a singular visible head and source of visible unity of the whole Church. A headless Church would not be able to stand the test of time.

Answer: 1. It can and has been argued for a very long time with plausibility that the papacy has been the greatest cause of division in the history of Christianity. For example the papacy is a principal cause of the schism between East and West in AD 1054, the sixteenth-century Protestant Reformation, the schism of the Old Catholics following Vatican I, and the present-day schism of the Sedevacantists following Vatican II. The fact is the Sedevacantists exist today only because Roman Pontiffs called for, ratified, and implemented contradictory reforms at Vatican II. **2.** As for the Church not being able to stand the test of time without a single visible, infallible head, the Eastern Orthodox Church has never had an infallible, singular, visible head, and yet remarkably it is not the Eastern Orthodox Church but rather the Roman Catholic Church that had a Protestant Reformation, a Vatican II, and a *Novus Ordo Missae*.[262] In fact it is often the case that the Sedevacantist Dimond brothers advise people who call their "monastery," asking for advice on where to receive sacraments, to approach the Eastern Catholic Churches that are in full communion with Rome. The question we should ask then is this: How well has an infallible, indefectible head served the Western Church when its members are advised to approach Eastern liturgies for grace? **3.** It can also be argued that the episcopacy was the intended visible head to Christ's Church and that it served that function even in the West during the early centuries of Christianity. Unlike a visible head in Dimond's *sporadic* papa-

---

[262] "New Order of Mass" was promulgated by Pope Paul VI in 1969.

The First Vatican Council (1869–1870)

cy, the episcopacy perpetually exists, every single moment, without interruption. Even while popes die and vacancies are created, the episcopal body remains.

Objection: Rome's selection for bishop is a heretic! He is not the true pope.

Answer: Anybody who truly believes this must come to terms with the Church's claims of indefectibility and infallibility. Unless they can identify the "real" Holy See and prove its legitimacy, Francis is their man.

Objection: You claimed that the Old Catholic Church is a predecessor of today's Sedevacantists, but that is a lie. The Old Catholics were heretics for rejecting the same papal dogmas that the Sedevacantists are defending. Sedevacantists do not reject any dogmas, they are not heretics, and they are not schismatics.

Answer: Historically, more often than not, heretics and schismatics denied that they were heretics and schismatics.

> 6. The chief deceit used to conceal the new schism is the name of "Catholic." The originators and adherents of the schism presumptuously lay claim to this name despite their condemnation by Our authority and judgment. It has always been the custom of heretics and schismatics to call themselves Catholics and to proclaim their many excellences in order to lead peoples and princes into error.[263]

---

263 "Quartus Supra," Papal Encyclicals Online, accessed May 3, 2015, http://www.papalencyclicals.net/Pius09/p9quartu.htm.

The question is, "Who has the authority to determine who is a heretic or a schismatic and make it stand?" The answer, of course, is Rome. The Sedevacantists are outside the Church for the same reason the Old Catholics are outside the Church—*Roma locuta; causa finita est.*[264] The comparison between Old Catholics and Sedevacantists is nearly identical.

---

264 "Rome has spoken, the cause if finished." Also refer to Guettée, *The Papacy*, 178–181, for an Eastern Orthodox Church perspective and translation of this often-cited but controversial phrase.

CHAPTER 4

Visibility of the Church

You are the light of the world. A city seated on a mountain cannot be hid.[265]

THE FIFTEENTH OBJECTION DIMOND ADDRESSES in his book is that the Sedevacantists deny the doctrine of visibility of the Church. My position is agreement with this objection; the Sedevacantists *do* deny the visibility of the Church, most especially concerning its intrinsic bonds of unity.

Although important aspects of the Church's visibility have already been addressed in previous objections, Dimond's arguments are so laden with errors that it is necessary to repeat certain points here. This chapter addresses the fourth and fifth principal heresies of the Sedevacantists: visible hierarchical unity is accidental to the Roman Catholic Church; apostolic authority is accidental to the episcopal order.

The Church's visibility includes two things by necessity: 1. The Church's essential material components must remain accounted for. 2. The Church's members must be in communion with those constituent parts. Another way to state these points is that the Holy See must remain physically intact, recognizable, and easily located, and the rest of the Catholic Church must be in communion with it. Obviously if the Holy See cannot be accounted for then the Sedevacantists certainly cannot

---

265 Matt. 5:14.

be in communion with it. Furthermore, as established in objection one, if the Holy See cannot be accounted for then it would have defected.

The doctrine of visibility corresponds to the doctrine of indefectibility in this important way: While indefectibility entails that the material structure of the Church cannot fail or defect, visibility means it cannot vanish or become unrecognizable. Although the Church may be forced underground or reduced enough in membership that her visible presence *seems* to vanish in certain geographical locations (e.g., where the Church may be persecuted or suppressed), the Church as a visibly unified, hierarchical organism can never cease to exist and manifest itself to the world in general.

These points must remain true in eras of great faith and in times when the world grows indifferent to religion. That is important to keep in mind because some Sedevacantists (previously identified as "school two") claim the Church remains visible to only a privileged few somewhere in the world but is no longer generally visible. The bottom line is that if the true Church cannot be located then a defection has occurred. We are now about to learn of another reason why Sedevacantism incontrovertibly involves a defection of the Church—an invisible Church is all that the Sedevacantists believe survived the Vatican II revolution.

Objection Fifteen

The Church and the hierarchy will always be visible. If the Vatican II Church is not the true Catholic Church, then the Church and hierarchy are no longer visible.[266]

---

266 Dimond, *The Truth*, 331.

Part I
Visible Unity

❦

VISIBILITY BELONGS TO THE ESSENCE of the Church and as such is an indefectible property. The Church cannot cease being visible unless it can cease to exist. The Baltimore Catechism explains why this must always remain so:

Q. 513. Why must the true Church be visible?

A. The true Church must be visible because its founder, Jesus Christ, commanded us under pain of condemnation to hear the Church; and He could not in justice command us to hear a Church that could not be seen and known.[267]

I will assume most Sedevacantists would agree with the Baltimore Catechism's explanation for *why* the Church must remain visible. In fact even Dimond does not deny that one of the Church's properties is visibility; he simply defines it in such a way that it can be used to support Sedevacantism—namely by omitting critical distinctions. The reader will recall how Dimond used this same strategy in defining *indefectibility* in objection one. Before we look at Dimond's definition of the Church's

---

267 "Baltimore Catechism No. 3—Lesson 11," Audio Sancto, accessed December 2, 2014, http://www.audiosancto.org/inc/BC3/bc3-11.html.

visibility, let us recall that each of the four objections addressed in this work overlies and corresponds to the Church's essential constitution. Because the Church is more than just a spiritual society, it must remain perceptible to the senses; otherwise it would be difficult if not impossible to distinguish it as the one true Church founded by Christ.

Dimond's response to objection fifteen begins with an attempted clarification of the doctrine of visibility. He wrote: "People misunderstand in what the visibility of the Church consists…"[268]

And the stage is now set for Dimond to clarify the doctrine of visibility, presumably so misguided authors of papal encyclicals (popes) and editors of Catholic encyclopedias will never misunderstand it again:

> No one denies that the Catholic Church could cease to exist in all the countries of the world except one. The visibility of the Church does not require that the faithful or the hierarchy be seen in every single geographical location around the globe. This has never been the case. Simply, the visibility of the Church signifies real Catholic faithful who externally profess the one true religion, even if they are reduced to a very small number. These faithful who externally profess the one true religion will always remain the visible Church of Christ, even if their ranks are reduced to just a handful.[269]

Please note that Dimond has just defined visibility of the Church as "real Catholic faithful who externally profess the one true religion." The first problem with Dimond's definition is that it is deficient. The second problem is that the deficiencies make it very misleading. The reader will recall a point made in objection one that when Sedevacantists such as Dimond speak of a remnant Church, they fail to keep the constitutions of their remnant Churches intact so that any of them could be considered Roman Catholic. Dimond repeats this error with visibility by omitting all it entails and once again has the wrong portion of the Church sustaining

---

268 Dimond, *The Truth*, 331.
269 Ibid.

whereas essential components have failed. Additionally Dimond claims that the Catholic Church could cease to exist in all geographical locations except one, and that location could be *anywhere* provided at least a handful of faithful exists. This is false. Remember, first and foremost, indefectibility of the Church pertains to Rome: "Only to One particular Church is indefectibility assured, viz. to the See of Rome. To Peter, and in him to all his successors in the chief pastorate, Christ committed the task of confirming his brethren in the Faith (Luke 22:32); and thus, to the Roman Church, as Cyprian says, 'faithlessness cannot gain access.'"[270]

What Dimond is really saying is that random groups of Sedevacantists scattered abroad, none of which possesses a legitimate connection to the Holy See, can potentially represent the visible Catholic Church. In order to understand all of the ways Dimond is wrong, we will delve into a deeper understanding of the Church's visibility. We begin with *The Catholic Encyclopedia*:

Visibility of the Church

In asserting that the Church of Christ is visible, we signify, first, that as a society it will at all times be conspicuous and public, and second, that it will ever be recognizable among other bodies as the Church of Christ. These two aspects of visibility are termed respectively "material" and "formal" visibility by Catholic theologians. The material visibility of the Church involves no more than that it must ever be a public, not a private profession; a society manifest to the world, not a body whose members are bound by some secret tie. Formal visibility is more than this. It implies that in all ages the true Church of Christ will be easily recognizable for that which it is, viz. as the Divine society of the Son of God, the means of salvation offered by God to men; that it possesses certain attributes which so evidently postulate a Divine origin that all who see it must know it comes from God...It is unnecessary to say more

---

270 Joyce, *The Catholic Encyclopedia*, 756.

in regard to the material visibility of the Church than has been said in sections III and IV of this article. It has been shown there that Christ established his Church as an organized society under accredited leaders, and that He commanded its rulers and those who should succeed them to summon all men to secure their eternal salvation by entry into it. It is manifest that there is no question here of a secret union of believers: the Church is a worldwide corporation, whose existence is to be forced upon the notice of all, willing or unwilling. Formal visibility is secured by those attributes which are usually termed the "notes" of the Church—her Unity, Sanctity, Catholicity, and Apostolicity (see below). The proof may be illustrated in the case of the first of these. The unity of the Church stands out as a fact altogether unparalleled in human history. Her members all over the world are united by the profession of a common faith, by participation in a common worship, and by obedience to a common authority...One and all hold the same belief, join in the same religious ceremonies, and acknowledge in the successor of Peter the same supreme ruler. Nothing but a supernatural power can explain this. It is a proof manifest to all minds, even to the simple and the unlettered, that the Church is a Divine society. Without this formal visibility, the purpose for which the Church was founded would be frustrated. Christ established it to be the means of salvation for all mankind. For this end it is essential that its claims should be authenticated in a manner evident to all; in other words, it must be visible, not merely as other public societies are visible, but as being the society of the Son of God.[271]

As seen, the doctrine of visibility is intimately connected to the doctrine of unity.[272] In fact it is quite correct to refer to the Church's first mark as *visible unity* or to say that the true Church will always be *visibly one.* Let us read more on this connection, beginning with some false notions of unity:

---

271 Ibid., 753
272 The unity of the Catholic Church is based in the Roman papacy.

All admit that unity of some kind is indispensable to the existence of any well-ordered society, civil, political, or religious. Many Christians, however, hold that the unity necessary for the true Church of Christ need be nothing more than a certain spiritual internal bond, or, if external, it need be only in a general way, inasmuch as all acknowledge the same God and reverence the same Christ. Thus most Protestants think that the only union necessary for the Church is that which comes from faith, hope, and love toward Christ; in worshipping the same God, obeying the same Lord, and in believing the same fundamental truths which are necessary for salvation. [273]

Similarly the Church has also identified what it considers a true notion of unity (emphasis added):

The Catholic conception of the mark of unity, which must characterize the one Church founded by Christ, is far more exacting. *Not only must the true Church be one by an internal and spiritual union, but this union must also be external and visible, consisting in and growing out of a unity of faith, worship, and government. Hence the Church which has Christ for its founder is not to be characterized by any merely accidental or internal spiritual union, but, over and above this, it must unite its members in unity of doctrine, expressed by external, public profession; in unity of worship, manifested chiefly in the reception of the same sacraments; and in unity of government, by which all its members are subject to and obey the same authority, which was instituted by Christ himself.*[274]

Again, notice how the Church's unity is inseparably linked with its visibility in the following excerpt:

---

273 Chas J. Callan, *The Catholic Encyclopedia* (New York: Robert Appleton Company, 1912), Vol. XV, 179–180.
274 Ibid.

It was the intention of Christ that his Church should be one, and that, *not in any accidental internal way, but essentially and visibly.* Unity is the fundamental mark of the Church, for without it the other marks would have no meaning, since indeed the Church itself could not exist. Unity is the source of strength and organization, as discord and schism are of weakness and confusion. [275]

Roman Catholic apologists Bryan Cross and Thomas Brown wrote:

Through baptism we are incorporated into a unity greater than ourselves, and so become one with the Head and other members, yet without losing our individual identity. *This unity of the Mystical Body is a visible unity, precisely because it is the unity of a Body. Bodies are visible and hierarchically organized, not invisible. Because the Church is a Body, the Church is essentially visible. The visibility of the Body is not reducible to the visibility of certain of its members; the Church* per se *is visible, just as your body* per se *is visible. Because the Church is a Body, it must also be something definite and perceptible to the senses.*[276]

Cross correctly pointed out that the visibility of the body cannot be reduced to the visibility of certain of its members, as Dimond erroneously believes. As we can see, the doctrine of visibility is not merely Catholic faithful who externally profess the true religion. If an external profession of religion among pockets of believers were all that defined the Church's visibility then any Christian Church has a legitimate claim to being the visible Church of Christ, and most, of course, do make this claim. Once again Dimond's definition of the Church's visibility is very similar to Protestantism's invisible Church ecclesiology. Ott wrote:

The visibility of the Church was denied by the Spiritualistic Sects of the Middle Ages, by Huss and the Reformers...Luther taught that

---

275 Ibid.
276 "Christ Founded a Visible Church."

> the Church is "the assembly of the saints (=the faithful), in which the Gospel is properly taught and the Sacraments are properly administered." *But without an authoritative teaching office there is no certain norm for the purity of doctrine or for the administration of the Sacraments. The rejection of the hierarchy inevitably led to the doctrine of the invisible Church.*[277]

Just like the Protestant Reformers, the Sedevacantists have also rejected the visible hierarchy of the Church. Regardless of the reasons *why* they have done it, the critical point is that they *have* done it, and the consequences are identical (i.e., without an authoritative teaching office there is no certain norm for the purity of doctrine or for the administration of the sacraments). The primary difference between the Sedevacantists and the Protestants is only in their choices of authority. While the Protestants recognize the Bible, the Sedevacantists recognize only pre–Vatican II magisterial teachings. Interestingly, neither "authority" managed to preserve the visible unity of its Church in any of the ways that a living body (Church) must be unified to be considered the true Church of Christ. Sedevacantists, like the Protestants, simply cannot agree on any number of issues.

Visible Unity of Hierarchy

The three ways in which a living body (the Church) is unified are unity of essence, unity of activity, and unity of hierarchy. Dimond's concept of visibility does not include these unities, for even if his concept of visibility does include a shared profession of faith, the three bonds of unity in the Catholic Church are interdependent; there cannot be one without the others. Cross and Brown described the third of these, unity of hierarchy, as follows (emphasis added):

> Third, an organism is unified in its hierarchy. Not every part of the organism is the head. The parts of a body are ordered hierarchically,

---
[277] Ott, *Fundamentals of Catholic Dogma*, 301.

in systems, organs, tissues, and so on…If there were no hierarchy, then the whole would not be a body; it would be like a pin-cushion, Christ being the cushion, and all believers the pins, each one individually, directly, and independently of the others, connected to Him. *That is why the Church, since it is a Body, must be hierarchically ordered. Members serve the Head* (and whole) by serving the part of the Body proximate to themselves, according to the gifts and capacities with which they have been equipped, and under the authority of the hierarchy according to their place within it. *The hierarchy of a body must be unified in the sense that each member of the hierarchy must be ordered to the head. If there were two or more hierarchies—that is, if there were two or more ultimate ends toward which members were ordered—there would either be two distinct organisms present, or something equivalent to a cancer within an organism. Because the existence of a body requires hierarchical unity among its members, so likewise the existence of the Mystical Body of Christ requires hierarchical unity among its members.*

These three modes of unity correspond also to Christ's three roles as prophet, priest, and king, respectively. Christ is the perfect prophet, and this entails *that the members of His Mystical Body share one faith*. Christ is the perfect high priest, and this entails that *the members of His Mystical Body participate in the same liturgical activity, and thus in the same sacraments*. And because Christ is the perfect king, this entails that *the members of His Mystical Body share one visible hierarchy, and thus one visible magisterium*. In this way, Christ's perfect fulfillment of the roles of prophet, priest, and king entails the three "bonds of unity" in the Church. *These are also the three ways in which the Church is visible. She is visibly united in her shared profession of faith, her shared celebration of the same sacraments, and in her shared ecclesial hierarchy, each of these three having been received and passed down by succession from the Apostles.*[278]

Cross and Brown continued their explanation of unity of hierarchy and why without this unity, Protestants confuse the unity of the Church as a plurality of things sharing something in common as opposed to a whole unified

---

278 "Christ Founded a Visible Church."

organism. The reader should infer that the Protestants' errors are identical to those of the Sedevacantists. Cross and Brown wrote (emphasis added):

> But when we come to the question of unity of hierarchy, Protestants and Catholics do not agree. Protestants either claim that the visible hierarchical unity Christ initially provided to His Mystical Body was accidental (i.e., non-essential) and hence capable of being lost (and was in fact eventually lost), or they claim that Christ's Mystical Body was never given visible hierarchical unity in the first place. *The Catholic position, on the other hand, is that visible hierarchical unity belongs to the essence of Christ's Mystical Body. For that reason, according to Catholic doctrine, hierarchical unity cannot be lost unless the Mystical Body ceases to exist. But since the Mystical Body cannot cease to exist, because it shares in the very life of the Son of God over whom death is powerless, therefore the visible hierarchical unity cannot be lost.* [279]

The writers just stated something very important about the Church: The only way union of hierarchy can be lost is if the Church ceases to exist.

Visible Head

Cross and Brown explained why a singular visible head is essential to a visible hierarchy and thus the very existence of the Church (emphasis added):

> *For there to be a visible hierarchy, it is not enough for each member to be ordered to an invisible Head.* Merely being ordered to an invisible Head is fully compatible with having no visible hierarchy...*Furthermore, for a visible hierarchy to be one, it must have a visible head. Only if each member of a visible hierarchy is ordered to one visible head can the visible hierarchy itself be one. And only if the visible head is essentially one can the visible hierarchy be essentially one. If the visible head of the hierarchy were plural, then the visible hierarchy would not be essentially unified, but at most only accidentally unified.*

---
279 Ibid.

And Pope Leo XIII says,

"Indeed no true and perfect human society can be conceived which is not governed by some supreme authority. Christ therefore must have given to his Church a supreme authority to which all Christians must render obedience. For this reason, as the unity of the faith is of necessity required for the unity of the Church, inasmuch as it is the body of the faithful, so also for this same unity, inasmuch as the Church is a divinely constituted society, unity of government, which effects and involves unity of communion, is necessary jure divino. The unity of the Church is manifested in the mutual connection or communication of its members, and likewise in the relation of all the members of the Church to one head."

The Church as a visible organism preserves the visible head established by Christ, and thus retains all three marks of unity. Without a visible head, the Mystical Body would be reduced to the ontological equivalent of visible pins invisibly connected to an invisible pin-cushion. That is because without a visible head, a visible hierarchy is only accidentally one, because intrinsically it is potentially many separate hierarchies. Many separate hierarchies are not a visible unity; they are ontologically equivalent to many separate individuals. They are a mere plurality, not an actual unity.

A "visible Church" made up of separate visible hierarchies would be equivalent in its disunity to a merely invisible Church having some visible members. *Therefore a visible head belongs to the essence of the Mystical Body, since a body cannot have mere accidental unity, but must have unity essentially.* In other words, an ecclesiology that is analogous to visible pins invisibly connected to an invisible pin-cushion is equivalent to a denial of the visibility of Christ's Mystical Body because such an ecclesiology denies the essentially unified hierarchy necessary for a body to be a body. It makes no difference whether the pins are individual Christians or individual congregations. Without an essentially unified visible hierarchy, a composite whole cannot be a *body, let alone a visible body. And when hierarchical unity is abandoned, nothing preserves unity of faith or unity of sacraments. In this way each one of the three "bonds of unity" depends on the other two.*[280]

By now the reader should easily infer that Sedevacantism is very similar to Protestantism in the sense that both commit the same philosophical errors the above article identified. There can be no question that a visible head belongs to the essence of the Church and that the Church's visibility is far more than a scattered remnant of believers in something. Yet Sedevacantists are forced to present just such a church. As to why Sedevacantists believe that their separated churches have visible unity *essentially*, Catholic apologist Bryan Cross identified their error as "[a]ssuming that unity of type is sufficient for unity of composition... things of the same type do not by that very fact compose a unified whole."[281]

Independent Sedevacantist churches *may* share "unity of type," but without an essentially unified hierarchy under Rome, they cannot possess a true "unity of composition." As addressed in objection six, according to Vatican I's Dogmatic Constitution *Pastor Aeternus*, the Church's *visible* unity is permanent. Moreover, that council stated how visible unity is realized: "The Roman Pontiff, as the successor of Peter, is the perpetual and visible source and foundation of the unity both of the bishops and of the whole company of the faithful."[282,283]

In defining the Mystical Body of Christ, Pope Pius XII wrote:

> 69. Now since its Founder willed this social body of Christ to be visible, the cooperation of all its members must also be externally

---

280 Ibid.
281 "Why Protestantism has no Visible Catholic Church," last modified December 2, 2014, http://www.calledtocommunion.com/2009/09/why-protestantism-has-no-visible-catholic-Church/.
282 Vatican Council II, *"Lumen Gentium,"* 31.
283 The Sedevacantist who rejects Vatican II's *Lumen Gentium* will recall the above quote from objection six and its corresponding endnote citing the First Vatican Council, which most Sedevacantists recognize as a valid council.

manifest through their profession the same faith and their sharing the same sacred rites, through participation in the same Sacrifice, and the practical observance of the same laws. *Above all, it is absolutely necessary that the Supreme Head, that is, the Vicar of Jesus Christ on earth, be visible to the eyes of all, since it is He who gives effective direction to the work which all do in common in a mutually helpful way towards the attainment of the proposed end.* As the Divine Redeemer sent the Paraclete, the Spirit of Truth, who in His name should govern the Church in an invisible way, so, in the same manner, *He commissioned Peter and his successors* to be His personal representatives on earth and *to assume the visible government of the Christian community.*[284]

The necessity of a singular visible head to the unity of hierarchy is so critical to the existence of the Church that readers can expect to find that even concise definitions of the Church or the Church's visibility include some reference to the Roman Pontiff, authority, or the hierarchy. For example St. Robert Bellarmine defined the Church as (emphasis added): "A body of men united together by the profession of the same Christian Faith, and by participation in the same sacraments, *under the governance of lawful pastors, more especially of the Roman Pontiff, the sole vicar of Christ on earth.*"[285]

Ott wrote (emphasis added):

> The inner saving task of the Church is stressed in J. A. Mohler's definition: "By the Church on earth Catholics understand the visible community of all the faithful, founded by Christ, in which are continued the activities developed by Him during His earthly life for the remission of sin and for the salvation of mankind under the direction of His Spirit until the end of the world, *by means of a continuous uninterrupted*

---

284 Pius XII, "*Mystici Corporis Christi*" 51.
285 Joyce, *The Catholic Encyclopedia*, 745.

Apostolate ordained by Him, and by which, in the course of time, all peoples will be brought back to God." [286]

Contemporary definitions contain similar language (emphasis added):

> Visibility—That quality of the Church by which she appears externally and can be recognized by the senses. Two kinds of visibility are distinguished. The Church is materially visible in that her members are human beings who can be identified as Catholic Christians. The Church is also formally visible in possessing certain sensibly perceptible properties, notably the required profession of a common faith, the practice of a definite ritual, and obedience to identifiable laws *under an authorized hierarchy*.[287]

We now know that unity is not comprised merely of a like faith among believers, as Dimond seems to believe, but also communion with an essentially unified, *visible* hierarchy. Additionally we now know why an essentially unified, visible hierarchy must include a singular head in the person of the Roman Pontiff.

While indefectibility of the Church assures the faithful that the Church will always continue *being* the Roman Catholic Church in time and space, visibility necessitates that *she will always be recognized* as the Roman Catholic Church in time and space. In short the Roman Catholic Church as a visibly unified, hierarchical institution under the Roman Pontiff must forever remain manifest to the world in general, and we have already established why this must be so: "Jesus Christ, commanded us under pain of condemnation to hear the Church; and He could not in justice command us to hear a Church that could not be seen and known."[288]

---

286 Ott, *Fundamentals of Catholic Dogma*, 271–272.
287 Hardon, *Modern Catholic Dictionary*, 564.
288 "Baltimore Catechism No. 3."

Part II

False Teachers

❦

Much of Dimond's response to objection fifteen is comprised of quotations. Let us have a look at some of Dimond's usage of quotations, including his ace cards—*prophecies.* In the third paragraph of his reply to objection fifteen, Dimond wrote (emphasis original):

> "And that is <u>precisely what is predicted to happen</u> at the end of the world."
>
>> St. Athanasius: "Even if Catholics faithful to tradition are reduced to a handful, they are the ones who are the true Church of Jesus Christ."[289]

A basic assumption must accompany the above quote or else St. Athanasius could be categorized along with Dimond under "those who denied Roman doctrines that should have existed from the foundation of the Church." Roman Catholics must presume that Athanasius's understanding of "the true Church of Jesus Christ" agrees with Roman doctrines of indefectibility, the Apostolic primacy of the Roman See, the necessity of the Roman Pontiff to the visibility and unity of the Church, and the other characteristics of the Church as addressed in objections

---
[289] Dimond, *The Truth,* 331.

one, five, six, and fifteen. Additionally, since Dimond claimed Athanasius was predicting the state of the Church at the end of the world, he should support his claim.

Next Dimond quoted scripture to support the "remnant Church" theory (emphasis original):

> Our Lord Himself indicates that the size of the Church will become frighteningly small in the last days.
>
> > Luke 18:8: "**But yet, when the Son of man cometh, shall He find, think you, faith on earth?**"[290]

Luke 18:8 would be useful for Dimond's purposes only if the Lord had said instead, "But yet, when the Son of Man cometh, shall He find, think you, *his Church* on earth?" Faith may indeed be scarce when the Lord returns, but the Church's constitution cannot be compromised in the least way without violating indefectibility.

Dimond continued:

> The Apocalypse of St. John seems to indicate the same.
>
> > Apocalypse 11:1–2: "And there was given me a reed like unto a rod, and it was said to me: Arise, and measure the temple of God, and *the altar*, and them that adore in it. But the court, which is without the temple, cast out, and measure it not, because it is given to the Gentiles…"
>
> The *Haydock version of the Douay-Rheims Bible*, a popular compilation of Catholic commentary on the Scriptures by Rev. Fr. Geo. Leo Haydock, contains the following comment on Apoc. 11:1–2.

---

290 Ibid.

Catholic Commentary on Apoc. 11:1–2, Haydock version of the Douay-Rheims Bible:

> **"The Churches consecrated to the true God, are so much diminished in number, that they are** represented **by St. John as one Church; its ministers officiate at one altar; and all the true faithful are so few, with respect to the bulk of mankind, that the evangelist sees them assembled in one temple, to pay their adorations to the Most High.—Pastorini."**[291]

Once again, to be seen as favorable for Dimond's purposes, one must presume the author understood the above scripture passage to mean that a visibly unified hierarchy under the Roman Pontiff, as well as the Church's other essential characteristics, are not present in the "one Church" referenced in Apocalypse 11, which, like Dimond and his version of Athanasius, would make this commentator equally guilty of proposing a heretical interpretation of scripture. Apocalypse 11 even makes a strong inference to unity of the Church, as in "one Church" gathered in "one temple," as well as apostolicity, as in "ministers who officiate at one altar"; these could presumably account for the first and fourth notes of the Church. Moreover, for this commentary to be favorable to the Sedevacantists so it is *they* who represent the "true faithful" in Apocalypse 11, they would require visible unity, which is impossible for reasons already addressed.

Dimond continued:

> Further, during the Arian crisis the true Faith was eliminated from entire regions, so much so that there were hardly any Catholic bishops to be found anywhere.
>
> Fr. William Jurgens: "At one point in the Church's history, only a few years before Gregory's [Nazianz] present preaching

---
[291] Ibid.

(+380 A.D.), <u>perhaps the number of Catholic bishops in possession of sees, as opposed to Arian bishops in possession of sees, was no greater than something between 1% and 3% of the total</u>. **Had doctrine been determined by popularity, today we should all be deniers of Christ and opponents of the Spirit.**"

Fr. William Jurgens: "In the time of the Emperor Valens (4th century), Basil was virtually the only orthodox Bishop in all the East who succeeded in retaining charge of his see…If it has no other importance for modern man, **a knowledge of the history of Arianism should demonstrate at least that the Catholic Church takes no account of popularity and numbers in shaping and maintaining doctrine:** else, we should long since have had to abandon Basil and Hilary and Athanasius and Liberius and Ossius and call ourselves after Arius."

The Arian heresy became so widespread in the 4th century that the Arians (who denied the Divinity of Christ) came to occupy almost all the Catholic Churches and appeared to be the legitimate hierarchy basically everywhere.

St. Ambrose (+382): "**There are not enough hours in the day for me to recite even the names of all the various sects of heretics**."

Things were so bad that St. Gregory Nazianz felt compelled to say what the Catholic remnant today could very well say.

St. Gregory Nazianz, "Against the Arians" (+380): "Where are they who revile us for our poverty and pride themselves in their riches? **They who define the Church by numbers and scorn the little flock?**"[292]

---

292 Ibid., 332.

Roman Catholics do not define the Church by numbers even today but rather by all of the indefectible characteristics, attributes, and properties addressed in this work. The Catholic Church is the whole package not fragmented parts of a whole.

ARIANISM AND INDEFECTIBILITY

The Arian heresy that spread through the Church in the fourth century raises an interesting issue. The popular opinion that Pope Liberius lost the faith during the Arian heresy has often forced Roman apologists to defend papal infallibility.[293] Apologists argue that Liberius did not breech infallibility because he did not attempt to bind heresy on the whole Church. While that may be true, what is most often overlooked by Protestants and Roman apologists alike actually concerns the Church's indefectibility, which property should have left the Holy See unscathed by the Arian heresy.

Interestingly it is the patriarch of Antioch, Athanasius, who is most often recognized in the East and West for having preserved the true Catholic faith against the Arians, whereas according to the doctrines of the papacy the rock of the Church should have been the Roman See. According to some popular accounts, Athanasius himself maintained that Pope Liberius consented to a heretical doctrine in order to gain his freedom from Arian captivity. Roman apologists claim that Athanasius was not in a position to know the truth and that he had received misinformation, but I find it difficult to believe that Athanasius was not in a better position to know exactly who betrayed the faith than Church

---

[293] Dimond asserted that Pope Liberius, who reigned during the Arian crisis, remained orthodox in the faith, and he quoted sources to support this. However, evidence also exists against Liberius having remained faithful, so an unresolved controversy remains. Catholic apologist Patrick Madrid wrote: "Did he [Pope Liberius] finally cave in and sign a heretical creed, condemning Athanasius? Or did the emperor realize the futility of keeping him captive? There is evidence for both positions. A number of figures contemporary to the time, St. Athanasius for one, claimed that Liberius did indeed give in and sign the defective creed..." [Patrick Madrid, *Pope Fiction* (Rancho Santa Fe, California, Basilica Press, 1999), 142–143.]

historians and apologists who wrote about these events long after his time. It seems unlikely that Athanasius would rashly accuse the Roman Pontiff of such a betrayal without certainty. It is one thing to bear false witness and calumniate another person and quite another to do the same against the Roman Pontiff, who, according to the Church, should have been acknowledged as the Vicar of Christ on Earth. Undoubtedly Athanasius deserves more credit for the accuracy of his information as well as the probability of his exercising extreme prudence in casting judgment on the pope.

Invisible Church Ecclesiology

Next Dimond continued promoting Protestantism's invisible Church ecclesiology (emphasis added):

> The Magisterium of the Catholic Church has never taught that there must always be a certain number of bishops or faithful for the Church to exist. **As long as there is at least one priest or bishop and at least a few faithful, the Church and the hierarchy are alive and visible**. Today there is much more than a handful of faithful left who maintain the unchanging Catholic Faith. Thus, the argument of our opponents from the standpoint of visibility lacks any merit and is contrary to the prophecies of Sacred Scripture.[294]

As covered in objections one, five, six, and fifteen, the Church must be identified by much more than one priest or bishop and a few faithful. Many Protestant churches as well as the Orthodox Churches can claim these as well. Yet for any church to be considered Roman Catholic, all of its essential constitutional components must be readily accounted for, beginning with the foundation. Next Dimond wrote (emphasis original):

---

294 Dimond, *The Truth*, 331.

This period of Church history, therefore, proves an important point for our time: If the Church's indefectible mission of teaching, governing and sanctifying <u>required</u> a *governing* (i.e., jurisdictional) bishop for the Church of Christ to be present and operative in a particular see or diocese, then one would have to say that the Church of Christ <u>defected</u> in all those territories where there was no governing Catholic bishop during the Arian heresy. However, it is a fact that in the 4th century, <u>where the faithful retained the true Catholic faith, even in those sees where the bishop defected to Arianism</u>, the faithful Catholic remnant constituted the true Church of Christ.[295]

As already addressed, Arianism is not a precedent to our times. As for the defection of Churches, indefectibility does not pertain to individual Churches or sees (emphasis added):

> The gift of indefectibility plainly does not guarantee each several part of the Church against heresy or apostasy. *The promise is made to the corporate body.* Individual Churches may become corrupt in morals, may fall into heresy, may even apostatize. Thus at the time of the Mohammedan conquests, whole populations renounced their faith; and the Church suffered similar losses in the sixteenth century. *But the defection of isolated branches does not alter the character of the main stem.*[296]

Once again, the "main stem" of the Church includes Rome:

> *Only to One particular Church is indefectibility assured, viz. to the See of Rome.* To Peter, and in him to all his successors in the chief pastorate, Christ committed the task of confirming his brethren in the Faith (Luke 22:32); and thus, to the Roman Church, as Cyprian says, "faithlessness cannot gain access.[297]

---

295 Ibid., 332.
296 Joyce, *The Catholic Encyclopedia*, 756.
297 Ibid.

Next Dimond wrote something that is self-defeating:

> By the way, the idea of an invisible Church—taught by the Vatican II sect—has been condemned at least three times:
>
> Pope Leo XIII, Satis Cognitum (#3), June 29, 1896; Pope Pius XI, Mortalium Animos (#10), Jan. 6, 1928, Pope Pius XII, Mystici Corporis Christi (#64), June 29, 1943.[298]

It is puzzling why any Sedevacantist would mention these papal encyclicals, which collectively refute Sedevacantism in various ways. *Satis Cognitum* is an excellent choice to demonstrate this, as it addresses most of the important issues addressed in this work. A few excerpts concerning the visibility of the Church should suffice to make the point. Pope Leo XIII wrote (emphasis added):

The Church Always Visible

3. From this it follows that those who arbitrarily conjure up and picture to themselves a hidden and invisible Church are in grievous and pernicious error: as also are those who regard the Church as a human institution which claims a certain obedience in discipline and external duties, but which is without the perennial communication of the gifts of divine grace, and without all that which testifies by constant and undoubted signs to the existence of that life which is drawn from God. It is assuredly as impossible that the Church of Jesus Christ can be the one or the other, as that man should be a body alone or a soul alone. *The connection and union of both elements is as absolutely necessary to the true Church as the intimate union of the soul and body is to human nature.* The Church is not something dead: it is the body of Christ endowed with supernatural life. As Christ, the Head and Exemplar, is not wholly in His visible human nature,

---

298 Dimond, *The Truth*, 333.

which Photinians and Nestorians assert, nor wholly in the invisible divine nature, as the Monophysites hold, but is one, from and in both natures, *visible and invisible*; so the mystical body of Christ is the true Church, *only because its visible parts draw life and power from the supernatural gifts and other things whence spring their very nature and essence. But since the Church is such by divine will and constitution, such it must uniformly remain to the end of time. If it did not, then it would not have been founded as perpetual, and the end set before it would have been limited to some certain place and to some certain period of time; both of which are contrary to the truth. The union consequently of visible and invisible elements because it harmonizes with the natural order and by God's will belongs to the very essence of the Church, must necessarily remain so long as the Church itself shall endure...*[299]

Satis Cognitum also refutes the particular branch of Sedevacantism (school two, discussed in objection one) that advances a heretical theory that the apostolic hierarchy and sacraments have disappeared from the world:

Also Augustine says: *"Unbelievers think that the Christian religion will last for a certain period in the world and will then disappear.* But it will remain as long as the sun—as long as the sun rises and sets: that is, as long as the ages of time shall roll, the Church of God—the true body of Christ on earth—*will not disappear"* (In Psalm. lxx., n. 8). And in another place: "The Church will totter if its foundation shakes; but how can Christ be moved?...Christ remaining immovable, it (the Church) shall never be shaken. *Where are they that say that the Church has disappeared from the world, when it cannot even be shaken?"*[300]

None of the above quotes or prophecies used by Dimond explicitly speaks of the Church losing its visible foundation or any of its essential

---

299 Leo XIII, "*Satis Cognitum*," 388.
300 Ibid., 388–389.

attributes or properties. But even if prophecies and commentaries infer a disappearance of the material structure of the Church founded, as it were, upon the papacy, it would not matter to Catholics because they are bound by Catholic dogma not prophecies or commentaries—even if they are drawn from sacred scripture. It is important to remember that Catholic dogma has solidified the Church's visible unity in the uninterrupted line of successors in the Roman See until the end of time. Regardless of the numerical size of the Church in eschatological times, she must retain her essential constitution. Sedevacantists are proposing that although the Church remained intact for two thousand years, it has been shattered in this, the final stretch.

I close part II of objection fifteen with the following excerpts from "The Pillar and Ground of the Truth" by Rev. Thomas E. Cox:

> Just one thought more. What sort of a society is this true Church of Christ? Can it be seen and known? Is it visible? Or is it an indeterminable, intangible, shadowy, subtle something, that escapes discovery and does not admit of identification? Is it like the lark which Europeans speak of, that soars amid the clouds till lost from human vision? Is it like the fabled serpent of the sea, a mystery or a misnomer? Is the Church a cuttle-fish institution, that addles the elements and eludes one's grasp? Is it the juggler's bean that is forever under the wrong thimble?
>
> Our purpose here is to prove that the Church which Christ established is a visible, tangible institution, capable of being known and pointed out. Christ and His Apostles were visible. The Apostles received their commission to teach by audible sounds and visible signs,—"He breathed on them; and he said to them." They discharged this office by words and acts. The Holy Ghost on the birthday of the Church came down in the form of tongues of fire upon the disciples. The Scriptures tell us that on that day three thousand persons were added to the Church,—"Pathians, and Medes, and Elamites, and inhabitants of Mesopotamia, Judea, and Cappadocia, Pontus, and Asia, Phrygia, and

Pamphilia, Egypt, and the parts of Lybia, about Cyrene, and strangers of Rome. Jews also, and proselytes, Cretes, and Arabians." How could it be said that these were added to the Church unless members could be known and numbered and visibly introduced?

The visibility of the Church follows of necessity if there exists an obligation to enter the Church. God could not command me to hear a Church that could not be known, nor to enter a Church that could not be found. But the Church is visible because its membership is made up of men who are visible; its authority is exercised by men who are known, upon subjects who are able to be located. Man belongs to human society. He is a social being. He must give public worship to God as a member and part of human society. All this implies that the organization or society in which he worships God must be, like human society, a visible institution.

Again, the visibility of the Church is proved from the mode of accession to and association with it. The idea of membership is full of visibility. We receive the knowledge of truth by definite instruction. The doctrines and laws presented are tangible things. "Faith…cometh by hearing." "And how shall they hear without a preacher?"

Baptism, by which we are born into the bosom of the Church, is a visible sign. The profession of faith, prescribed as a condition for Baptism, falls under the organs of sense. All the rites and ceremonies employed by the Church appeal to the soul only through the senses of the body. From the cradle to the grave our existence in the Church is nourished by the Sacraments, all of which are visible signs.

There is not one phrase in the whole Scripture, not one word applied to the Church, which does not aptly suit it as a visible institution. All the figures and parables which so admirably portray its character refer to something visible. The Church is called "a flock," "a field," "a city seated upon a mountain" which "cannot be hid," a light "upon a candle stick" (not "under a bushel"), "a grain of mustard-seed" that "becometh a tree" and furnishes shelter to the birds of the air, "a stone…cut out of a mountain" that will fill the whole earth. It is "the mountain of the house of the Lord…prepared on the top of mountains." It is likened to a "house," a "body," the "body of Christ."

There is no stronger way to express the visibility of the Church than to call it a body. St. Paul gives us to understand that Christ instituted the Church as a kind of reincarnation of Himself; Christ is the very life and soul of it, men are the members, the body of it. He says: "Now you are the body of Christ, and members of member," and: "He hath subjected all things under his feet: and hath made him head over all the Church, which is his body, and the fullness of him, who is filled all in all."

Although the Church is a visible society, we must not forget that it has within it something that is invisible. It is a spiritual and supernatural society as well. Hence the extreme error of saying that the Church is all body or all soul, or that it is all visible or all invisible.

The last argument I shall adduce for the visibility of the Church is the strongest of all. There is nothing that proves a fact so well as the fact itself. Both the existence and the visibility of the Church are demonstrated by pointing out the very Church itself, visibly present in the world. History tells of that Church, of its venerable antiquity, its splendid equipment, its precise and powerful action. That Church challenges our admiration and invites our study. It is of that Church the Canticle speaks when it says, "Who is she that cometh forth as the morning rising, fair as the moon, bright as the sun, terrible as an army set in array?" And Isaias, when he says, "The Mountain of the house of the Lord shall be prepared on the top of mountains, and it shall be exalted above the hills, and all nations shall flow unto it." The study of the Church is a profitable thing. It is little less than a crime against our intellectual nature to remain ignorant of her splendid story. For a Catholic, especially, to ignore her prerogatives, and not to glory in her greatness, is, to my mind, a thing to be deeply deplored.

One word to those who are not of the Catholic faith. No trivial business is before us. The Church of Christ is an institution great and grand enough to claim your most thoughtful study. Let me tell you that there are many who do not know the old Church. The bias of early training, inherited prejudices that are hard to lay aside, and the scandals caused by unworthy members of the Church, have conspired to give wrong notions of her. But I put the question to you, Are not your eternal interests and present obligations respecting the truth just the same as are mine? Are we not all children of one Father? "Hath not one God created us?" Have we different destinies, or are we provided with unlike means for reaching our end? If Christ founded a Church, there is an obligation for you to find it. "He that believeth not, shall be condemned." "He that is not with me, is against me." What doth it profit a man, if he gain the whole world, and suffer the loss of his own soul?" Christ knew, however, that "not all would obey the Gospel," and His heart went out towards the obstinate and the erring,—"Other sheep I have that are not of this fold," He said, "them also I must bring, and they shall hear my voice, and there shall be one fold, and one shepherd," The Church of Christ is visible. "Seek, and you shall find: knock, and it shall be opened to you." If you are assailed by doubts in this matter, or wrapped in insensible slumber, as a friend of your souls I bid you arise; take courage, and wrestle with the angel of doubt. When you have fully awakened to the light of truth, you will exclaim with Jacob of old, "Indeed the Lord is in this place, and I knew it not...This is no other but the house of God, and the gate of heaven."[301]

---

301 Thomas E. Cox, *The Pillar and Ground of the Truth, A Series of Lenten Lectures on the True Church, Its Marks and Attributes* (Chicago: J. S. Hyland & Company, 1900), 36–43.

Part III
...and Apostolic Church

❦

WE HAVE NOW ARRIVED AT the point in objection fifteen where Dimond assaulted the fourth mark of the Church—apostolicity. As we proceed we will see how Dimond's understanding of the relationship between the Church and its authority is identical to his understanding of the relationship between the Church and the Vicar of Christ—meaning that he understands these relationships as incidental or nonessential. Here we encounter the fifth principal Sedevacantist heresy: Apostolic authority is accidental to the episcopal order.

Dimond promoted the first school of Sedevacantism mentioned in objection one.[302] For those who may not remember, the first school argues that men who obtain episcopal consecrations and priestly ordinations *of their own volition* constitute the legitimate, visible hierarchy of the Roman Catholic Church. Dimond advocated the continued reception of sacraments from schismatics, heretics, and self-appointed clergymen in order to avoid contradictions with the doctrines of visibility and indefectibility. Otherwise he would have to explain why the Church disappeared and left the faithful without the sacraments—precisely the problem for all those who subscribe to the second school of Sedevacantism.

---

302 The two schools of Sedevacantism are as follows: 1. The apostolic hierarchy and sacraments continued after Vatican II by way of self-constituted men. 2. The apostolic hierarchy and sacraments have been lost indefinitely.

To account for the indefectibility of the hierarchy and sacraments, the first school of Sedevacantists must accept *self-appointed* men as carriers of the fourth mark of the Church for the simple reason that their only other choice is the Vatican II hierarchy. They will argue that the Church's present "emergency situation" justifies self-appointment to the episcopacy and the priesthood through lengthy treatises built around terms such as *supplied jurisdiction*[303] and *epikeia*.[304] What these ecclesiastical terms essentially mean for the Sedevacantists is that the Church's laws restricting the transmission of apostolic authority during normal times have ceased to bind and that the Church *supplies* authority directly to Sedevacantists in order to perpetuate apostolicity and the sacraments. Allegedly, for Sedevacantists who manage to obtain for themselves the sacrament of orders, it entitles them to open public chapels; offer sacraments; preach; establish religious chapters and new religious orders; accept donations from the public; open seminaries; confer ordinations; and, in some notable cases, elect their own Roman Pontiffs. For the Sedevacantists this particular "crisis" in the Church, stemming from Vatican II, justifies a free-for-all, and anyone who desires to become the visible hierarchy of the Roman Catholic Church is at liberty to do so because it is purportedly for the common good of the Church. Notwithstanding the fact that these practices have been going on in the traditional Catholic movement for decades,[305] nothing could be more contrary to the established order of the Church.

---

303 In ecclesiastical law s*upplied jurisdiction* is defined as "a form of delegation supplied by the Church, enabling a priest who is otherwise unauthorized to validly absolve penitents in the sacrament of penance. Thus jurisdiction is supplied in the case of common error (when people think that the priest has jurisdiction); in doubt of law or fact, assuming that the doubt is sincere; and if a priest's jurisdiction had inadvertently expired." (Hardon, *Modern Catholic Dictionary*, 526–527.)

304 *Epikeia* is defined as "[a] liberal interpretation of law in instances not provided by the letter of the law. It presupposes sincerity in wanting to observe the law, and interprets the mind of the lawgiver in supplying his presumed intent to include a situation that is not covered by the law. It favors the liberty of the interpreter without contradicting the express will of the lawgiver." (Hardon, *Modern Catholic Dictionary*, 190.)

305 "Sedevacantism," last modified November 5, 2014, http://en.wikipedia.org/w/index.php?title=Sedevacantism&oldid=600207158.

In the Catholic Church, authority is hierarchical and descends from the top town. Hence one does not become a bishop, priest, deacon, or member of a religious order by self-appointment regardless of the severity of a crisis. All episcopal consecrations, priestly ordinations, religious orders, administration of sacraments, etc., must be authorized, and they are strictly regulated. In fact the act of consecrating a bishop without a papal mandate carries a penalty of automatic excommunication.

But would the laws governing the transmission of apostolic authority and the dispensing of sacraments cease to bind if there is no identifiable authority from whom to receive it? According to Dimond and his band of Sedevacantists, the answer is yes—on the grounds that the salvation of souls is the supreme law of the Church and because bishops, priests, and sacraments are necessary to that end. On the surface their argument appears to make sense, for we recall from objection one that the hierarchy and the sacraments cannot disappear on the universal level without violating the indefectibility of the Church. However, the stated question is based on a false premise that such a situation could ever exist in the first place. According to Catholic teaching, it absolutely cannot.

We recall from objection one that the Catholic Church is a juridical Church and that apostolic authority belongs to its essential constitution. Thus it *should be* impossible for this authority to disappear. If it could disappear so that self-appointed clergymen become the best choice to account for and preserve apostolicity from expiration, the Roman Catholic Church would have defected. This means that what the Sedevacantists are proposing is supposed to be impossible.

Moreover, the power to dispense valid sacraments, which derives from the power of orders, should never be misconstrued with the authority to do so, which derives from the hierarchy of jurisdiction. Thus sacraments will never exist without the Church; the Church will never exist without Rome; the Church will never exist without a visibly unified hierarchy; the hierarchy will never exist without the fullness of apostolic power; and apostolic authority will never exist without uninterrupted human succession. This is the order instituted by Jesus Christ from the foundation of the Church, and it cannot cease unless the Church could cease to exist. In a moment we will see exactly what apostolic succession entails and why no Sedevacantist sect has it.

Furthermore *The Catholic Encyclopedia* states that during times of constitutional disturbances (e.g., papal interregnums), the supreme law of the Church actually shifts from being the salvation of souls to the safety of the Church, without which the sacraments would be of no value. The Church's highest priority following a vacancy of the Holy See is to elect a pope, not to consecrate bishops or ordain priests for the continuation of the sacraments. *The Catholic Encyclopedia* states (emphasis added):

> A council not only acting independently of the Vicar of Christ, but sitting in judgment over him, is unthinkable in the constitution of the Church; in fact, much assemblies have only take place in times of great constitutional disturbances, when either there was no pope or the rightful pope was indistinquishable from antipopes. *In such abnormal times the safety of the Church becomes the supreme law, and the first duty of the abandoned flock is to find a new shepherd, under whose direction the existing evils may be remedied.*[306]

Of course the first duty of the flock is to find a new shepherd. That is why the Church government in Rome shuts down and Cardinals are immediately summoned to Rome following a papal vacancy. Let us now consult with *The Catholic Encyclopedia* on the fourth mark of the Church—apostolicity (emphasis added).

Apostolicity

In explaining the concept of Apostolicity, then, special attention must be given to Apostolicity of mission, or Apostolic succession. Apostolicity of mission means that the Church is one moral body, possessing the mission entrusted by Jesus Christ to the Apostles, *and transmitted through them and their lawful successors in an unbroken chain to the present representatives of*

---

306 Wilhelm, *The Catholic Encyclopedia*, 426.

Christ upon earth. This authoritative transmission of power in the Church constitutes Apostolic succession. This Apostolic succession must be both material and formal; the material consisting in the actual succession in the Church, through a series of persons from the Apostolic age to the present; *the formal adding the element of authority in the transmission of power. It consists in the legitimate transmission of the ministerial power conferred by Christ upon His Apostles. No one can give a power which he does not possess.* Hence in tracing the mission of the Church back to the Apostles, no lacuna can be allowed, no new mission can arise; *but the mission conferred by Christ must pass from generation to generation through an uninterrupted lawful succession.* The Apostles received it from Christ and gave it in turn to those *legitimately appointed by them,* and these again selected others to continue the work of the ministry. *Any break in this succession destroys Apostolicity, because the break means the beginning of a new series which is not Apostolic.* "How shall they preach unless they be sent?" (Romans 10:15). An authoritative mission to teach is absolutely necessary, *a man-given mission is not authoritative.* Hence any concept of Apostolicity that excludes authoritative union with the Apostolic mission robs the ministry of its Divine character. Apostolicity, or Apostolic succession, then, means that the mission conferred by Jesus Christ upon the Apostles *must pass from then to their legitimate successors, in an unbroken line, until the end of the world.* This notion of Apostolicity is evolved from the words of Christ himself, the practice of the Apostles, and the teaching of the Fathers and theologians of the Church.[307]

The Catholic Encyclopedia made several key distinctions that must not be overlooked. Because we know that apostolic succession is *"the authoritative transmission of power stemming from the Apostles through their lawful successors in an unbroken chain to the present representatives of Christ upon Earth,"* we can rule out any defense of the Sedevacantist thesis based upon epikeia and supplied jurisdiction immediately. The reason is that the means of apostolic succession as instituted by Christ is indefectible, so it can never

---

307 Thomas C. O'Reilly, *The Catholic Encyclopedia* (New York: Robert Appleton Company, 1907), Vol. 1, 648.

cease as long as the Church exists, while epikeia and supplied jurisdiction presuppose that what Christ instituted has suffered a lapse.

Again, what is the means for this transmission of apostolic authority that Christ instituted? It is through *"an uninterrupted series of persons from the apostolic age to the present."* But there is something else that this transmission must include: its formal element—authority. "Formal element" means a legitimate transmission of the ministerial power originally conferred by Christ upon his apostles. If, according to the Sedevacantists, the Church as an entity distinct from its human composition has to supply the components of apostolic succession in order to prevent its expiration, then the means instituted by Christ for its transmission and perpetuation (i.e., series of persons) has ended. In other words if the Church must step in to preserve apostolic succession by transmitting its formal element directly to Sedevacantist clergy because legitimate human successors who should possess it perished, defected, or disappeared and cannot be located, then succession is broken, unity destroyed, indefectibility contravened, and in all cases of Sedevacantist episcopal consecrations- a new series of bishops begun.

According to the doctrine of apostolicity, Sedevacantist bishops must be considered a new series of bishops because they possess at best only a material element to apostolic succession and must depend on the Church instead of human succession to supply the deficiencies. Moreover, even the material element of apostolicity is dubious among Sedevacantist clergymen, as the validity of entire lineages of episcopacies are greatly contested among the various factions within the Sedevacantist movement.

The Reverend Thomas R. Cox wrote:

> Apostolicity is the fourth mark of the true Church, and one of its essential attributes…It is not enough for it (Apostolicity) to teach all of the doctrines of the Apostles, if it lacks either their orders *or their jurisdiction*. Nor is it enough to have the orders of the Apostles if either their doctrine or mission is wanting…Finally *no Church is Apostolic that is not authorized and commissioned by apostolic continuity.*

> *Those who have lost the line of valid ministers leading back to apostolic times, cannot plead the possession of Apostolicity.* Where there is no ordination, no priesthood, no authority, no power, Apostolicity is out of the question. *Even if valid orders exist, where jurisdiction is lacking there is no real Apostolicity.*[308]

Nevertheless, scattered, headless Sedevacantists march forward with the belief that the Church supplies authority for their actions. While it may be argued that the necessity for sacraments supersedes the necessity for authority *in certain instances,* which may be seen in the canon law[309] that allows priests without jurisdiction to hear confessions in the case of imminent death, it cannot be said that this law (Canon 882) exists because the identifiable, lawful authority in the Church could ever cease to exist. The Church supplies jurisdiction to priests only in the case of imminent death because it recognizes that situations can arise when there is a *lack of time* to obtain it. Not so for the Sedevacantists, who are now approaching the sixth decade without the Holy See from which all authority emanates.

Obviously there is a significant difference between there being a *lack of time* to obtain authority and the belief that *no identifiable source of apostolic authority exists,* especially being that one of these contradicts the Church's indefectibility and visibility and the other does not. It must also be noted that Sedevacantists cannot find a law of the Church similar to Canon 882 that would supply jurisdiction for the consecration of bishops without a papal mandate. Because the Church has endured vacancies of the Roman See for two thousand years, it cannot be argued with reason that the Church did not foresee the necessity of such a law. It is only reasonable to assume that the law does not exist because the Church understands something that the entire Sedevacantist movement exemplifies—such a law would threaten the unity of the Church each time there was a vacancy of the Holy See.

---

308   Cox, *The Pillar,* 168.
309   Refer to Canon 882 in the 1917 Code of Canon Law.

If nothing else, in each of the four objections addressed thus far, Dimond has been consistent in dividing doctrines of the Church in order to make them fit his version of Sedevacantism. To this point of objection fifteen, Dimond argued that partial specifications of apostolicity (material) conserves the whole (material and formal). Dimond continued to argue that parts equal the whole by classifying apostolic succession into *ordinary jurisdiction* and *supplied jurisdiction* as though the latter could exist in the Church without the former. Dimond was teaching that because the ordinary power of the apostles has ceased to exist; virtually anyone in the world can assign himself the required authority to function as a member of the hierarchy and claim that his authority came from the Church, which allegedly *supplies* it. Dimond began by referencing Fr. William Jurgens, St. Ambrose, and St. Gregory Nazianz, each of who spoke of the greatly diminished size of the Church during the Arian crisis, and interpreted these accounts in favor of his heretical "remnant Church" theory. Dimond quoted Fr. Jurgens and then commented (emphasis original):

> Fr. William Jurgens: "At one point in the Church's history, only a few years before Gregory's [Nazianz] present teaching (+380 A.D.), <u>perhaps the number of Catholic bishops in possession of sees, as opposed to Arian bishops in possession of sees, was no greater than something between 1% and 3% of the total</u>. **Had doctrine been determined by popularity, today we should all be deniers of Christ and opponents of the Spirit."**
>
> ...This period of Church history, therefore, proves an important point for our time: If the Church's indefectible mission of teaching, governing and sanctifying required a governing (i.e., jurisdictional) bishop for the Church of Christ to be present and operative in a particular see or diocese, then one would have to say that the Church of Christ defected in all those territories where there was no governing Catholic bishop during the Arian heresy...[310]

---
310 Dimond, *The Truth*, 332.

Dimond was confused. Indeed the Church of Christ *did* defect in all of those territories where governing Catholic bishops became Arian. Particular churches (sees) defect if their hierarchies (i.e., governing bishops) defect, not because the members of the faithful defect. That is because only the bishops represent the hierarchy of the Church, and only the bishops are considered essential to the Church's constitution (see objection one). Furthermore the fact that individual sees defected to Arianism does not contradict the Church's doctrine of indefectibility. We recall from objection one that indefectibility does not protect individual sees but only the Roman See.

> *The gift of indefectibility plainly does not guarantee each several part of the Church against heresy or apostasy. The promise is made to the corporate body.* Individual Churches may become corrupt in morals, may fall into heresy, may even apostatize. Thus at the time of the Mohammedan conquests, whole populations renounced their faith; and the Church suffered similar losses in the sixteenth century. *But the defection of isolated branches does not alter the character of the main stem.*
>
> *Only to One particular Church is indefectibility assured, viz. to the See of Rome.* To Peter, and in him to all his successors in the chief pastorate, Christ committed the task of confirming his brethren in the Faith (Luke 22:32); and thus, to the Roman Church, as Cyprian says, "faithlessness cannot gain access."[311]

Dimond continued:

> ...In that remnant, the Catholic Church existed and endured in her mission to teach, govern and sanctify without a governing bishop, thus proving that the Church of Christ's indefectibility and mission to teach, govern and sanctify does not require the presence of a jurisdictional bishop.[312]

---

311 Joyce, *The Catholic Encyclopedia*, 756.
312 Dimond, *The Truth*, 332.

Dimond's statement is vague and misleading. First, the Church does not endure in her mission to teach, govern, and sanctify without governing bishops. Only bishops are anointed to teach, govern, and sanctify the Church, not a remnant of Catholic faithful. Second, particular dioceses defect when their governing bishops defect. Third, a visibly unified hierarchy under Rome will exist and endure as long as a remnant of Catholic faithful exists and endures. When a unified hierarchy under Rome ceases to exist and endure, it will be because the salvific mission of the Church has ended. Fourth, if a remnant of faithful in the Arian sees were still able to receive the sacraments from Catholic priests, it was because those priests previously had or subsequently received the necessary authority from the visibly unified Catholic hierarchy to administer them. The hierarchy, albeit a greatly diminished hierarchy, existed at all times and retained the ordinary power of the apostles. Fifth, if a remnant of Catholic faithful were able to sanctify themselves in an Arian see, it was not because the Church supplied jurisdiction to laymen in order to teach, govern, and sanctify themselves, nor was it because the Church supplied jurisdiction to laymen to receive illicit priestly and episcopal ordinations. If Dimond was implying that these things occurred during Arianism then he ought to produce the evidence.

Dimond continued his search for ways to support the first school of Sedevacantism and found something from Pope Pius XII. Dimond wrote (emphasis original):

> It should also be noted that the hierarchy can be defined in two ways: the jurisdictional hierarchy and the ecclesiastical hierarchy.
>
> > Pope Pius XII, *Ad Sinarum gentum* (# 13), Oct. 7, 1954: "Besides—as has also been divinely established—**the power of orders (through which the ecclesiastical hierarchy is composed of bishops, priests, and ministers) comes from receiving the Sacrament of Holy Orders.**"

Only those who have ordinary jurisdiction (i.e., jurisdiction which is attached to an office) constitute the jurisdictional hierarchy. All valid Catholic priests, on the other hand, constitute parts of the ecclesiastical hierarchy. It is possible that as long as the ecclesiastical hierarchy remains the hierarchy exists.[313]

Dimond argued that as long as Catholic priests exist, the "hierarchy" has not defected. There are at least three problems with Dimond's reasoning, but before I address them, I should mention that the above encyclical from which Dimond quoted *(Ad Sinarum Gentum)* is number twelve, not number thirteen.[314] Furthermore Dimond did not quote number twelve in its entirety. Later we will see why this omission is important.

The first problem with Dimond's argument is that priests do not comprise the Church's hierarchy. Technically speaking a valid Catholic priest is *part* of the ecclesiastical hierarchy in virtue of the sacrament of orders, but when we read that indefectibility pertains to the hierarchy[315] we understand that hierarchy must include successors of the apostles, in whom Christ entrusted the teaching, pastoral, and sacerdotal powers in the Church. Pius XII, referencing Gregory the Great, called bishops "principal parts of the members of the Lord."[316] Because one is technical-

---

313 Ibid., 332–333.
314 Pius XII, "*Ad Sinarum Gentem* (Encyclical Letter on the Supranationality of the Church)," in *The Papal Encyclicals*, (Raleigh, McGrath Publishing Company, 1981), 266–267.
315 Hierarchy: "The successors of the Apostles under the Pope as successor of St. Peter. Three powers are included under the Catholic hierarchy: teaching, pastoral, and sacerdotal. They correspond to the threefold office laid on Christ as man for the redemption of the world; the office prophet or teacher, the pastoral or royal office of ruler, and the priestly office of sanctifying the faithful. Christ transferred this threefold office, with the corresponding powers, to the Apostles and their successors. A man enters the hierarchy by episcopal ordination when he receives the fullness of the priesthood. But he depends on collegial union with the Bishop of Rome and the rest of the Catholic hierarchy for actually being able to exercise the two other powers of teaching divine truth and of legitimately ruling the believers under his jurisdiction." (Hardon, *Modern Catholic Dictionary*, 249–250.)
316 Pius XII, "*Mystici Corporis Christi*," 45.

ly considered a member of the hierarchy by way of episcopal ordination, which priests do not receive, priests are not considered the hierarchy of the Church. Accordingly, even a Church reduced to a remnant of faithful must include bishops who possess full apostolic authority.

The second problem with Dimond's argument is that even bishops do not comprise hierarchy in the Catholic Church. Bishops are principal parts, but they are still only *parts* of the hierarchy. To complete the hierarchical structure of the Church necessitates a visible head to which it is both adjoined and subordinate. Only by this union of body and head can the true hierarchy exist. Therefore, in addition to requiring bishops, Dimond's remnant Church requires a visible head, or else a body of bishops would remain disconnected, divided, and impotent.

The third problem with Dimond's argument is that *illicit* ordinations and episcopal consecrations do not automatically produce legitimate members of the Roman Catholic ecclesiastical hierarchy. We must remember that Dimond would like his readers to believe that men who obtain the sacrament of orders through the Sedevacantist underworld, those who convert to the Sedevacantist position from elsewhere, and those possessing valid orders who secede from the modern Roman See instantly obtain status as the Roman Catholic ecclesiastical hierarchy. That is false. The legitimate ecclesiastical hierarchy must possess the ordinary authority of the apostles. This is addressed in the portion of Pope Pius XII's encyclical *Ad Sinarum Gentum* #12 that Dimond omitted. Let us now review *Ad Sinarum Gentum* # 12 in totality (emphasis added):

Orders and Jurisdiction

12. By virtue of God's Will, the faithful are divided into two classes: the clergy and the laity. By virtue of the same Will is established the twofold sacred hierarchy, namely, of orders and jurisdiction. Besides— as has also been divinely established—the power of orders (through which the ecclesiastical hierarchy is composed of Bishops, priests, and

ministers) comes from receiving the Sacrament of Holy Orders. *But the power of jurisdiction, which is conferred upon the Supreme Pontiff directly by divine rights, flows to the Bishops by the same right, but only through the Successor of St. Peter, to whom not only the simple faithful, but even all the Bishops must be constantly subject, and to whom they must be bound by obedience and with the bond of unity.*[317]

The italicized sentence above indicates the portion Dimond omitted from #12. Self-appointed bishops and priests who possess the power of orders alone (material element) cannot be considered the legitimate ecclesiastical hierarchy of the Catholic Church unless they receive the right to exercise the power of order. That is what Pope Pius XII means by *"twofold sacred hierarchy."* Both hierarchies (orders and jurisdiction) are essentially two facets of a single hierarchy of the Church. In other words members of the Church who constitute the hierarchy of orders should simultaneously rank somewhere in the hierarchy of jurisdiction. If that were not true, then it would be correct to consider bishops of the Eastern Orthodox Church and the Old Catholic church legitimate members of the hierarchy. Again, Dimond attempts to divide teachings to make them fit his theory. Here he attempts to divide the twofold hierarchies so that self-appointed clergymen who do not receive the right to exercise the power of order could still be considered the legitimate hierarchy of the Church in virtue of the power of orders alone. That is false. *The Catholic Encyclopedia* states (emphasis added):

> *Furthermore, with the power of jurisdiction there should be connected the right to exercise the power of order.* The acts of the power of order are, it is true, always valid (except in the sacrament of Penance, which requires in addition a power of jurisdiction). However, in a well-ordered society like the Church, *the right to exercise the power of order could never be a mere matter*

---

317 Pius XII, *"Ad Sinarum Gentem,"* 266–267.

of choice. For its legitimate exercise the Church requires either jurisdiction, or at least permission, even of a general character.[318]

Sedevacantists will argue that since there is no Roman Pontiff, they are entitled, in fact obliged as a matter of divine law, to obtain and exercise the power of orders on their own volition for the common good of the Church.[319] However, this theory contradicts indefectibility and apostolicity, which teach that the means instituted by Christ for the perpetuation of apostolic mission and sacraments will never expire. Again, the means instituted by Christ is by an uninterrupted series of persons. For Sedevacantists to be correct, there would have to be a lapse in apostolic succession because the indefectible component of authority is missing in all Sedevacantist ordinations, which is why they claim the Church supplies it. We recall from objection one that indefectibility belongs to the apostolic hierarchy:

> ...nor can it (the Church) ever lose the apostolic hierarchy, or the sacraments through which Christ communicates grace to men...By the hierarchy and the sacraments, Christ, further, made the Church the depositary of the graces of the Passion. Were it to lose either of these, it could no longer dispense to men the treasures of grace.[320]

There is no such a thing in the Roman Catholic Church as an apostolic hierarchy that lacks authority such as Sedevacantists openly confess. We recall the following from *The Catholic Encyclopedia*:

> An authoritative mission to teach is *absolutely necessary*, a man-given mission is not authoritative. Hence any concept of Apostolicity that

---

318 A. Van Hove, *The Catholic Encyclopedia* (New York: Robert Appleton Company, 1910), Vol. 7, 323.
319 See Rev. Anthony Cekada's article "Home Alone?" located here: http://www.traditionalmass.org/articles/article.php?id=55&catname=14.
320 Joyce, *The Catholic Encyclopedia*, 756.

excludes authoritative union with the Apostolic mission robs the ministry of its Divine character.[321]

Dimond wrote:

> If it's true that there must be one bishop with ordinary jurisdiction somewhere (which is something that has not been proven), then he is somewhere. But it doesn't change the fact that Benedict XVI and his apostate bishops are not Catholic and therefore not part of the hierarchy. Against a fact there is no argument; against this fact there is no argument.[322]

Dimond required proof that bishops with ordinary jurisdiction exist in the world. Both the Council of Trent as well as the First Vatican Council explicitly taught that the powers bestowed on the apostles have descended to the bishops (de fide). Pope Leo XIII reaffirmed this (emphasis added):

Bishops Belong to the Essential Constitution of the Church

But if the authority of Peter and his successors is plenary and supreme, it is not to be regarded as the sole authority. For He who made Peter the foundation of the Church also "chose, twelve, whom He called apostles" (Luke vi., 13); *and just as it is necessary that the authority of Peter should be perpetuated in the Roman Pontiff, so, by the fact that the bishops succeed the Apostles, they inherit their ordinary power, and thus the episcopal order necessarily belongs to the essential constitution of the Church.* Although they do not receive plenary, or universal, or supreme authority, they are not to be looked as *vicars* of the Roman Pontiffs; because they exercise a power really their own, and are

---

321 O'Reilly, *The Catholic Encyclopedia*, 648.
322 Dimond, *The Truth*, 333.

most truly called the *ordinary* pastors of the peoples over whom they rule.[323]

It remains true that as long as bishops succeed the apostles, ordinary jurisdiction exists in the Church because Jesus Christ instituted both from the foundation of the Church. The fact that Sedevacantist bishops do not have ordinary jurisdiction is just one more proof that they are not legitimate successors of the apostles but only counterfeits.

Recognizably frustrated that he cannot account for ordinary jurisdiction in the Church, Dimond wrote:

> Non-sedevacantists who raise this objection cannot point to one real Catholic bishop with ordinary jurisdiction. To whom are they going to point? Are they going to point to "Bishop" Bruskewitz, who conducted an interfaith Seder Supper with a group of rabbis in his own cathedral during Holy Week? Are they going to point to "Cardinal" Mahony or "Cardinal" Keeler?[324]

I must point out that neither can Sedevacantists point to any bishops with ordinary jurisdiction. With only a few exceptions, Sedevacantist clergymen deny that they have ordinary jurisdiction, and of the few who do, they could have received it only by circumventing a Roman Pontiff, which contradicts the established order. But if ordinary jurisdiction is integral to apostolicity, and if apostolicity must always exist and remain identifiable, where did it go? To whom will Dimond point who carries on real apostolicity if ordinary jurisdiction is absent in all of the men he claims are successors of the ordinary authority of the apostles? If the episcopal order belongs to the essential constitution of the Church *(Satis Cognitum)*; if bishops inherit the ordinary power of the apostles *(Satis Cognitum)*; if the power of jurisdiction flows to the bishops only through the successor of St. Peter *(Ad Sinarum Gentum)*

---

323 Leo XIII, "*Satis Cognitum*," 400.
324 Dimond, *The Truth*, 333.

then three conclusions regarding Roman Catholic bishops may be stated:

1. They must exist.
2. They must possess ordinary jurisdiction.
3. One and two came by way of a Roman Pontiff.

It is contrary to the teachings of the Catholic Church to theorize that the episcopacy exists without ordinary jurisdiction. Consequently Sedevacantist bishops who unabashedly disclaim their right (i.e., nearly all of them) to the ordinary power of the apostles should in no way be considered representatives of the legitimate apostolic hierarchy. Nearly all Sedevacantists of the first school claim an impotent hierarchy for themselves. In his syllabus of Modernist Errors, *Lamentabili Sane*, Pope St. Pius X wrote:

> The elders who fulfilled the office of watching over the gatherings of the faithful were instituted by the Apostles as priests or bishops to provide for the necessary ordering of the increasing communities *and not properly for the perpetuation of the Apostolic mission and power—condemned.*[325]

Nevertheless there are in fact a few Sedevacantist bishops who *do* claim to possess the ordinary power of the apostles. Members of these sects are actually closer to upholding the Church's teachings and yet *still* incorrect in how they could have received it, for legitimate transmission of power must come through the Roman Pontiff.

The following are additional excerpts from Leo XIII's encyclical *Satis Cognitum* on the perpetuity and immutability of the fourth mark of the Church (emphasis added):

> The Magisterium (or Teaching Authority) of the Church to be Perpetual

---
325 "Lamentabili Sane."

8. It was consequently provided by God that the Magisterium instituted by Jesus Christ should not end with the life of the Apostles, but that it should be perpetuated. We see it in truth propagated, and, as it were, *delivered from hand to hand.* For the Apostles consecrated bishops, and each one appointed those who were to succeed them immediately "in the ministry of the word."

Nay more: they likewise required their successors to choose fitting men, *to endow them with like authority, and to confide to them the office and mission of teaching.* "Thou, therefore, my son, be strong in the grace which is in Christ Jesus: and the things which thou hast heard of me by many witnesses, the same command to faithful men, who shall be fit to teach others also" (2 Tim. ii., 1–2). *Wherefore, as Christ was sent by God and the Apostles by Christ, so the Bishops and those who succeeded them were sent by the Apostles.* "The Apostles were appointed by Christ to preach the Gospel to us. Jesus Christ was sent by God. Christ is therefore from God, and the Apostles from Christ, *and both according to the will of God...* Preaching therefore the word through the countries and cities, when they had proved in the Spirit the first—fruits of their teaching they appointed bishops and deacons for the faithful...They appointed them and then ordained them, so that when they themselves had passed away other tried men should carry on their ministry" (S. Clemens Rom. Epist. I ad Corinth. capp. 42, 44). On the one hand, therefore, *it is necessary that the mission of teaching whatever Christ had taught should remain perpetual and immutable,* and on the other that the duty of accepting and professing all their doctrine should likewise be perpetual and immutable.[326]

Leo XIII reaffirmed that the transmission of apostolic authority is carried out hand to hand. Of course nobody would argue that hand to hand entails human succession.

---

326 Leo XIII, "*Satis Cognitum,*" 393.

Una Cum Antichrist?

If apostolicity must always exist, if ordinary jurisdiction is integral to apostolicity, if the Sedevacantist clergy do not have ordinary jurisdiction, where did apostolicity go? Dimond is essentially left with one choice: apostolicity is perpetuated in the post–Vatican II Church, which Dimond considers the false Church of the Antichrist. Dimond's intuition must tell him this is true, for of all the Sedevacantist clergymen he could choose to receive sacraments from, does he approach any of them? I do not know of his current practices, but it is well known that Dimond had been attempting to pilfer grace from his local Antichrist's diocese.[327] By that action it is only reasonable to conclude that Dimond tacitly recognizes, albeit correctly, apostolicity in the post–Vatican II Church under Pope Francis.

As for attempting to make sense of Dimond's sacramental theology that claims one can communicate sacramentally with the Antichrist and Jesus Christ simultaneously, I will leave that for his disciples to work out. We may also say that Dimond's incapacity to identify one bishop with ordinary jurisdiction remaining in the whole Church is trumped only by his incapacity to identify a single bishop anywhere in the free world that he does not believe is a heretic. Because bishops with the ordinary power of the Apostles belong to the essential constitution of the Church, and because the Church's hierarchy must remain visibly unified and known, it should not be very difficult for Dimond to name them.

By combining the Church's indefectible property of visibility with the teachings of the papal encyclicals *Ad Sinarum Gentum* and *Satis Cognitum*, Catholics must know with certainty that an apostolic hierarchy possessing ordinary jurisdiction obtained through a Roman Pontiff is manifest to the world in general at this very moment. This, of course, means that the apostolic hierarchy is right in front of us and has been all the while. Aside from Dimond, who tacitly recognizes them in the local Antichrist's diocese, most Sedevacantists do not recognize them

---

[327] Furthermore, Dimond attends an Eastern Rite liturgy.

because they have not yet figured out who they should be looking for. Dimond "gets it."

I conclude objection fifteen on apostolicity with some words from the Reverend Cox, who wrote so eloquently on this subject. Because the Sedevacantist movement is comprised of self-constituted individuals who assume the responsibilities of "saving the Church," ironically from itself as it turns out, his words are far more relevant to our times than those of either Father William Jurgens or Father Edmund O'Reilly. Reverend Cox wrote (emphasis added):

> *They (the Apostles) were not self-constituted leaders*, "desiring to be teachers of the law, understanding neither the things they say, nor whereof they affirm."[328]
>
> It is an error, therefore, to suppose that the preacher gets his power from the people. This same St. Paul, who was so miraculously converted, and so singularly called to the ministry, *did not begin his work of his own motion, but had recourse to the established authority of the Church. He was duly ordained and commissioned by the Church*…St. Paul did not establish an independent community, nor a people's Church, nor a Paul's Church, simply because he was called differently from the rest.[329]
>
> *A careful study of the manner in which Christ instituted the Church, and the way in which He selected and commissioned His Apostles, ought to settle forever the assumptions of self-constituted teachers.* It was of self-appointed preachers God spoke by the mouth of Jeremias: "I did not send prophets, yet they ran: I have not spoken to them, yet they prophesied." Christ is the door. The shepherd of the sheep entereth by the door. *"He that entereth not by the door into the sheepfold,"* says our Lord, *"but climbeth up another way, the same is a thief and a robber."*[330]

---

328 Cox, *The Pillar*, 162.
329 Ibid., 165–166.
330 Ibid., 166–177.

The pretensions to an extraordinary mission, independent of apostolic authority, by would-be guides of mankind, is but one phase of a human insanity that is more common than many of us have any idea of. The world has held, and does hold, no small number of false prophets, cranks, and humbugs. *Scarcely a parish exists in which some one cannot be found who is perfectly sure of having had a divine call to regulate and run everything religious,* political, social and domestic, according to his own whim. In my experiences I have met three or four persons each pretending to be Christ, and half a dozen claiming to be the Blessed Virgin Mary, but they were all hopelessly insane. Now, is it to be wondered at that some of these people, rising above the rest in madness and deception, have succeeded in making considerable noise here and there in the world?[331]

---

331 Ibid., 167–168.

Summary

Non-Sedevacantists object to Sedevacantism because *"[t]he Church and the hierarchy will always be visible. If the Vatican II Church is not the true Catholic Church, then the Church and hierarchy are no longer visible."*[332] My position is agreement with this objection; the Sedevacantists *do* deny the visibility of the Church, most especially concerning the Church's intrinsic bonds of unity.

Visibility belongs to the essence of the Church and as such is an indefectible property. While indefectibility entails that the Church will always *be* the Roman Catholic Church, visibility entails that it will always *be recognized* as the Roman Catholic Church. The Baltimore Catechism explains that the true Church must be visible because its founder, Jesus Christ, commanded us under pain of condemnation to hear the Church, which He could not in justice do if the Church could not be seen or known.[333]

The Catholic Encyclopedia explains the Church is a society that will always be conspicuous and public and that it will always be recognized among other bodies as the Church of Christ. *Material visibility* means it must be a public profession and a society manifest to the world. *Formal visibility* is secured by the four notes of the Church—unity, sanctity, catholicity, and apostolicity. Visible unity entails that the Church's members throughout the world will always be united by the profession of the same

---

332 Dimond, *The Truth*, 331.
333 "Baltimore Catechism No. 3."

faith, participation in common worship, and obedience to a common authority. All hold the same belief, join in the same religious ceremonies, and acknowledge the successor of Peter as their supreme ruler. The Church must be one essentially and visibly.[334]

Catholic apologists Bryan Cross and Thomas Brown explained that the Church's unity is visible since it is the unity of a body, and bodies are both visible and hierarchically organized. The Church's visibility is not reducible merely to the visibility of its members; the Church per se is visible like a human body and must remain perceptible to the senses.[335]

Three interdependent bonds of unity are essence, activity, and hierarchy. Unity of the Church must include an essentially unified, visible hierarchy.[336] The fourth principal heresy of Sedevacantism is that visible hierarchical unity is accidental to the Catholic Church. Cross and Brown also explained why hierarchical unity requires a singular visible head in collaboration with the Church's teachings that the Roman Pontiff, as Peter's successor, is the perpetual and visible source and foundation of the unity of the whole Church.[337]

Dimond divided doctrines in order to make them fit his version of Sedevacantism, such as defining the Church's visibility as *"real Catholic faithful who externally profess the one true religion."*[338] Dimond's definition is deficient, misleading, and similar to Protestantism's invisible Church ecclesiology. Dimond also stated that the Church could cease to exist in all geographical locations provided a handful of faithful exists somewhere. Dimond erred about the geographical locations in which the Church may or may not defect and in his understanding of what constitutes defection. Individual sees may defect but never the Roman See. Geographical territories or dioceses defect when their governing sees defect, not necessarily the faithful. Bishops, not the faithful, form

---

334 Joyce, *The Catholic Encyclopedia*, 753.
335 "Christ Founded a Visible Church."
336 Ibid.
337 Vatican Council II, *"Lumen Gentium,"* 31.
338 Dimond, *The Truth*, 331.

an essential part of the Church's constitution. Even if the Holy See relocated to a satellite location, it must remain visible and identifiable.

Because visibility is a permanent property belonging to the Church, Roman Catholic faithful must dismiss prophecies or commentaries interpreted in a way that undermines the Church's indefectible constitution. I addressed and refuted Dimond's contradictory interpretations in favor of the Sedevacantist thesis.

Dimond promotes the first school of Sedevacantism, which is that self-appointed men constitute the legitimate hierarchy of the Catholic Church. Self-appointed men do not belong to the ecclesiastical hierarchy of the Church even if they attain the power of orders. Apostolicity must include both material and formal elements. The formal element includes full apostolic power. Sedevacantist clergy are deficient of the necessary elements of apostolicity and must rely on an intangible conception of the Church to supply it. If the Church has to supply the components of apostolic succession in order to prevent its expiration, the means instituted by Christ for its transmittance—*succession via a series of persons*—has ended, and the Church would have defected. Sedevacantism destroys apostolic succession and unity, contravenes indefectibility, and begins a new series of bishops. The fifth principal Sedevacantist heresy is that apostolic authority is accidental to the episcopal order.

Dimond proposed that ordinary jurisdiction disappeared from the true Church, leaving only supplied jurisdiction. However, the Church teaches that the authority of the apostles and the episcopal order belong to the essential constitution of the Church. At present an apostolic hierarchy possessing ordinary jurisdiction is visibly identifiable to the world in general, or the Catholic Church has defected according to its own terms. Dimond tacitly, albeit correctly, recognized apostolicity in the Vatican II hierarchy under Pope Francis, with whom he communicates.

Objections

Objection: When the Church was born on Pentecost, only the closest disciples could see the Church, whereas the rest of the world could not. This proves that the Church's visibility does not mean all must always see the Church. It has also been predicted that in the end-times, the Church would be unseen by the majority of the world.

Answer: 1. On Pentecost three thousand souls were baptized and added to the Church[339] *because* the Church was visible and known. **2.** If scripture or prophecies are interpreted in any way that contradicts Catholic doctrines, the faithful must dismiss them—*even if the interpretation is true.*

Objection: In your last answer, you erred in saying that interpretations of prophecies could contradict Roman doctrines and still be true.

Answer: Prophecies and scripture passages that contradict Catholic doctrines could be true when Catholic doctrines are false. Furthermore, not all prophecies or quotes Catholics use are from periods or personages that would have recognized the doctrines of the papacy.

Objection: There have been numerous periods of persecution in the history of the Church where the faithful were deprived of the sacraments.

---
339 Acts 2:41.

The Japanese persecution[340] is one example where the faithful did not have a visible Church for a very long time. This proves the Church is not always visible.

Answer: It is reasonable to assume that the Japanese persecution does not contradict visibility when one considers that a Japanese Catholic would easily have found the Catholic Church if he or she left Japan, as the Catholic Church remained visible to the world in general.

Objection: You criticize Sedevacantists for using prophecies, but prophecies are an important part of both the Old and New Testaments. Moreover, Our Lord predicted that in the end-times the deception would be so great even the elect would be deceived.[341] This fits perfectly with what Sedevacantists claim has happened to the Church in the twentieth century.

Answer: 1. Sedevacantists must decide which takes precedence, prophecies or doctrines of the faith. If the answer is doctrines of the faith then prophecies that apparently contradict them cannot be used to support the Sedevacantists. For example many Sedevacantists cite the messages of *La Salette* in order to claim that the Roman See has or will become the seat of the Antichrist. However, that alleged prophecy is heretical. 2. The scriptural prophecy that in the end-times *"even the elect could be deceived"* (Matthew 24:24) could never be applicable to the faithful who are believing and practicing what God commands them to believe and practice. In other words if the Roman Catholic Church is the one true Church of Christ, it is impossible for the faithful to be

---

340 "Kakure Kirishitan, (Japanese: 'Hidden Christians'), descendants of the first Japanese converts to Christianity who, driven underground by 1650, managed to maintain their faith in secret for more than two centuries." ("Kakure Kirishitan," *Encyclopædia Britannica Online*, accessed March 05, 2015, http://www.britannica.com/EBchecked/topic/309931/Kakure-Kirishitan.)

341 Matt. 24:24: "For there shall arise false Christs and false prophets, and shall shew great signs and wonders, insomuch as to deceive (if possible) even the elect."

tricked into following the Antichrist while maintaining unity with the Roman See.

Objection: Yes, you are right that the elect could never be tricked into following the Antichrist by maintaining unity with the Roman See, which is exactly why Sedevacantists are not deceived into maintaining unity with the false claimants to the papacy! Sedevacantists are the elect of which Our Lord speaks.

Answer: It is de fide that the faithful are to remain in communion with the Roman See; it is not de fide that the faithful are to be in communion with the Roman See only when it is occupied by a Catholic. The reason is that the Church teaches elsewhere that the Roman See cannot defect, lose the faith, disappear, or be taken over by enemies, apostates, heretics, or the Antichrist. Furthermore if dogmas are infallible, divinely revealed truths then it is impossible for the faithful to be deceived when adhering to them. If any Sedevacantist disagrees, let him produce the dogma that states the faithful must examine, pass judgment on, and monitor the Holy See for orthodoxy *before* establishing communion and consenting to its authority. Second, being that the Church must be visible, let the Sedevacantists identify the real one. Until convincing proofs are produced of the material existence of the Holy See, we can be certain that if heretics, apostates, or the Antichrist himself is presently ruling the Roman See, the Catholic Church defected.

Objection: Sedevacantists are in communion with the Holy See. The Holy See is synonymous with all of the true doctrines defined by true popes and councils up until 1958.

Answer: Let us briefly review the correct understanding of the Holy See:

> **Holy See:** The term means, in a general sense, the actual seat (i.e., residence) of the supreme pastor of the Church, together with the various ecclesiastical authorities who constitute the central administration…

In the canonical and diplomatic sense, the term is synonymous with "Apostolic See," "Holy See," "Holy Apostolic See," "Roman Church," "Roman Curia."[342]

The Code of Canon Law (1983)
Can. 360 The Supreme Pontiff usually conducts the business of the universal Church through the Roman Curia, which acts in his name and with his authority for the good and for the service of the Churches. The Curia is composed of the Secretariat of State or Papal Secretariat, the Council for the public affairs of the Church, the Congregations, the Tribunals and other Institutes. The constitution and competence of all these is defined by special law.[343]

Can. 361 In this Code the terms Apostolic See or Holy See mean not only the Roman Pontiff, but also, unless the contrary is clear from the nature of things or from the context, the Secretariat of State, the Council for the public affairs of the Church, and the other Institutes of the Roman Curia.[344]

The **Holy See** (Latin: *Sancta Sedes*) is the episcopal jurisdiction of the Roman Catholic Church in Rome. The primacy of Rome makes its bishop, commonly known as the Pope, the worldwide leader of the Church. Since Rome is the preeminent episcopal see of the Roman Catholic Church, it contains the central government of the Church, including various agencies essential to administration. Diplomatically, the Holy See acts and speaks for the whole Roman Catholic Church. The Pope governs the Catholic Church through the Roman Curia. The Roman Curia consists of a complex of offices that administer Church affairs at the highest level, including the Secretariat of State, nine Congregations, three Tribunals, eleven Pontifical Councils, and seven Pontifical Commissions.[345]

---

342 Baumgarten, *The Catholic Encyclopedia*, Vol. 7, 424.
343 "The Code of Canon Law 1983," last modified February 27, 2011, http://www.holyrosaryprovince.org/2011/media/essencial/code_of_canon_law_1983.pdf.
344 Ibid.
345 "Holy See."

Roman Curia: Strictly speaking, the ensemble of departments or ministries which assist the sovereign pontiff in the government of the Universal Church. These are the Roman Congregations, the tribunals, and the offices of Curia (*Ufficii di Curia*).[346]

As we can see, the Sedevacantists are certainly not in communion with the Holy See. In fact according to the Sedevacantist thesis, the Holy See no longer exists. For example consider that Sedevacantists do not possess a Roman Pontiff, a College of Cardinals, or a single member of the Roman Curia. The Sedevacantists cannot even identify a cardinal camerlengo[347] who should be responsible for important affairs of the Church during a legitimate period of sede vacante. Sedevacantists believe that all of the aforementioned components of the Holy See are in the possession of heretics, apostates, or the Antichrist. With the exception of Dimond and others who receive sacraments from priests in communion with Pope Francis, the strictest of the Sedevacantists do not have any legitimate, material connection to the Holy See and are certainly not in communion with it.

Objection: Sedevacantists do not deny that jurisdiction still exists in the Church; they only deny that ordinary jurisdiction exists. Clearly the Church supplies jurisdiction to bishops and priests in the traditional Catholic movement during this unprecedented crisis for the good of souls.

Answer: If the Church must *supply* jurisdiction in order to preserve apostolicity because it ran out of men who could legitimately pass it on,

---

346 Ojetti, *The Catholic Encyclopedia*, Vol. 13, 147.
347 An Italian chamberlain. There are three ecclesiastical persons in Rome who carry this title: 1. camerlengo of the Holy Roman Church, who administers the revenue and property of the Holy See, verifies the death of the Pope, directs preparations, and manages the conclave for election of a new pontiff; 2. camerlengo of the Sacred College, who is in charge of property and revenues of the college, pontificates at Mass for deceased cardinals, and registers all consistorial business; and 3. camerlengo of the Roman clergy, elected by canons and parish priests of Rome, who presides over their conferences and is arbiter in questions of precedence. (Hardon, *Modern Catholic Dictionary*, 77.)

then apostolicity or apostolic succession as instituted by Jesus Christ and as defined by the Church has officially ended. That, of course, would constitute defection.

Objection: You claimed that the First Vatican Council teaches that the power of the apostolic primacy is an arrested power without a Roman Pontiff to exercise it, but you are wrong. One example proving you are wrong is that the Church can sometimes supply jurisdiction for clergy in the absence of a pope. This proves that the power of the primacy can be exercised without a pope and that your interpretation of the First Vatican Council is wrong.

Answer: First, I supported my understanding of the First Vatican Council. Second, if the primacy can be exercised when there is no pope in office then the Church does not *really* need a pope. True as that may be, it is certainly contradictory to the dogmatic doctrines on the papacy. In this example supplied jurisdiction essentially separates the primacy of the Roman See from that of the Roman Pontiff. However, the teaching of the Church on the relationship between the authority of the Roman See and the Roman Pontiff is that no separation is permitted.[348] Essentially the chair and the pope are considered one and the same, which should make access and utilization of the primacy impossible when no pope exists. Accordingly, supplied jurisdiction ought to be impossible

---

[348] "From ancient times a distinction has been made between the Apostolic See and its actual occupant: between *sedes* and *sedens*. The object of the distinction is not to discriminate between the two nor to subordinate one to the other, but rather to set forth their intimate connection. The See is the symbol of the highest papal authority; it is, by its nature, permanent, whereas its occupant holds that authority but for a time and inasmuch as he sits in the Chair of Peter. It further implies that take supreme authority is a supernatural gift, the same in all successive holders, independent of their personal worth, and inseparable from their ex-officio definitions and decisions. The Vatican definition of the pope's infallibility when speaking *ex cathedra* does not permit of the sense attached to the distinction of *sedes* and *sedens* by the Gallicans, who claimed that even in the official use of the authority vested in the See, with explicit declaration of its exercise, the *sedens* was separate from the *sedes*." (Wilhelm, *The Catholic Encyclopedia*, Vol. 1, 641.)

when there is no pope in office. Third, I am not an apologist for Catholic doctrinal contradictions, of which there are many to be found.

Objection: If you accept St. Vincent Ferrer as a licit priest despite the fact that he received his mission to preach and hear confessions from an antipope during the Great Western Schism then you cannot hold that no independent priests hold jurisdiction today.[349]

Answer: The above objection comes from Dimond's refutation article against those who argue that Sedevacantist priests and bishops do not have jurisdiction. Obviously Dimond does not realize that he refutes his own argument in that very same article (emphasis added): "Even though he [St. Vincent Ferrer] was never 'sent' or commissioned to preach in the official and normal fashion by any ordinary, *Our Lord specifically called him to preach…*"[350]

Vincent Ferrer allegedly received an extraordinary mission from God and proved it by miracles. God gave a similar mission to St. Paul. Let any Sedevacantists prove their extraordinary mission from God by performing miracles, and I will concede this argument. I nominate Dimond to go first.

Objection: Concerning jurisdiction, you are confusing human ecclesiastical laws with divine laws. The crucial distinction is between the necessity to have jurisdiction, which is divine law, and the way that jurisdiction is dispensed in the Church, which is of ecclesiastical law.[351] Therefore there is no contradiction in the fact that the Church can suspend its laws on how jurisdiction is normally

---

349 "Facts Which Demolish the 'No Independent Priest Today Has Jurisdiction' Position," last modified September 1, 2011, http://www.mostholyfamilymonastery.com/jurisdiction.pdf.
350 Ibid., 18.
351 Ibid., 12–13.

dispensed and supply it directly to Sedevacantist clergy in this unprecedented situation.

Answer: The argument's premise is bogus. That the Church can endure catastrophic crises that may warrant *supplied jurisdiction* to its lawfully ordained clergy in certain instances via the Church's apostolic hierarchy is very different from saying the Church can endure catastrophic crises that warrant the Church *supplying an apostolic hierarchy*. The former is not the reason jurisdiction is not supplied to Sedevacantist clergy; rather it is because the perceived crisis (i.e., that there is no lawful authority from whom to receive authority remaining in the Church) is impossible. According to indefectibility, the Church cannot have a crisis that would necessitate self-appointment to the hierarchy of orders or hierarchy of jurisdiction. In other words if self-constituted men must step in and govern the Church, the reason is that the Church would have defected in its authority, hierarchy, and sacraments. As stated repeatedly in this work, the Sedevacantists erroneously believe they can have the doctrine of indefectibility *and* a great apostasy. For the Sedevacantists, however, either no lawful authority exists from whom to receive authority because the Church defected or else the Vatican II hierarchy under Francis is it.

Objection: Bishops do not always receive ordinary jurisdiction, as in the case of titular bishops, thus proving that ordinary jurisdiction is not a permanent attribute in the Church.

Answer: 1. Jesus Christ instituted ordinary jurisdiction at the foundation of the Church, and it belongs to the Church's essential constitution; it can never be lacking. **2.** Apostolic authority is transmitted by way of human successors because that is how Christ arranged it. Accordingly a need could never arise for groups such as the Sedevacantists to claim that the Church supplies jurisdiction to them. **3.** Sedevacantists employ backward thinking in that the Church supplies jurisdiction to self-appointed men who in turn will have to restore ordinary jurisdiction (heresy) once they find a way to restore the papacy (heresy). The correct Catholic thinking is that the papacy will never need restoration, and men with ordinary jurisdiction will always exist. Accordingly a need for self-constituted Sedevacantists should never exist. The only reason they do exist is that the Catholic Church defected in reality.

Objection: The Vatican II Church altered the rites of the sacraments. In several cases they tampered with the sacramental form, matter, and intention, which clearly invalidates them per the teaching of the "true" Church prior to Vatican II. Therefore, aside from Eastern Rite Roman Catholic sacraments, the Vatican II hierarchy cannot possibly carry on apostolicity. In many cases they are not even valid priests and bishops due to a defect in the new rites of priestly and episcopal ordinations.

Answer: 1. It is true that the Catholic Church altered its sacraments following Vatican II in such a way that the changes conflict with pre–Vatican II theology as well as the "required" *form, matter,* and *intention* for validity.[352] Such changes constitute a defection. **2.** It is also true that none of the various Sedevacantist sects is the true Catholic Church unless the Sedevacantists are willing to forego the Roman Church's divinely laid foundation as well as several of its other properties, attributes, and characteristics addressed in this work. **3.** Because it is true that the Vatican II Church defected and that the Sedevacantists cannot be considered the true Church, each Sedevacantist must decide for himself or herself whether it is more plausible to believe that the Catholic Church contradicted itself or that the Catholic Church invalidated itself. Either way Sedevacantism is out of the question.

---

352 For a comprehensive analysis on the changes to the New Mass, see the Rev. Anthony Cekada's book *Work of Human Hands—A Theological Critique of the Mass of Paul VI* (West Chester, OH: Philothea Press, 2010).

Conclusion

THE FOUR OBJECTIONS TO SEDEVACANTISM that I chose to address correlate to the Catholic Church's essential constitution. As established, the Sedevacantist thesis cannot explain the contradictions between the pre– and post–Vatican II Church without contradicting fundamental doctrines specific to the Church's essential constitution. Among other things these doctrines include *indefectibility of the Church, the necessity of the Vicar of Christ, the Roman Papacy as the Church's foundation, visible hierarchical unity,* and *apostolicity.* Furthermore the Sedevacantists' responses to these objections contained principal heresies upon which the Sedevacantist thesis lies. These heresies were identified as follows:

In response to objection one, Dimond argued that Sedevacantism does not entail a defection of the Church provided at least a remnant of faithful exists *somewhere*. I refuted Dimond's position with an examination of the doctrine of indefectibility and an overview of the Church's essential constitution, which above all else must include the Church's divinely laid foundation comprised of four mutually dependent components identified as the papacy. I demonstrated that regardless of how the Sedevacantists attempt to justify their theory, Sedevacantism fails because it always entails a defection of the Church to its foundation. In remarkable similarity to the Eastern Orthodox Church, the Sedevacantists condemn the Roman Church for its fall into heresy and apostasy, which fundamental premise incontrovertibly entails a defection of the Church according to its own terms. Sedevacantist heresy: A defection of the Church occurred in fact.

In response to objection five, Dimond argued that a forty-year papal interregnum does not contradict the Church's indefectibility, but I exposed Dimond's strategy of using the term *interregnum* as an attempt to camouflage the Sedevacantists' real position that the Church defected. Because the Sedevacantists argue that the Church has no teaching or law that puts a limitation on how long papal interregnums can last, it follows that the Sedevacantists must also believe papal interregnums can last indefinitely, even a thousand or more years, in order to remain consistent. I demonstrated why the Vicar of Christ belongs to the Church's essential constitution and why indefinite vacancies of the papacy would be contradictory. If the Church could exist and function without a Vicar of Christ then by definition he is not essential but accidental. Regardless of whether that is true in reality, an accidental Vicar of Christ was shown to be completely incongruent with the dogmatic teachings on the papacy.

Additionally the Sedevacantist theory based on papal interregnums opened the door for criticisms of the papacy. The occurrence of all papal vacancies undermines the papacy and supports the Eastern Orthodox Church's position that the later rendition of the Roman papacy was a fabrication that evolved over the centuries as opposed to being the divinely laid foundation of the Church. Sedevacantist heresy: The Vicar of Christ is accidental to the Church.

In response to objection six, Dimond argued that the First Vatican Council's dogmatic constitution *Pastor Aeternus* is not contradictory to the Sedevacantist thesis, but an examination of the dogmatic constitution proved that it is. The first two passages Dimond cited required the Sedevacantists to disclaim the necessity of a connection to the Church's material foundation for the important reason that they cannot account for it. Aside from the fact that the disintegration of the Holy See constitutes a defection of the whole Catholic Church, I demonstrated why the Sedevacantists also cannot account for the other constituent components of the papacy. Because the primacy functions through a mutually dependent system comprised of the Apostle Peter, Rome, and the Roman Pontiff, it cannot stand alone without frustrating the end for which it exists—unity of the Church.

Sedevacantism's fundamental premise, which is based on the defection of Rome, forces its adherents, such as Dimond, to improvise a heretical ecclesiology that I have termed "the papacy of desire." We saw how Dimond's papacy of desire erred in two ways: first by dividing the components of the papacy in order to claim some portion of it, second by falsely teaching that the Holy See need not exist materially, only spiritually. Thus Dimond's ecclesiology is that membership and unity of the Church are attained by one's *desire* to be united to what is essentially an invisible Church. Thus with the assistance of Dimond, who provided an example of Eastern Orthodox conversions to the Sedevacantist position, I demonstrated how and why Sedevacantism always ends in schism.

The third and final passage Dimond addressed contradicted the Sedevacantists because the term *perpetual* in the dogmatic constitution's canon that declared "perpetual successors in the primacy" is equivalent to *uninterrupted* succession (i.e., popes will follow each other in an unbroken chain). Of course the Sedevacantists' theory of six successive antipopes ruling the Holy See contradicts the council's intended meaning of "perpetual successors." Lastly the dogmatic teachings on the papacy contradicted themselves as well as the actual papacy, once again lending support to the Eastern Orthodox Church and its stance against the papacy since AD 1054. Sedevacantist heresy: Papacy of desire is sufficient for membership in and visible unity of the Church.

In response to objection fifteen, Dimond argued that a handful of faithful constitutes the Church's visible unity and that a self-appointed, impotent episcopacy constitutes apostolicity. However, I refuted Dimond's definition of the Church's visibility, as visibility is far more than just a remnant of faithful who externally profess the Catholic religion. Visibility requires material and formal elements and a visibly unified hierarchy under Rome, not merely scattered faithful, priests, or bishops.

Conclusion

Dimond also erred in arguing that apostolicity could exist without the fullness of apostolic authority or the means of transmission as established by Jesus Christ from the foundation of the Church. The means of transmission of apostolic authority established by Christ is human succession, which the Sedevacantists must deny for the reason that their theory proposes that the Church ran out of men who could legitimately pass it on. Sedevacantist heresies: 1. Visible hierarchical unity is accidental to the Catholic Church. 2. Apostolic authority is accidental to the episcopal order.

Overall the Sedevacantist thesis that proposes the existence of two Churches (i.e., a "true" Church versus a false/imposter sect) is heretical because its premise necessitates that a defection of the Roman Church occurred in any capacity. Among other things, this conclusion is confirmed by the fact that the Sedevacantists cannot demonstrate an uninterrupted existence of the Holy See from the moment a papal vacancy purportedly first began to the present day as well as how any Sedevacantist sect possesses all of the Catholic Church's indefectible properties, attributes, and essential components addressed in this work.

Even still, the Catholic Church contradicted itself and promulgated numerous heresies with the documents and reforms of Vatican II. How can this be explained? The only explanation that does not require the faithful to hold contradictory positions is that the Catholic Church is not now nor ever has been the infallible Church it claims to be. Sedevacantism is especially supportive of this assertion because its adherents must eventually challenge the historical papacy itself if they are to stay consistent. In fact this trend can already be seen by certain Sedevacantists who now propose the purported papal interregnum began as early as Pope Pius IX (1846–1878). However, the most reasonable starting point for challenging the papacy is neither Vatican II nor Pope Pius IX but rather the East-West schism. Thus Sedevacantism followed to its logical conclusion challenges the papacy over the course of a millennium and effectively nails the blame for the AD 1054 schism between

Rome and the Eastern Orthodox Church onto the doors of St. Peter's Basilica.

And so if an entity exists today that could be called "the true Church of Christ," the Sedevacantists have provided an invaluable service to Eastern Orthodox Christianity by exposing the Roman Church's defection with Vatican II while simultaneously disqualifying themselves and every other purported "substitute" Roman Catholic Church in the process. Ironically the Sedevacantists now find themselves in the same boat (i.e., schism) as the Eastern Orthodox Church for essentially the same reason—each refused to let Rome get away with changing core doctrines of the Catholic faith that had already been defined, unanimously understood, and so imparted to the universal Church for centuries.

In conclusion, the Catholic Church contradicted itself at Vatican II because it can. Not only *can* the Church contradict itself, *it has done* so, yet it remains the Roman Catholic Church of the ages. Only in that sense can it be truthfully stated that the Catholic Church is indefectible.

Afterword

INFORMATION TECHNOLOGY HAS INTRODUCED AN unprecedented opportunity for ordinary people to substantiate the claims of powerful institutions such as churches and governments. Were our societies not cultivated to idealize and revere our institutions, the power of information sharing might go a long way in advancing the cause of freedom. Even still, I anticipate that freedom of information will vanish in a whirlwind once it has solidified our transition into the *Novus Ordo Saclorum*. At least for the time being, those who do endeavor to look where they are not supposed to look can have some satisfaction in knowing how their cherished institutions have been lying to them all along. Consequently I often find myself wondering how in the New Age we will be less free.[353]

The Second Vatican Council was a pivotal event in the history of Christianity. From that time forward, the faithful will be trained to look back on the transformation of the Catholic Church as they do the transformation of the one true religion of the Old Testament to the religion of the New Testament (i.e., by divine ordinance, what was is no more and never shall be again). Interestingly the Sedevacantists have played no small part in mending *Church past* with *Church present* despite each side's disdain for the other.

---

[353] German philosopher and poet Johann Wolfgang von Goethe wrote, "None are more hopelessly enslaved than those who falsely believe they are free." Essentially, then, my work has been about coming to terms with reality.

Afterword

The great irony here is that the Sedevacantist movement, which ostensibly exists for defending the "true" Church, should eventually earn the recognition it deserves for its outstanding contributions against it.[354] This explains why most Catholics pretend that the Sedevacantist movement does not exist, for those who have attempted to dance with the Sedevacantists have surely discovered why it is impossible to refute them without incriminating themselves along with the entire Catholic Church. Of course, as I was able to demonstrate, the Sedevacantists face the identical problem, although to this point they have not understood. Hence if Vatican II is viewed through the correct lenses, we can see that the modern Church dug up more than a few important skeletons while leveling its beautiful cathedrals in order to make way for its New Age temples, and the Sedevacantists tried to hide them before they could be seen. However, the Sedevacantists only exposed the bones all the more by pretending they are the "true" Church *after* proving Rome's defection. This is precisely why Vatican II's collision with the Sedevacantists ultimately lends tremendous support to Eastern Orthodoxy. You see, when one finally determines that neither the Sedevacantists nor the modern Roman Church is what they claim themselves to be, it becomes imperative to revisit the historical origins of the claims.

In light of the facts, what are the Sedevacantists supposed to do? Am I proposing that the Sedevacantists should rush to convert to the Eastern Orthodox Church? I am proposing no such thing. Every person's faith journey is his or her own business. However, what I do wish to point out is that Sedevacantism teaches an important lesson about the risk of idealizing our institutions, be they churches, governments, or other. The lesson is that we should remain watchful for cues that signal the time to quit, exit, or withdraw from controlling systems. The risk in missing those cues is that we will continue mistaking illusions for reality. Withdrawing from a system essentially means to cease participating in a transfer of power. While it may not always be necessary or possible

---

354 As new Sedevacantist sects enter the fray with a primary directive to seek and destroy rival Sedevacantists, this movement will eventually destroy itself.

to exit a system in a physical way, withdrawal can still be achieved completely or in part by severing emotional and intellectual attachments to the illusions a system projects in order to protect and maintain its power.

In general a necessity to quit or exit a controlling system arises if two conditions are simultaneously present. First, when it is impossible to win or attain a desired outcome (e.g., truth, justice, inerrancy, etc.) while honoring that system's established rules and leadership. Second, and more importantly, when remaining attached to a system becomes harmful to one's quality of life. When both conditions are present, the transfer of power is always negative (i.e., disempowering) for the individual because not only is he or she supporting a system that cannot fulfill its obligations or its stated purpose for being, but also the individual is forced to bear the system's fault because it cannot do so.

In the realm of religion, government, and even family, transferring the fault for a system's failures to individual members is a necessary action; otherwise the system would be exposed. This is especially observable among the Sedevacantists and other traditional Catholics who never cease accusing *the members* of the Church for the Vatican II revolution instead of the infallible institution as a whole. Their mind-set is that if only the members of the Church were not such horrible sinners, if only individual Catholics had not failed to pray, tithe, do penance, and sacrifice more, none of this would have happened.[355] A poisonous, shame-based mentality that says we are never good enough or holy enough is internalized and subsequently transmitted onto others while the faulty system is always given an exemption.

---

355 One notorious example of guilt-driven self-punishment proliferating among traditional Catholics today is in response to the so-called "messages of Our Lady of Fatima," whereby these faithful continue praying earnestly for a conversion of Russia while petitioning the Holy See to consecrate Russia to the Immaculate Heart of Mary. Oddly enough the next consecration of Russia by a pope would mark the eighth consecration dating to 1942. Evidently the "messages of heaven" were of such urgent importance that popes seem to have struggled repeatedly with following "heaven's" instructions. This, of course, has fostered a never-ending Fatima saga and allowed the Fatima enterprise to thrive for a hundred years despite the probability that the messages and alleged miracles of Fatima were a hoax all along.

Afterword

The Sedevacantists have gone quite far in challenging the Church of Rome and taken their licks from the mainstream for doing so. Even still, they ultimately forfeit their power by maintaining emotional and intellectual attachments to the very system that created their plight.[356] The Sedevacantists' refusal to let go of the concept of an infallible Church in the aftermath of Vatican II is why all Sedevacantists maintain the delusion that *they* are that Church; after all, in their minds, it *had to go somewhere*. In reality it never existed.

And so at least the first criterion for the necessity of quitting a system is present for all Sedevacantists, as it is impossible to win or attain their desired outcome while simultaneously honoring and upholding that system's established rules or leadership. Whether or not the second criterion for exiting that system (when remaining in it becomes harmful to quality of life) is simultaneously present for the Sedevacantists is not something on which I could or would presume to make a general judgment.[357] That determination is personal to each Sedevacantist who endeavors to conduct a personal inventory of all of the ways the Sedevacantist ideology affects his or her life. My point is that we can now understand that *if* both conditions exist, emotional and intellectual detachment from the system is the most profitable action.

Elisabeth Kübler-Ross identified five stages of grief following significant loss: denial, anger, bargaining, depression, and acceptance. For the Sedevacantists the significant loss is obvious—the "true" Church. Unfortunately the Sedevacantists have not passed through the first

---

356 In a similar vein, many astute Americans who become aware of the plethora of contradictions, falsifications, and impossible physics concerning the so-called 9/11 terrorist attacks continue casting their votes in national elections and writing letters to their elected representatives and to the media, demanding that the government conducts another investigation. Here, similar to the Sedevacantists, the "9/11 truther" remains attached to the system and its illusions of free elections and the press, but his or her time could be used more profitably watching comedian Carlin's skit on not voting.

357 I do not agree that maintaining the Sedevacantist delusion is necessarily detrimental to one's life. Sedevacantists can surely make a convincing argument that observance of a traditional Catholic lifestyle, with its strict code of morals and values, is a better and safer alternative to the modern culture. Nevertheless Sedevacantism is still a delusion.

stage: denial. They are in denial that the "true" Church, which simply means *the Church as they subjectively understand it*, defected somewhere between 1958 and 1965 and that because it defected, they are not it. In reality the pre- and post-Vatican II Churches are different facets of the same Church. Moreover, all Sedevacantists are heretics and schismatics for attempting to hold the Church to its own doctrines.

The Sedevacantists will pass through the denial stage when they realize *why* both they and the modern Church of Rome are simultaneously wrong and right. This was the objective of this work, and if I have been successful in conveying it, it should bring a certain peace to the Sedevacantists because it effectively transfers the contradictions that the Church unjustly imposes upon its faithful members back to the Church, where they emanated from and so deservedly belong. Perhaps the Sedevacantists will then understand that Vatican II was the work of neither Satan nor the Holy Ghost but rather, like the great schism between the East and the West, the First Vatican Council and numerous other landmark moments throughout the ages…just politics.

Lastly, the acceptance stage for the Sedevacantists may eventually follow in either of two very different ways. The first is that they will accept that the Church is still the Church, forgive it for its fallibility, and enter into communion with modern Rome.[358] In this way they will be able to detach from certain illusions that the Roman system projects and cease participating in a negative transfer of power and yet not have to exit the system entirely if they do not want to. Instead they will be able to use the system for all of the good they perceive it to be worth (e.g., hope, fellowship, worship, charity, morality, solace, forgiveness, the sacraments) while simultaneously acknowledging its obvious failures and limitations.

---

358 In numerous ways the post-Vatican II Church has openly conceded the Church's fallibility and many modern Catholics appreciate their Church's willingness to confess its limitations. The faithful's acceptance of the Church's fallibility comes with a strange twist: what they have always freely taken from the Church—forgiveness for their sins—must ultimately be returned to the Church in kind for its own.

Afterword

The second way acceptance may follow is that they will begin their individual searches for God elsewhere. Either way the Sedevacantists must advance beyond denial in order to emancipate themselves from a delusional state that allows them to continue believing that *they* are the "true" Church of Christ.

APPENDIX

Appendix

The Sedevacantist Argument in Brief[359]

1. Officially sanctioned Vatican II and post–Vatican II teachings and laws embody errors and/or promote evil.
2. Because the Church is indefectible, her teaching cannot change, and because she is infallible, her laws cannot give evil.
3. It is therefore impossible that the errors and evils officially sanctioned in Vatican II and post–Vatican II teachings and laws could have proceeded from the authority of the Church.
4. Those who promulgate such errors and evils must somehow lack real authority in the Church.
5. Canonists and theologians teach that defection from the faith, once it becomes manifest, brings with it automatic loss of ecclesiastical office (authority). They apply this principle even to a pope who, in his personal capacity, somehow becomes a heretic.
6. Canonists and theologians also teach that a public heretic, by divine law, is incapable of being validly elected pope or obtaining papal authority.
7. Even popes have acknowledged the possibility that a heretic could one day end up on the throne of Peter. In 1559 Pope Paul IV decreed that the election of a heretic to the papacy would be invalid and that the man elected would lack all authority.
8. Since the Church cannot defect, the best explanation for the post-Vatican II errors and evils we repeatedly encounter is that they proceed from individuals who, despite their occupation of the Vatican and of various diocesan cathedrals, publicly defected from the faith, and therefore do not objectively possess canonical authority.

---

[359] "Sedevacantism: A Quick Primer," last modified July 2015, http://www.fathercekada.com/2013/11/19/sedevacantism-a-quick-primer/.

A Doctrinal Catechism

Q. Must not Catholics believe the Pope in himself to be infallible?

A. This is a Protestant invention; it is no article of the Catholic faith; no decision of his can oblige, under pain of heresy, unless it be received and enforced by the teaching body, that is, by the Bishops of the Church.[360]

---

360 Stephen Keenan, *A Doctrinal Catechism* (New York: Edward Dunigan & Brother, 1848), 305–306.

Appendix

MORTALIUM ANIMOS[361]
ON RELIGIOUS UNITY
ENCYCLICAL OF POPE PIUS XI JANUARY 6, 1928

To Our Venerable Brethren the Patriarchs, Primates, Archbishops, Bishops, and other Local Ordinaries in Peace and Communion with the Apostolic See.

Venerable Brethren, Health and Apostolic Benediction.

Never perhaps in the past have we seen, as we see in these our own times, the minds of men so occupied by the desire both of strengthening and of extending to the common welfare of human society that fraternal relationship which binds and unites us together, and which is a consequence of our common origin and nature. For since the nations do not yet fully enjoy the fruits of peace—indeed rather do old and new disagreements in various places break forth into sedition and civic strife—and since on the other hand many disputes which concern the tranquillity and prosperity of nations cannot be settled without the active concurrence and help of those who rule the States and promote their interests, it is easily understood, and the more so because none now dispute the unity of the human race, why many desire that the various nations, inspired by this universal kinship, should daily be more closely united one to another.

2. A similar object is aimed at by some, in those matters which concern the New Law promulgated by Christ our Lord. For since they hold it for certain that men destitute of all religious sense are very rarely to be found, they seem to have founded on that belief a hope that the nations, although they differ among themselves in certain religious matters, will without much difficulty come to agree as brethren in professing certain doctrines, which form as it were a common basis of the spiritual life. For which reason conventions, meetings and addresses are frequently arranged by these persons, at which a large number of listeners are present, and at which all without distinction are invited

---
361 "*Mortalium Animos*," Papal Encyclicals Online, accessed May 4, 2015, http://www.papalencyclicals.net/Pius11/P11MORTA.HTM.

to join in the discussion, both infidels of every kind, and Christians, even those who have unhappily fallen away from Christ or who with obstinacy and pertinacity deny His divine nature and mission. Certainly such attempts can nowise be approved by Catholics, founded as they are on that false opinion which considers all religions to be more or less good and praiseworthy, since they all in different ways manifest and signify that sense which is inborn in us all, and by which we are led to God and to the obedient acknowledgment of His rule. Not only are those who hold this opinion in error and deceived, but also in distorting the idea of true religion they reject it, and little by little. turn aside to naturalism and atheism, as it is called; from which it clearly follows that one who supports those who hold these theories and attempt to realize them, is altogether abandoning the divinely revealed religion.

3. But some are more easily deceived by the outward appearance of good when there is question of fostering unity among all Christians.

4. Is it not right, it is often repeated, indeed, even consonant with duty, that all who invoke the name of Christ should abstain from mutual reproaches and at long last be united in mutual charity? Who would dare to say that he loved Christ, unless he worked with all his might to carry out the desires of Him, Who asked His Father that His disciples might be "one." [John xvii, 21.] And did not the same Christ will that His disciples should be marked out and distinguished from others by this characteristic, namely that they loved one another: "By this shall all men know that you are my disciples, if you have love one for another"? [John xiii, 35.] All Christians, they add, should be as "one": for then they would be much more powerful in driving out the pest of irreligion, which like a serpent daily creeps further and becomes more widely spread, and prepares to rob the Gospel of its strength. These things and others that class of men who are known as pan-Christians continually repeat and amplify; and these men, so far from being quite few and scattered, have increased to the dimensions of an entire class, and have grouped themselves into widely spread societies, most of which are directed by non-Catholics, although they are imbued with varying doctrines concerning the things of faith. This undertaking is so actively promoted as in many places to win for itself the adhesion of a number of

citizens, and it even takes possession of the minds of very many Catholics and allures them with the hope of bringing about such a union as would be agreeable to the desires of Holy Mother Church, who has indeed nothing more at heart than to recall her erring sons and to lead them back to her bosom. But in reality beneath these enticing words and blandishments lies hid a most grave error, by which the foundations of the Catholic faith are completely destroyed.

5. Admonished, therefore, by the consciousness of Our Apostolic office that We should not permit the flock of the Lord to be cheated by dangerous fallacies, We invoke, Venerable Brethren, your zeal in avoiding this evil; for We are confident that by the writings and words of each one of you the people will more easily get to know and understand those principles and arguments which We are about to set forth, and from which Catholics will learn how they are to think and act when there is question of those undertakings which have for their end the union in one body, whatsoever be the manner, of all who call themselves Christians.

6. We were created by God, the Creator of the universe, in order that we might know Him and serve Him; our Author therefore has a perfect right to our service. God might, indeed, have prescribed for man's government only the natural law, which, in His creation, He imprinted on his soul, and have regulated the progress of that same law by His ordinary providence; but He preferred rather to impose precepts, which we were to obey, and in the course of time, namely from the beginnings of the human race until the coming and preaching of Jesus Christ, He Himself taught man the duties which a rational creature owes to its Creator: "God, who at sundry times and in divers manners, spoke in times past to the fathers by the prophets, last of all, in these days, hath spoken to us by his Son."[Heb. i, I seq.] From which it follows that there can be no true religion other than that which is founded on the revealed word of God: which revelation, begun from the beginning and continued under the Old Law, Christ Jesus Himself under the New Law perfected. Now, if God has spoken (and it is historically certain that He has truly spoken), all must see that it is man's duty to believe absolutely God's revelation and to obey implicitly

His commands; that we might rightly do both, for the glory of God and our own salvation, the Only-begotten Son of God founded his Church on earth. Further, We believe that those who call themselves Christians can do no other than believe that a Church, and that Church one, was established by Christ; but if it is further inquired of what nature according to the will of its Author it must be, then all do not agree. A good number of them, for example, deny that the Church of Christ must be visible and apparent, at least to such a degree that it appears as one body of faithful, agreeing in one and the same doctrine under one teaching authority and government; but, on the contrary, they understand a visible Church as nothing else than a Federation, composed of various communities of Christians, even though they adhere to different doctrines, which may even be incompatible one with another. Instead, Christ our Lord instituted his Church as a perfect society, external of its nature and perceptible to the senses, which should carry on in the future the work of the salvation of the human race, under the leadership of one head, [Matt. xvi, 18 seq; Luke xxii, 32; John xxi, 15–17.] with an authority teaching by word of mouth, [Mark xvi, 15.] and by the ministry of the sacraments, the founts of heavenly grace; [John iii, 5; vi, 48–59; xx, 22 seq; cf. Matt. xviii, 18, etc.] for which reason He attested by comparison the similarity of the Church to a kingdom, [Matt. xiii.] to a house, [cf. Matt. xvi, 18.] to a sheepfold, [John x, 16.] and to a flock. [John xxi, 15–17.] This Church, after being so wonderfully instituted, could not, on the removal by death of its Founder and of the Apostles who were the pioneers in propagating it, be entirely extinguished and cease to be, for to it was given the commandment to lead all men, without distinction of time or place, to eternal salvation: "Going therefore, teach ye all nations." [Matt. xxviii, 19.11] In the continual carrying out of this task, will any element of strength and efficiency be wanting to the Church, when Christ himself is perpetually present to it, according to His solemn promise: "Behold I am with you all days, even to the consummation of the world?" [Matt. xxviii, 20. 12] It follows then that the Church of Christ not only exists to-day and always, but is also exactly the same as it was in the time of the Apostles, unless we were to say, which God forbid, either that Christ our Lord could not effect His purpose, or that He erred when He asserted that the gates of hell should never prevail against it. [Matt. xvi, 18.]

7. And here it seems opportune to expound and to refute a certain false opinion, on which this whole question, as well as that complex movement by which non-Catholics seek to bring about the union of the Christian Churches depends. For authors who favor this view are accustomed, times almost without number, to bring forward these words of Christ: "That they all may be one... And there shall be one fold and one shepherd," [John xvii, 21; x, 16.] with this signification however: that Christ Jesus merely expressed a desire and prayer, which still lacks its fulfillment. For they are of the opinion that the unity of faith and government, which is a note of the one true Church of Christ, has hardly up to the present time existed, and does not to-day exist. They consider that this unity may indeed be desired and that it may even be one day attained through the instrumentality of wills directed to a common end, but that meanwhile it can only be regarded as mere ideal. They add that the Church in itself, or of its nature, is divided into sections; that is to say, that it is made up of several Churches or distinct communities, which still remain separate, and although having certain articles of doctrine in common, nevertheless disagree concerning the remainder; that these all enjoy the same rights; and that the Church was one and unique from, at the most, the apostolic age until the first Ecumenical Councils. Controversies therefore, they say, and longstanding differences of opinion which keep asunder till the present day the members of the Christian family, must be entirely put aside, and from the remaining doctrines a common form of faith drawn up and proposed for belief, and in the profession of which all may not only know but feel that they are brothers. The manifold Churches or communities, if united in some kind of universal federation, would then be in a position to oppose strongly and with success the progress of irreligion. This, Venerable Brethren, is what is commonly said. There are some, indeed, who recognize and affirm that Protestantism, as they call it, has rejected, with a great lack of consideration, certain articles of faith and some external ceremonies, which are, in fact, pleasing and useful, and which the Roman Church still retains. They soon, however, go on to say that that Church also has erred, and corrupted the original religion by adding and proposing for belief certain doctrines which are not only alien to the Gospel, but even repugnant to it. Among the chief of these they number that which concerns the

primacy of jurisdiction, which was granted to Peter and to his successors in the See of Rome. Among them there indeed are some, though few, who grant to the Roman Pontiff a primacy of honor or even a certain jurisdiction or power, but this, however, they consider not to arise from the divine law but from the consent of the faithful. Others again, even go so far as to wish the Pontiff Himself to preside over their motley, so to say, assemblies. But, all the same, although many non-Catholics may be found who loudly preach fraternal communion in Christ Jesus, yet you will find none at all to whom it ever occurs to submit to and obey the Vicar of Jesus Christ either in His capacity as a teacher or as a governor. Meanwhile they affirm that they would willingly treat with the Church of Rome, but on equal terms, that is as equals with an equal: but even if they could so act. it does not seem open to doubt that any pact into which they might enter would not compel them to turn from those opinions which are still the reason why they err and stray from the one fold of Christ.

8. This being so, it is clear that the Apostolic See cannot on any terms take part in their assemblies, nor is it anyway lawful for Catholics either to support or to work for such enterprises; for if they do so they will be giving countenance to a false Christianity, quite alien to the one Church of Christ. Shall We suffer, what would indeed be iniquitous, the truth, and a truth divinely revealed, to be made a subject for compromise? For here there is question of defending revealed truth. Jesus Christ sent His Apostles into the whole world in order that they might permeate all nations with the Gospel faith, and, lest they should err, He willed beforehand that they should be taught by the Holy Ghost: [John xvi, 13.] has then this doctrine of the Apostles completely vanished away, or sometimes been obscured, in the Church, whose ruler and defense is God Himself? If our Redeemer plainly said that His Gospel was to continue not only during the times of the Apostles, but also till future ages, is it possible that the object of faith should in the process of time become so obscure and uncertain, that it would be necessary to-day to tolerate opinions which are even incompatible one with another? If this were true, we should have to confess that the coming of the Holy Ghost on the Apostles, and the perpetual indwelling of the same Spirit in the Church, and the very preaching of Jesus Christ, have several

Appendix

centuries ago, lost all their efficacy and use, to affirm which would be blasphemy. But the Only-begotten Son of God, when He commanded His representatives to teach all nations, obliged all men to give credence to whatever was made known to them by "witnesses preordained by God,"[Acts x,41.] and also confirmed His command with this sanction: "He that believeth and is baptized shall be saved; but he that believeth not shall be condemned." [Mark xvi, 16.] These two commands of Christ, which must be fulfilled, the one, namely, to teach, and the other to believe, cannot even be understood, unless the Church proposes a complete and easily understood teaching, and is immune when it thus teaches from all danger of erring. In this matter, those also turn aside from the right path, who think that the deposit of truth such laborious trouble, and with such lengthy study and discussion, that a man's life would hardly suffice to find and take possession of it; as if the most merciful God had spoken through the prophets and His Only-begotten Son merely in order that a few, and those stricken in years, should learn what He had revealed through them, and not that He might inculcate a doctrine of faith and morals, by which man should be guided through the whole course of his moral life.

9. These pan-Christians who turn their minds to uniting the Churches seem, indeed, to pursue the noblest of ideas in promoting charity among all Christians: nevertheless how does it happen that this charity tends to injure faith? Everyone knows that John himself, the Apostle of love, who seems to reveal in his Gospel the secrets of the Sacred Heart of Jesus, and who never ceased to impress on the memories of his followers the new commandment "Love one another," altogether forbade any intercourse with those who professed a mutilated and corrupt version of Christ's teaching: "If any man come to you and bring not this doctrine, receive him not into the house nor say to him: God speed you." [11 John 10.] For which reason, since charity is based on a complete and sincere faith, the disciples of Christ must be united principally by the bond of one faith. Who then can conceive a Christian Federation, the members of which retain each his own opinions and private judgment, even in matters which concern the object of faith, even though they be repugnant to the opinions of the rest? And in what manner, We ask, can men who follow contrary opinions, belong to

one and the same Federation of the faithful? For example, those who affirm, and those who deny that sacred Tradition is a true fount of divine Revelation; those who hold that an ecclesiastical hierarchy, made up of bishops, priests and ministers, has been divinely constituted, and those who assert that it has been brought in little by little in accordance with the conditions of the time; those who adore Christ really present in the Most Holy Eucharist through that marvelous conversion of the bread and wine, which is called transubstantiation, and those who affirm that Christ is present only by faith or by the signification and virtue of the Sacrament; those who in the Eucharist recognize the nature both of a sacrament and of a sacrifice, and those who say that it is nothing more than the memorial or commemoration of the Lord's Supper; those who believe it to be good and useful to invoke by prayer the Saints reigning with Christ, especially Mary the Mother of God, and to venerate their images, and those who urge that such a veneration is not to be made use of, for it is contrary to the honor due to Jesus Christ, "the one mediator of God and men." [Cf. I Tim. ii, 15.] How so great a variety of opinions can make the way clear to effect the unity of the Church We know not; that unity can only arise from one teaching authority, one law of belief and one faith of Christians. But We do know that from this it is an easy step to the neglect of religion or indifferentism and to modernism, as they call it. Those, who are unhappily infected with these errors, hold that dogmatic truth is not absolute but relative, that is, it agrees with the varying necessities of time and place and with the varying tendencies of the mind, since it is not contained in immutable revelation, but is capable of being accommodated to human life. Besides this, in connection with things which must be believed, it is nowise licit to use that distinction which some have seen fit to introduce between those articles of faith which are fundamental and those which are not fundamental, as they say, as if the former are to be accepted by all, while the latter may be left to the free assent of the faithful: for the supernatural virtue of faith has a formal cause, namely the authority of God revealing, and this is patient of no such distinction. For this reason it is that all who are truly Christ's believe, for example, the Conception of the Mother of God without stain of original sin with the same faith as they believe the mystery of the August Trinity, and the Incarnation of our Lord just as they do the infallible teaching authority of the Roman Pontiff, according to the sense in which it was defined by the Ecumenical Council of the Vatican. Are these truths not equally certain, or not equally to be believed, because the Church has solemnly sanctioned and defined them, some in one age and some in another, even in those times immediately before our own? Has not God revealed them all? For the teaching authority of the Church, which in the divine wisdom was constituted on earth in order that revealed doctrines might remain intact for ever, and that they might be brought with ease and security to the knowledge of men, and which is daily exercised through the Roman Pontiff and the Bishops who are in communion with him, has also the office of defining, when it sees fit, any truth with solemn rites and decrees, whenever this is necessary either to oppose the errors or the attacks of heretics, or more clearly and in greater detail to stamp the minds of the faithful with the articles of sacred doctrine which have been explained. But in the use of this extraordinary teaching authority no newly invented matter is brought in, nor is anything new added to the number of those truths which are at least implicitly contained in the deposit of Revelation, divinely handed down to the Church: only those which are made clear which perhaps may still seem obscure to some, or that which some have previously called into question is declared to be of faith.

10. So, Venerable Brethren, it is clear why this Apostolic See has never allowed its subjects to take part in the assemblies of non-Catholics: for the union of Christians can only be promoted by promoting the return to the one true Church of Christ of those who are separated from it, for in the past they have unhappily left it. To the one true Church of Christ, we say, which is visible to all, and which is to remain, according to the will of its Author, exactly the same as He instituted it. During the lapse of centuries, the mystical Spouse of Christ has never been contaminated, nor can she ever in the future be contaminated, as Cyprian bears witness: "The Bride of Christ cannot be made false to her Spouse: she is incorrupt and modest. She knows but one dwelling, she guards the sanctity of the nuptial chamber chastely and modestly." [De Cath. Ecclesiae unitate, 6.] The same holy Martyr with good reason marveled exceedingly that anyone could believe that "this unity in the Church which arises from a divine foundation, and which is knit together by heavenly sacraments, could be rent and torn asunder

by the force of contrary wills." [Ibid.] For since the mystical body of Christ, in the same manner as His physical body, is one, [I Cor. xii, 12.] compacted and fitly joined together, [Eph. Iv, 16.] it were foolish and out of place to say that the mystical body is made up of members which are disunited and scattered abroad: whosoever therefore is not united with the body is no member of it, neither is he in communion with Christ its head. [Cf. Eph. v, 30; 1, 22.]

11. Furthermore, in this one Church of Christ no man can be or remain who does not accept, recognize and obey the authority and supremacy of Peter and his legitimate successors. Did not the ancestors of those who are now entangled in the errors of Photius and the reformers, obey the Bishop of Rome, the chief shepherd of souls? Alas their children left the home of their fathers, but it did not fall to the ground and perish for ever, for it was supported by God. Let them therefore return to their common Father, who, forgetting the insults previously heaped on the Apostolic See, will receive them in the most loving fashion. For if, as they continually state, they long to be united with Us and ours, why do they not hasten to enter the Church, "the Mother and mistress of all Christ's faithful"? [Conc. Lateran IV, c. 5.] Let them hear Lactantius crying out: "The Catholic Church is alone in keeping the true worship. This is the fount of truth, this the house of Faith, this the temple of God: if any man enter not here, or if any man go forth from it, he is a stranger to the hope of life and salvation. Let none delude himself with obstinate wrangling. For life and salvation are here concerned, which will be lost and entirely destroyed, unless their interests are carefully and assiduously kept in mind." [S. Cypr. Ep. 48 ad Cornelium, 3.]

12. Let, therefore, the separated children draw nigh to the Apostolic See, set up in the City which Peter and Paul, the Princes of the Apostles, consecrated by their blood; to that See, We repeat, which is "the root and womb whence the Church of God springs," [I Tim. iii, 15.] not with the intention and the hope that "the Church of the living God, the pillar and ground of the truth" [I Tim. ii, 4.] will cast aside the integrity of the faith and tolerate their errors, but, on the contrary, that they themselves submit to its teaching and government. Would that it were Our happy

lot to do that which so many of Our predecessors could not, to embrace with fatherly affection those children, whose unhappy separation from Us We now bewail. Would that God our Savior, "Who will have all men to be saved and to come to the knowledge of the truth," [Divin. Instit. Iv, 30. 11–12.] would hear us when We humbly beg that He would deign to recall all who stray to the unity of the Church! In this most important undertaking We ask and wish that others should ask the prayers of Blessed Mary the Virgin, Mother of divine grace, victorious over all heresies and Help of Christians, that She may implore for Us the speedy coming of the much hoped-for day, when all men shall hear the voice of Her divine Son, and shall be "careful to keep the unity of the Spirit in the bond of peace." [Eph. iv, 3. 30]

13. You, Venerable Brethren, understand how much this question is in Our mind, and We desire that Our children should also know, not only those who belong to the Catholic community, but also those who are separated from Us: if these latter humbly beg light from heaven, there is no doubt but that they will recognize the one true Church of Jesus Christ and will, at last, enter it, being united with us in perfect charity. While awaiting this event, and as a pledge of Our paternal good will, We impart most lovingly to you, Venerable Brethren, and to your clergy and people, the apostolic benediction.

Given at Rome, at Saint Peter's, on the 6th day of January, on the Feast of the Epiphany of Jesus Christ, our Lord, in the year 1928, and the sixth year of Our Pontificate.

BIBLIOGRAPHY

Audio Sancto. "Baltimore Catechism No. 3—Lesson 11." Accessed December 2, 2014. http://www.audiosancto.org/inc/BC3/bc3-11.html.

Baumgarten, P. M. "Holy See." In *The Catholic Encyclopedia*, Vol. 7. New York: Robert Appleton Company, 1910.

Baumgarten, P. M. "Old Catholics." In *The Catholic Encyclopedia*, Vol.11. New York: Robert Appleton Company, 1911.

Berkhof, Louis. *Systematic Theology*. Grand Rapids, MI: Wm. B. Eerdmans Publishing Company, 1953.

Called to Communion. "Christ Founded a Visible Church." Last modified December 1, 2014. http://www.calledtocommunion.com/2009/06/christ-founded-a-visible-Church/.

Called to Communion. "Why Protestantism Has No Visible Catholic Church." Last modified December 2, 2014. http://www.calledtocommunion.com/2009/09/why-protestantism-has-no-visible-catholic-Church/.

Carlen, Claudia. *The Papal Encyclicals*. Raleigh, NC: McGrath Publishing Company, 1981.

Catechism of the Catholic Church, 2nd ed. Washington, DC: United States Catholic Conference, 1994.

Catholic Answers. "What Is a 'Cafeteria Catholic'?" Last modified December 3, 2014. http://www.catholic.com/quickquestions/what-is-a-cafeteria-catholic.

Bibliography

CatholiCity. "The First Commandment of God." Accessed March 14, 2015. http://www.catholicity.com/baltimore-catechism/lesson16.html.

Cekada, Anthony. *Work of Human Hands—a Theological Critique of the Mass of Paul VI.* West Chester, Ohio: Philothea Press, 2010.

Cox, Thomas E. *The Pillar and Ground of the Truth: A Series of Lenten Lectures on the True Church, Its Marks and Attributes.* Chicago: J. S. Hyland & Company, 1900.

Denzinger, Henry. *The Sources of Catholic Dogma,* 30th ed. New Hampshire: Herder & Co., 1954.

Devine, Arthur. *The Creed Explained; or, An Exposition of Catholic Doctrine According to the Creeds of Faith and the Constitutions and definitions of the Church,* 4th ed. New York: Benziger Bros, 1903.

Devivier, W. *Christian Apologetics: A Defense of the Catholic Faith.* New York: Benziger Brothers, 1903.

Dimond, Peter. *Outside the Catholic Church There Is Absolutely No Salvation,* 2nd Edition. New York: Most Holy Family Monastery, 2006.

Dimond, Michael, and Peter Dimond. *The Truth about What Really Happened to the Catholic Church after Vatican II.* New York: Most Holy Family Monastery, 2007.

Encyclopædia Britannica. "Kakure Kirishitan." Accessed March 5, 2015. http://www.britannica.com/EBchecked/topic/309931/Kakure-Kirishitan.

Fleming, David L. *The Spiritual Exercises of St. Ignatius: A Literal Translation and a Contemporary Reading.* St. Louis: The Institute of Jesuit Sources, 1978.

Fordham University. "Modern History Sourcebook: The Apparitions at La Sallette, 1846." Accessed May 17, 2015. http://legacy.fordham.edu/halsall/mod/1846sallette.asp.

The Franciscan Friars. "Who Are We?" Last modified January 6, 1999. http://friarsminor.org/whoarf2.html.

Google Books. "Dr. J.J.I. Von D Döllinger's Fables Respecting the Popes in the Middle Ages." Accessed May 17, 2015. https://books.google.com/books?vid=0o5gZXZPy84SyfDX7wo&id=JucQAAAAIAAJ&pg=PA337&dq=%252522other+Apostles+to+have+expired%252522&as_brr=1&hl=en#v=onepage&q&f=false.

Guettée, Abbé. *The Papacy: Its Historic Origin and Primitive Relations with the Eastern Churches.* Blanco, TX: New Sarov Press, 1866.

Hardon, John A. *Modern Catholic Dictionary.* Garden City, NY: Doubleday and Company, Inc., 1980.

Hebermann, Charles G., et al., eds., *The Catholic Encyclopedia: An International Work of Reference on the Constitution, Doctrine, Discipline and History of the Catholic Church.* New York: Robert Appleton Co., 1907–1912, 15 vols.

IntraText. "Chapter IV: The Roman Curia." Last modified August 26, 2007. http://www.intratext.com/IXT/ENG0017/_P19.HTM.

Joyce, George. "The Pope." In *The Catholic Encyclopedia,* Vol. 12. New York: Robert Appleton Company, 1911.

Keenan, Stephen. *A Doctrinal Catechism: Catholic Faith and Practice Assailed by Modern Heretics,* 1st Amer. ed. New York: Edward Dunigan & Brother, 1848.

Küng, Hans. *Infallible? An Inquiry.* Translated by Edward Quinn. Garden City, NY: Doubleday & Company, 1983.

Madrid, Patrick. *Pope Fiction: Answers to 30 Myths & Misconceptions about the Papacy.* Rancho Santa Fe, CA: Basilica Press, 1999.

Mgh-bibliothek.de. "The Sacred College of Cardinals: Size and Geographical Composition (1099–1986)." Accessed May 7, 2015. http://www.mgh-bibliothek.de/dokumente/z/zsn2a045837.pdf.

Most Holy Family Monastery. "Facts Which Demolish the 'No Independent Priest Today Has Jurisdiction' Position." Last modified September 1, 2011. http://www.mostholyfamilymonastery.com/jurisdiction.pdf.

New Advent. "Holy See." Accessed March 6, 2015. http://www.newadvent.org/cathen/07424b.htm.

New Advent. "Old Catholics." Accessed March 5, 2015. http://www.newadvent.org/cathen/11235b.htm.

New Advent. "The Epistle of Ignatius to the Smyrnaeans." Accessed May 17, 2015. http://www.newadvent.org/fathers/0109.htm.

New Advent. "The Pope." Accessed March 3, 2015. http://www.newadvent.org/cathen/12260a.htm.

OrthodoxChristianity.net. "The Vatican Dogma." Accessed December 2, 2014. http://www.orthodoxchristianity.net/articles/39-the-vatican-dogma.

Orthodox Wiki. "Church of Jerusalem." Last modified March 19, 2012. http://orthodoxwiki.org/index.php?title=Church_of_Jerusalem&oldid=108084.

Ott, Ludwig. *Fundamentals of Catholic Dogma,* 2nd ed., edited by James Canon Bastible, translated by Patrick Lynch. Cork, Ireland: The Mercier Press Limited, 1957.

Our Lady of the Rosary Province. "Code of Canon Law." Last modified February 27, 2011. http://www.holyrosaryprovince.org/2011/media/essencial/code_of_canon_law_1983.pdf

Papal Encyclicals Online. "Decrees of the First Vatican Council." Accessed March 3, 2015. http://www.papalencyclicals.net/Councils/ecum20.htm.

Papal Encyclicals Online. "*Lamentabili Sane.*" Accessed May 7, 2015. http://www.papalencyclicals.net/Pius10/p10lamen.htm.

Papal Encyclicals Online. "*Quartus Supra.*" Accessed May 7, 2015. http://www.papalencyclicals.net/Pius09/p9quartu.htm.

Papal Encyclicals Online. "*Satis Cognitum.*" Accessed May 7, 2015. http://www.papalencyclicals.net/Leo13/l13satis.htm.

Papal Encyclicals Online. "*Unam Sanctam.*" Accessed May 7, 2015. http://www.papalencyclicals.net/Bon08/B8unam.htm.

Papal Encyclicals Online. "*Pascendi Dominici Gregis.*" Accessed May 7, 2015. http://www.papalencyclicals.net/Pius10/p10pasce.htm.

Papal Encyclicals Online. "*Mortalium Animos.*" Accessed May 7, 2015. http://www.papalencyclicals.net/Pius11/P11MORTA.HTM.

Papal Encyclicals Online. "*Mystici Corporis Christi.*" Accessed May 7, 2015. http://www.papalencyclicals.net/Pius12/P12MYSTI.HTM.

Bibliography

Pius XII. "*Ad Sinarum Gentem* (Encyclical Letter on the Supranationality of the Church)." In *The Papal Encyclicals*. Raleigh, NC: McGrath Publishing Company, 1981.

Quidlibet. "Sedevacantism: A Quick Primer." Last modified November 19, 2013. http://www.fathercekada.com/2013/11/19/sedevacantism-a-quick-primer/.

Radecki, Francisco and Radecki, Dominic. *Tumultuos Times: The Twenty General Councils of the Catholic Church and Vatican II and its Aftermath*. MI: Saint Joseph's Media, 2004.

The Real Presence Association. "Christ to Catholicism." Last modified March 28, 2014. http://www.therealpresence.org/archives/Church_Dogma/Church_Dogma_027.htm.

The-pope.com. "Contra Haereses Feeneyism." Last modified March 8, 2011. http://www.the-pope.com/BOB_BOD_BOK.html.

Traditionalmass.org. "Baptism of Desire and Theological Principles." Accessed May 7, 2015. http://www.traditionalmass.org/images/articles/BaptDes-Proofed.pdf.

Traditionalmass.org. "Canon 188.4 or Where Is the Church." Accessed December 1, 2013. http://www.traditionalmass.org/articles/article.php?id=12&catname=10.

Traditionalmass.org. "Response to Bishop Williamson on the Subject of the Vacancy of the Roman See." Last modified March 3, 2014. http://www.traditionalmass.org/images/articles/williamson_response.pdf.

Vatican Council II. "*Lumen Gentium* (Dogmatic Constitution on the Church)." In *Vatican Council II: the Basic Sixteen Documents*. Edited by Austin Flannery. Northport, NY: Costello, 1996.

Vatican Council II. *"Unitatis Redintegratio* (Decree on Ecumenism)." In *Vatican Council II: the Basic Sixteen Documents*. Edited by Austin Flannery. Northport, NY: Costello, 1996.

Wathen, James F. *I Know Mine and Mine Know Me: The Voice of a Faithful Catholic Priest to His Flock*, Vol. I. Louisville, KY: The James F. Wathen Traditional Catholic Foundation, 2012.

Wikipedia. "Cum ex apostolates officio." Last modified February 3, 2015. http://en.wikipedia.org/w/index.php?title=Cum_ex_apostolatus_officio&oldid=575778370.

Wikipedia. "Ecumenism." Last modified February 16, 2015. http://en.wikipedia.org/w/index.php?title=Ecumenism&oldid=617151791.

Wikipedia. "Essence." Last modified January 27, 2015. http://en.wikipedia.org/w/index.php?title=Essence&oldid=601926247.

Wikipedia. "Filioque." Last modified February 6, 2015. http://en.wikipedia.org/w/index.php?title=Filioque&oldid=599606019.

Wikipedia. "Holy See." Last modified February 21, 2015. http://en.wikipedia.org/w/index.php?title=Holy_See&oldid=601690896.

Wikipedia. "Leonard Feeney." Last modified February 14, 2015. http://en.wikipedia.org/w/index.php?title=Leonard_Feeney&oldid=602557677.

Wikipedia. "Most Holy Family Monastery." Last modified October 1, 2014. http://en.wikipedia.org/w/index.php?title=Most_Holy_Family_Monastery&oldid=627871630.

Wikipedia. "Mortalium Animos." Last modified January 29, 2015. http://en.wikipedia.org/w/index.php?title=Mortalium_animos&oldid=550013375.

Wikipedia. "Pope." Last modified February 12, 2015. http://en.wikipedia.org/w/index.php?title=Pope&oldid=646849753.

Wikipedia. "Sedevacantism." Last modified February, 2015. http://en.wikipedia.org/w/index.php?title=Sedevacantism&oldid=600207158.

Wikipedia. "Tiara of Pope Paul VI." Last modified November 12, 2014. http://en.wikipedia.org/w/index.php?title=Tiara_of_Pope_Paul_VI&oldid=633550992.

WordNet. "Delusion." Accessed May 7, 2015. http://wordnetweb.princeton.edu/perl/webwn?s=delusion.